THE SEXUAL CODE

WOLFGANG WICKLER
THE
SEXUAL CODE
The Social Behavior of Animals and Men

With an Introduction by KONRAD LORENZ
Illustrated by HERMANN KACHER
Translated from the German by FRANCISCA GARVIE

ANCHOR BOOKS
Anchor Press/Doubleday, Garden City, 1973

THE SEXUAL CODE was originally published under the title SIND WIR
SÜNDER? by Droemer Knaur, Munich, in 1969. The Doubleday edition
is published by arrangement with Droemer Knaur and is the first publica-
tion of this translation. Copyright © 1969 Droemersche Verlagsanstalt Th.
Knaur Nachf.

Anchor Books edition: 1973

ISBN: 0-385-08112-x
Translation Copyright © 1972 by Doubleday & Company, Inc.

Wolfgang Wickler is Professor of Zoology at Munich University and a noted ethologist who has spent years in the study of animal and human behavior. Professor Wickler is the author of numerous journal articles and books including *Mimicry,* previously published in the United States; he also serves as editor of the *Journal of Comparative Ethology,* published in Berlin.

Professor Wickler's continuing research in animal social behavior leads him often to Eastern Africa for field studies; presently he is investigating the ecological and evolutionary implications of animal monogamy, in continuation of his study of animal family relationships upon which THE SEXUAL CODE is based.

CONTENTS

PART III

PART IV

INTRODUCTION

Konrad Lorenz

I have very good reasons for attaching great topical interest and great value to this book by my long-standing friend and colleague. These reasons are of a general nature and I shall have to go far back in order to explain them. But I believe that this may help the reader, and especially those readers who are not very familiar with biology, to appreciate the work more fully.

Every species of animal and plant has adapted itself to its environment in a process of adjustment lasting eons; in a sense each species is the image of its environment. The form of the horse's hoof is just as much an image of the steppe it treads as the impression it leaves is an image of the hoof. The process by which a species adapts to an extraspecific reality is a *one-sided* process only if this reality is determined by the immovable laws of inorganic nature. The fin of the fish, its undulating motion, and the streamlined shape of the fish body are an image of the water and of its physical characteristics, which the presence of fish has in no way affected. A species of living thing generally only causes limited changes in the inorganic world. Admittedly corals can alter entire coastlines and themselves build up the reefs on which they settle; plants can turn large expanses of water into land; burrowing rodents can cause landslides, etc. But all these effects are negligible compared to the extent that every animal or plant species influences its *living* environment. All species that live together in the same place are necessarily adapted *to one another* and are dependent on one another, even if they appear to be hostile, as in the relationship between the eater and the eaten. The hoofed animals that graze there and the hard grass of the steppe very largely owe their present form and mode of life to their reciprocal adaptation to each other. As students of phylogeny well know, a kind of armed competition has been taking place between the two since the early Tertiary Age; the grass acquired a harder and harder armor of silicates in order to be eaten less easily, while the grazing animals developed ever stronger teeth and enamel crowns in order to overcome the plants' defenses. For their part, the grazing animals are useful to the grass, by preventing the steppe from turning into forest. Naturally they are not the only partners in this community of life; both are, for instance, dependent on soil bacteria, which break up animal excretions, dead plants, and dead animals into substances that in turn nourish the plants. The final source of energy that keeps everything in motion is the sun, whose rays enable the plants to synthesize nourishing carbohydrates from carbon dioxide. This type of living community, or biocoenosis, involving innumerable species of animals and plants, is like an extraordinarily complicated piece of machinery in which everything interlocks with everything else and the loss of even the tiniest, apparently useless little cogwheel would cause unforeseeable destruction. Above all, of course, it is any sudden change that leads to the collapse of a biocoenosis; apart from rare natural disasters, these are caused almost exclusively by *man.*

Man upsets the equilibrium in which biocoenoses exist because he evolves at a very much faster rate than any other living thing. While the changes in body structure and mode of life to which living things are subject in the course of their phylogenetic development are all based on the same processes of mutation and recombination of genes, and on natural selection, man, thanks to his capacity of conceptual thought and speech, has become able to transmit to posterity the experiences and inventions of individuals as well as the insights that individuals have gained in their own life. So man is the only living thing with the ability to transmit acquired characteristics; the word "transmit" must, however, be taken in the original, juridical sense of heritage here, and not in the genetic sense more familiar to modern biologists.

Man has changed the biocoenosis in which he lives more than any other living thing. He has created his own environment and has scarcely allowed any species of animal or plant to survive other than those whose usefulness to his own well-being was immediately apparent. Unfortunately only a dwindling minority of the holders of political and economic power today knows enough about the character of biocoenoses and their dependence as a whole on the parts of which they are made up. This is why man is well on the way, or rather hell-bent, to destroying the community of life in and on which he lives.

If the fruits of the tree of knowledge drove man from Paradise, that is because he plucked them while they were unripe and has nowhere near digested them yet. Instead, they have given him spiritual indigestion so that all his opinions and ideals pass through him too quickly. It has led to that curious race of man against himself that is our curse and that leads to high blood pressure, cirrhosis of the liver, heart attacks, and premature death. Yet, paradoxically, the majority of people consider this to be progress. Briefly, man has succeeded in transforming his world in such a way that he has made himself unhappy in it and has indeed become *guilt*-laden. So in fact the story in the Bible is quite true.

The problems that beset us today are *ethical* problems.

The reason they are so difficult to solve is that it is quite impossible to discover firm criteria in the kaleidoscopic world of man with its lightning changes. As long as mankind still evolved more slowly it was easier, and at least people *believed* they had some idea of what was good and what was bad. But the devil lies by definition, and the serpent's promise that men would know good from evil once they had eaten from the tree of knowledge proved the most disgraceful lie of all. Men seem to know this less and less the farther their so-called knowledge advances. But this was not inevitable; it is so chiefly because the devil has given man a far too inflated opinion of himself, which prevents him from knowing *himself*. There are no such obstacles, however, to his knowledge of the world around him. Knowledge is power, and man has gained great power over the universe around him, but not over himself and his own behavior. This is a highly dangerous state of affairs.

Proverbially, pride comes before a fall, and man in his pride is only too eager to see himself not as a part of nature but as something at the opposite pole, if not actually superior to nature. Indeed, the term "nature" is itself a product of this pernicious attitude. The delusion of man and nature as opposites has resulted in senseless questionings. A great deal of fruitless effort has been devoted to discussing what is or is not "natural" to man.

By being contrasted to a number of entirely different things as its polar opposite, the concept of "natural" is being robbed of any pertinence or definition. One moment it is mankind as a whole as opposed to nature; the next it is only man's spirit; then his culture; or, finally, "unnatural," the abnormal in the sense of something diseased, is considered the opposite of nature. Accordingly, the term "natural" also assumes a series of entirely different meanings. First, "natural" can mean the nonspiritual—as in Klage's *Der Geist als Widersacher der Seele* (*The Spirit as Enemy of the Soul*); second, it can mean all that is peculiar to man, not on the basis of cultural tradition but because of the hereditary factors of our species; third, it is simply equated with "healthy."

The value judgments made on the content of this scintillating concept are, of course, even more muddled and contradictory. According to Kantian moral philosophy, everything natural is of indifferent value; the best action is free of all value if it is born of natural inclination and not of categoric self-analysis. Civilization has imposed on man the need to control some of his instincts, and this has led, through excessive exaggeration in certain pietistic and puritanical cultural circles, to the appalling delusion that all natural drives are *ipso facto* inspired by the devil, especially if they give pleasure. Yet, on the other hand, it is considered a legitimate excuse for highly reprehensible behavior patterns if they are "natural." In terms of the object of their drives, some otherwise upstanding men consider themselves free of all moral responsibility. The English proverb runs "all is fair in love and war"; so the loved one can be treated just like an enemy. Few people blamed Goethe for seducing, betraying, and—if truth be told—killing Friederike von Sesenheim in the most shameful manner.

Unfortunately this confusion in the concept of what is natural, due to the fallacy of opposites, is so familiar to us all now that we are scarcely able to see what misleading and dangerous results it has. Arnold Gehlen cut through the Gordian knot with the opposite phrase that man is by nature a civilized being. Broca's area in the supramarginal gyrus of the left temporal lobe, where praxis and gnosis, experience and knowledge, collaborate in such wonderful fashion and form the basis of conceptual thought and speech, is just as much a physical and natural organ of man as his lungs or kidneys, although there are no comparable organs in the animal kingdom. And nothing is more natural than disease! No living system is free from these disturbances to its function, and small, disease-breeding organisms are just as much part of the realm of nature as man himself.

In order to solve the problems that are currently troubling us and to obviate the dangers looming from all sides we need a *new ethics,* springing from a mode of thought quite different from that concept of opposites we have just criticized. This mode of thought, which sees man not as a contrapuntal opposite but as *part* of a single universe based on natural laws, is not new. Its statements and methods are those that have been accepted in biology since the days of Charles Darwin. This approach to the universe also posits values—and pairs of opposites. The widespread idea that science is "value-free" is entirely misleading. The biologist knows that in the course of phylogeny, the new, that has never existed before, is constantly being created, and that it is more than the original elements from which it sprang; so he also recognizes the existence of lower and higher stages of organic being. And with the knowledge that every organic system can step out of order, i.e., fall ill and die, the biologist is also aware of the opposites of health and disease.

The question of what is a lower and what a higher stage is just as meaningful as the other question of whether a course of life is diseased or healthy. When we consider passages of human civilized life we often find ourselves in the position of having to decide these questions. The reply to the second question is particularly difficult and lays great responsibility on us. For health and disease are concepts that can only be defined in the context of the living area of the organism in question. Sickle-cell anemia, a hereditary malformation of the red blood corpuscles, not only reduces their number but also their ability to carry oxygen. In a pure genetic, "homozygous" state, the tendency to sickle-cell formation is a so-called lethal factor, and, even if it exists in a "heterozygous" (split gene) state, it severely affects man in his normal environment: Even the heterozygous sickle-cell anemic person is "ill" in northern latitudes. In certain regions of Africa, however, which are particularly plagued by malaria, *he* is healthy while the possessor of "normal" blood corpuscles inevitably falls ill. For, curiously enough, the destructive malaria plasmodia cannot penetrate the malformed blood corpuscles; so their possessors are immune against the disease that makes residence in these parts impossible to any "healthy" person.

This makes it very clear that the almost synonymous attributes "healthy" or "adaptive" (meaningful in terms of the survival of the species) can only be applied in relation to a definite living area and a definite structure or function. In the case of phylogenetically evolved structure and functions of prehuman living things, this condition is still relatively easy to fulfill; but it becomes very difficult if we want to decide on the culturally based norms of human social behavior. The increasingly rapid alteration of his environment that man brings about by his culture and above all by his technology means that the traditional behavior norms of a culture can lose their adaptive powers almost "overnight"; moreover, other norms, that only recently were quite unadaptive, abnormal, and hostile to survival can henceforth serve the preservation of the individual and the community. Patriotic and militant enthusiasm for national ideals was still an essential behavior norm a few centuries ago, whereas today it is entirely reprehensible. A profound skepticism of time-honored ideals used to be harmful, whereas today it is essential to our survival.

This state of affairs, which is becoming more acute from decade to decade, has caused great ethical and moral confusion. The young generation of extremists believes that it must completely throw overboard all the traditions that have been handed down by its parents, and arrogantly deludes itself that it can construct a whole new civilization quite by itself. It does not realize that in terms of the history of civilization it is doing its best to regress to the level of a hypothetical pre-Stone Age or, in ontogenetic terms, to the stage of development of a pre-Struwelpeter. The older generation confronts the young with outraged rejection, seeing itself, not unjustifiably, as the sole defender of civilization; but by so doing it is also insisting, unawares, on dragging on traditions that have long since become outdated and are, if anything, detrimental now. The danger of a particularly narrow-minded form of fascism looms over America.

In no area of human life is the confusion and perplexity so great as in the sexual field. The primordial and proverbial power of the sexual drives is very liable to bring the behavior of the individual into conflict with the demands the community imposes on him. That is why, in all human cultures, sexual life in particular is regulated by very definite traditional norms, whose prime intention is quite obviously to bring up the children to be healthy and culturally mature members of society. It is still a truth valid for all cultures that the family is the elementary unit of every nation and civilization. These norms differ very widely in different cultural circles, from which we may deduce that man has devised no detailed, phylogenetically adaptive program for building up a family. But at the same time all the families of all the nations also have a whole number of traits in common, which clearly indicates the presence of certain common, culturally independent human and instinctive fundamentals.

There is scarcely another field of human social behavior where the idea of the so-called "natural" has been used in such contradictory fashion as that of love and family life. Either it is used as a pseudo-legitimate excuse for reprehensible behavior and as a passport to uncivilized excesses, or it serves to devaluate, if not forbid, healthy behavior patterns necessary to the survival of the species. There are few fields where clarification of this kind is as essential to the continuity of our civilization. The answer to the question whether a certain behavior norm, which seems pernicious or even abnormal to the older generation, which is more closely tied to tradition, may not in fact be system-preserving and therefore "healthy" in the present social environment, can be just as important as the answer to the reverse question, whether traditional behavior norms, which seem to have stood the test of age-old custom, are not extremely harmful under present conditions.

The solution to the question whether a certain behavior norm is healthy or diseased, whether it is beneficial or harmful to the survival of mankind and his civilization, is closely related, although by no means identical, to the question of good and evil. Certainly, the preservation of the living system of mankind and his civilization is a *value*, and we have a great ethical responsibility to uphold it. Certainly everything that can tend to the destruction of this value is undoubtedly bad. But we bear an even greater responsibility, namely for all that could still *become* of our descendants, in what will, God willing, be a better future. The great organic process of becoming, that has transformed unicellulars into multicellulars and animals into men from pre-Cambrian times, is continuing, so we firmly believe, in human civilization. We are duty bound to preserve it, above all because this is essential to its further evolution.

PREFACE

It was the encyclical *Humanae vitae* that occasioned this book. For the encyclical very clearly shows where theology is deficient in knowledge of nature and why the instructions it has given under the aegis of natural laws are suspect. This does not mean that the instructions are necessarily wrong—merely that they are questionable and therefore impose no obligation. Primarily this is because, even where they call on the nature of man, they in fact spring from an *idea* of man that is derived from a static concept of nature, in which history and evolution have no part. The same once applied to natural science. But a constant confrontation with nature forced natural science into a dynamic, historical mode of thought. For evolution exists, and the nature of man, to which ethical norms relate, moves with it.

It lies in the nature of man that he can do more than he may. Natural science and in particular biology can indicate what is biologically useful to man, and can check whether the ethical norms set up by others agree with the laws of biology. If they do not, usually it is because they derive from an abstract, metaphysical view of the nature of man; then a reason has to be found why people reach different conclusions—according to whether they start from the physical or the metaphysical nature of man. One test is the evidence about nonhuman beings, since it is assumed that they cannot act against their nature. If these organisms act

otherwise than expected, the false expectation must be due
to an error of method. It would be mere arbitrariness rather
than method, and a question not of science but of ideology
—and therefore outside the realm of any real discussion—
to attempt to conceal this error by holding that the damage
that man, by his fall, has also done to nonhuman creation
is responsible for the fact that this creation does not live
up to the nominal value of man's expectations. This does
not, however, mean that such ideas are wrong; but neither
does it allow one to discover whether they are right. All such
discussions should be concerned with the behavior of man
and of animals and with comparisons of the two, not with
humanized, anthropomorphic observations of animals or an
animalized, theomorphic view of man. Biologists and ethologists have brought to light facts that surprised the moral
theologians. It is to be expected that the latter will re-
examine their views in the light of these facts.

Humanae vitae requires that human behavior be subordinated to the purposes of nature, declares that it is a sin
if personal relations are not subordinated to (licit) bodily
behavior, and transforms a number of biological laws into
ethical ones. This can only be done on a metaphysical
basis. As long as this basis is circumvented, the requirement
cannot be understood properly; it is, therefore, not an ethical requirement—unless it pertains to an ethics of mystery.

I have not attempted to list theological authorities that
have proved wrong; rather I have tried to show as clearly
as possible how one can arrive at scientific statements on
the behavior on animals. The reconstruction of phylogenetic
developments is of major importance here. The methodology
for this was originally created for the forms of organs
(morphology). This is why I used it first for comparative
studies of organs, then applied it to simple forms of behavior—such as locomotion and foraging—and only then,
after a few necessary amendments, applied it to social be-

havior and communication among animals.[123]* My knowledge of the behavior of many of the animals discussed here is due to ten years of research work at the Max Planck Institut für Verhaltensphysiologie (Max Planck Institute of Behavior Physiology) and long observation of tropical animals in the wild. I have to thank my teacher and friend, Dr. Konrad Lorenz, for making this possible.

Theology and natural law

A number of theologians tend to react almost allergically to scientific discoveries that alter our image of mankind, even though many theological views largely coincide with those of biology. For example, it would contravene the teachings both of biology and theology to assume that natural drives have no good use. Theology teaches that God created nature and it was good. But both sciences also teach that it is not true that automatically *only* what is fitting and good comes about in the world. The biologist knows that changes in the environment can make new demands on a living thing to which its existing system of construction and function are not adapted. In some cases a single organism or an entire species can founder on this unfitness. Moreover, among higher animals and even more among men, the functional plan of behavior is not already determined at the egg stage but can and must be completed in the course of the individual's life, through experience and learning; and here too it may happen that the living thing learns something wrong. The theologian knows that evil impairs nature, which was created good, and that man at least is able to act contrary to the will of the Creator. So both sciences accept that man can act in accordance

---

* Where appropriate I have indicated recent specialist literature by means of small numbers in the text that correspond to the numbers in the bibliography, in order to give the interested reader the opportunity to go deeper into certain individual questions.

with nature or against nature, do good or evil. Consequently, both must try to establish criteria as to what is "natural" or "good." If we assume that the created world is the realization of divine ideas and that the Creator orders nonrational creatures in terms of the purpose he has set them by the law of nature, then "natural" and "good" can be equated in the realm of nonrational creatures. If this is meant to imply anything at all for man, who is endowed with reason, then it is that "to do evil" means the same as "to act contrary to (human) nature."

Since they agree on so many things, it is astonishing how often scientists and theologians still contradict each other, massively contradict each other in fact. In some fields the contradiction is increasing rather than diminishing, although one would expect the opposite if our knowledge really is advancing. The most recent important document of the teaching authority of the Catholic Church, the encyclical *Humanae vitae*, has been subject to more contradiction by natural scientists than any other. This is strange, considering that the document is directly concerned with "a teaching founded on the Natural Law." This "Natural Law" relates to reproduction and the conjugal life of human sexual partners, so it is also of extreme interest to biologists. It was formulated rather like this: Although reproduction also serves to unite the partners, besides serving procreation, these two meanings are inseparably connected, so that each marriage act is open to the transmission of life. I consider this the correct version, translated into biological terms, of what in theological language reads as follows: *That teaching . . . is founded upon the inseparable connection, willed by God and unable to be broken by man on his own initiative, between the two meanings of the conjugal act: the unitive meaning and the procreative meaning.* True, this is immediately preceded by: *No believer will wish to deny that the teaching authority of the Church is competent to interpret even the natural moral law.* So the encyclical is not only concerned with a natural law but also with its interpretation.

But the quarrel is obviously not sparked off by the interpretation alone, but by the somewhat unusual situation that this law of nature was laid down not by biologists but by theologians who, however, have omitted to tell how they came by it. This is why natural scientists and medical men competent in this field are now trying to examine the natural law in question. It is probably common knowledge by now that they have not yet been able to verify it, that is to say, that they seriously doubt whether there is any such natural law.

Specialists are not the only ones interested in this problem. In fact, there are countless laymen into whose daily conjugal life the Church has intervened heavily with its instructions. Many people find themselves simply incapable of following these instructions. Yet they are not satisfied with a purely emotional disagreement, as I have found from frequent conversations with engineers, teachers, soldiers, students, theologians, and university professors, but they try to form their own judgment in the controversy. Where theological statements of immediate interest contradict those of natural science and medicine, it is indeed up to the "consumer" to decide which to believe. Naturally he cannot hope to master all the knowledge of the two branches of science—normally not even scientists can do so. But what he can do is examine the methods that lead to the different conclusions. According to theological teaching, he is in fact obliged to do so; he cannot avoid the decision, which he must then somehow substantiate to himself, since "whatsoever is not of faith is sin," even if one blindly obeys the instructions of the Church.

No doubt it may seem bad manners to find fault with another instead of putting one's own house in order. Yet it is permissible here, not because we want to reprimand the theologians, but in order to get closer to the truth. Biolo-

gists and theologians are both concerned with the law of
nature. And even if what they are seeking is not necessarily
identical, it does at least coincide in part. At least the man
who hears the instructions of the moral theologians and
who inquires into natural laws is the same person. If he
should now elaborate a stringent method for exploring
natural laws and arrive at findings that do not coincide
with the statements of theology, he will have to doubt the
latter. It is no secret that many statements on man made
by theologians and learned churchmen have become very
suspect, whether they deal with the relationship between
man and animal or with original sin.

But who made it all become suspect? It was those theologians and learned churchmen who did not know their
method. This is fairly easy to demonstrate.

The first pages of the Bible give two accounts of the
Creation with contradictory details. The first lists the following sequence of creation: heaven and earth, plants, animals, man; but the second states explicitly that man was
created before the plants and the animals. It is quite legitimate for the natural scientist to examine the discrepancy
and to clarify the different points described; at least one
of the two statements must be wrong factually. But quite
apart from the question of fact, very different basic attitudes to the accounts of the Creation are possible, and this
is decisive for our discussion and many similar debates. On
the one hand we could point to the striking discrepancies
in details, thereby exposing the whole thing as hearsay if
not deception. The *sine qua non* of this entirely legitimate
method is distrust. But distrust is unfitting in the eye of
God; he demands faith. And this gives rise to the other
basic attitude one can take, which assumes that the two
accounts with their different details were given deliberately,
as an indication that it is not the details that count but
something more general that can be expressed one way or
another. So the contradictory details would be expressly

meant to prevent the reader from paying too much attention to superficial details and contenting himself with them.
Accordingly theology says the Bible is not a manual of
natural science but contains the tidings, clothed in a particular form of language, *that* God created the world, but
not *how* he created it.

But the natural scientist is particularly interested in the
how. And he will soon find that in this respect neither of the
two divergent accounts of the Creation is correct. This
makes many people doubt whether there is any truth at
all in the account of the Creation and whether it would not
be more advisable, if not necessary, for the natural scientist
to dismiss the Bible entirely. But anyone who gives way to
this doubt, be he natural scientist or theologian, is clinging
to details like a Pharisee and is overlooking the possibility
that the natural scientist may have found yet another way
of putting it, that expresses the essentials equally well. The
more such methods of portrayal there are, the easier it
should be clearly to distinguish the essential from the inessential.

Unfortunately the theologians have overlooked this again
and again. In order to remove any doubts people might
have and to sustain man's faith, theologians have tried to
defend the Bible against natural scientists, i.e., to compile
scientific counterarguments. Of course it can happen for a
natural scientist to assert that he has disproved that the
world was created by God; but he cannot put this forward
as a scientific finding, for his methods cannot yield any such
thing. The believer must not let himself be shaken by such
statements. The theological doctrine of the salvation is not
under attack by natural science; anyone who wants to defend it in spite of this would be falsely accusing natural
science of trespassing outside its territory—but this would
mean he himself was trespassing in the opposite direction
by trying to prove the doctrine of salvation with scientific
arguments. That is a rather tragic confusion. But it is not

the business of theology to decide whether scientific evidence is conclusive.

A tragic case of mistaken method having grievous results that still vex us today is the traditional teaching of the Catholic Church on monogenism, i.e., the doctrine that all mankind is descended from a single parent couple. Genesis only mentions the creation of orders of animals (birds, fish, etc.), not of individuals; similarly it says: "Let us make man." The doctrine of a single pair of progenitors cannot be deduced from the Biblical account of the Creation. The Church accounts for it in other ways too, for instance basing it on the theological doctrine of original sin; here the Church states dogmatically that the sin of Adam was passed down to all his descendants by descent, not by imitation; "original sin is transmitted through propagation." Hence the theologians deduced that the whole of mankind is descended from a single human couple. Admittedly this is not strict dogma but merely a "theologically certain doctrine" that can be revised as soon as there are sufficient grounds to do so. But these grounds existed from the outset, even within theology. Several notable theologians are now disputing the fact, that for theological reasons, monogenism must be encouraged under any circumstances, as was believed for a long time.[37] But there is no need to be a theologian to see that the assertion that all mankind descends from one pair of progenitors is a cogent biological statement. In principle, natural science can check such statements; whether our researches have furnished enough evidence for us to do so now is another question. But in any case it is a statement that belongs in principle to the field of natural science. So it is up to the natural sciences to decide whether it is correct. Theology is neither willing nor able to make positive statements in the field of natural science that are binding on the conscience of the faithful. Yet here theology is actually submitting a dogmatic statement to the judgment of natural science, thus risking that the statement will be refuted. Since theological statements lie outside the field of natural science, the statement on monogenism must be untheological. The duty of the theologian is to preach the doctrine of salvation, and here they must keep their statements independent of the current state of knowledge of natural science; otherwise, whether they wish it or not, they will become advocates of the theses of natural science. So it was not only untheological but in fact illogical for Pope Paul VI to declare, as recently as July 1966:

> *Thus it is quite clear that you* (the twelve theologians who had come to Rome for a symposium on original sin) *will regard the explanations of original sin given by some modern authors as irreconcilable with genuine Catholic doctrine. Starting out from the undemonstrated hypothesis of polygenism, they deny, more or less clearly, that the sin from which this great trash heap of ills in mankind is derived was first of all the disobedience of Adam, "the first man," a figure of the man to come—a sin that was committed at the beginning of history. As a consequence, such explanations do not agree with the teaching of Sacred Scripture, Sacred Tradition, and the Church's magisterium, according to which the sin of the first man is transmitted to all his descendants not through imitation but through propagation. . . . The theory of evolution will not seem acceptable to you whenever it is not decisively in accord with the immediate creation of each and every human soul by God, and whenever it does not regard as decisively important for the fate of mankind the disobedience of Adam, the universal first parent.*

The reference to the "undemonstrated hypothesis" betrays uncertainty of scientific method; the Pope is drawing limits to knowledge in the realm of natural science: *These limits are marked out by the living magisterium of the Church, which is the proximate norm of truth for all the faithful . . .*

In the context of the above mistake of method, the Pope's instructions to medical men in the encyclical *Humanae vitae* are, to say the least, misleading: *In this way scientists and especially Catholic scientists will contribute to demonstrate the fact that, as the Church teaches, "a true contradiction cannot exist between the divine laws pertaining to the transmission of life and those pertaining to the fostering of authentic conjugal love."* Natural scientists cannot prove that a theological doctrine must be right. Even if the Pope's wish is granted, namely that *medical science succeeded in providing a sufficiently secure basis for a regulation of birth, founded on the observance of natural rhythms* to determine the likelihood of conception more and more exactly, this is still no proof of the accuracy of any Church doctrine. There can be differences between natural laws and what theology has proclaimed as divine law. The theologians' explanations of nature and, in particular, the nature of man, are so impregnated with outdated scientific views that it requires natural scientists to work out what the theological nucleus of these explanations is.[93] But half of all the scientists history has produced are alive today. And our knowledge is growing apace. Of course, theology will always have to speak in the language of the times if it wants to be understood; but it must also develop alongside the insights of natural science if it does not want to be misunderstood in the future. It will have to take note of the fact that not only is man changing the world, but he is changing it more and more rapidly.

This is why it behooves the theologian to take an interest in the bases of the natural law in question (if it is one) too. And he does. The papal encyclical on birth control is subject to more controversy, even within Catholic theology, than any other. Unfortunately, the often rather heated dispute suffers greatly from ignorance of facts, without which one simply cannot work or argue. On the whole these facts are, however, widely accessible—except in theological textbooks; and, moreover, the subject is by no means one of dry academic scholarship but on the contrary very entertaining, because it deals with the family life and social life of all

kinds of animals for whom man has a great deal of interest
and affection in any case. I hope I will be able to offer at
least entertainment to some, and food for thought to as
many others as possible in this attempt to collate what the
ethologist has to say on the question of reproduction and
pair-bonding.

In the case of the more important animals, I have given
both the English and the scientific name (in parentheses and
italics), since different writers tend to christen exotic animals with various imaginative names that make it difficult
to identify them.

I have concentrated on a few striking examples in each
section; usually there are also a number of other familiar
examples. This is not meant as a handbook, however, but
as a definite scheme of argument. I trust the reader will
credit me with giving examples from which one can gener-
alize. Distrustful readers can check this from the bibliography. The earlier examples include more details on the life
of the relevant animal species in order to indicate other
biological connections; the later ones, for the sake of simplicity, concentrate on the elements of behavior under discussion. The word "marriage" as used here is purely descriptive and denotes the bond between partners of different
sex; it is also applied to animals. This is common practice
in scientific literature addressed to the layman too and it is
intended neither to deny man the special, supernatural features of his form of marriage nor to falsely attribute them to
animals.

The book is divided into four parts. The first deals with
the predicate value of natural laws, the second with the
specific natural laws of reproduction, the third with the
natural law of pair-bonding in the context of reproduction,
and the fourth with a few conclusions important to man.

Sternberg, May 1969   Wolfgang Wickler

THE SEXUAL CODE

I

1. Natural Inclination and Conscience

> *But beware instinct . . .*
> *Instinct is a great matter.*
>
> Shakespeare

Like Falstaff in Part 1 of *Henry IV* (Act 2, Scene 4), many people use instinct as an excuse for actions of which they are ashamed later, or at least actions of which their fellow men do not approve. Does behavior research, which is bringing more and more instinctive behavior to light for man too, therefore provide collective excuses for every situation in life? Is it true that we are well on the way to blaming failures on demons again—not, of course, on demons and evil spirits hovering somewhere in the world about us, but on demons within ourselves? If there is any truth in the notion that our traditional set of instincts is no longer adapted to the demands of the mass societies of today, if, as Konrad Lorenz says, what we call the voice of temptation is in fact the discrepancy between the demands of modern civilization and the instinctive drives that were created for age-old, perhaps prehuman conditions of life but which still cling to us today as a hereditary historical burden—do we not then have a good excuse? Cain did indeed slay Abel; but were not his aggressive drives really to blame?

This kind of argument seems to forget that, like the fratricidal Cain, perhaps Peter, who used his sword on the

servant of the Caiph, also acted instinctively. If we can
hold the polygamous tendency of man responsible for a
broken marriage, we can equally well hold an instinctive
tendency to monogamy responsible for marital fidelity, or
the brood-tending drive responsible for maternal devotion,
and so on. The reference to instincts can serve to extenuate
reprehensible behavior as well as praiseworthy actions,
although, of course, the latter usually need no excuse. The
only question is what this "extenuation" really means.

Our judges and spiritual advisers, when they deliberate
on guilt and sin, are not the only ones to be plagued by
the worry that motor drives in man, which take effect along
with conscious decisions, could put in question the responsibility of the individual. The same did and still does worry
those who want to or ought to propound positive moral
norms. Schiller's words are often quoted in this context:
"I like to serve my friends, but unfortunately I do so out
of inclination; and so it often worries me that I am not
really moral." These words allude to the fact that actions
that have been performed *against* natural inclinations are
nearly always considered worth particular merit. Lorenz
has repeatedly pointed out that in their choice of friends
people prefer those whose friendly behavior does not spring
from purely rational considerations but from natural affection alone. He explains this as follows:

> *The man who behaves socially from natural inclination
> normally makes few demands on the controlling mechanism
> of his own moral responsibility. Thus, in times of stress, he
> has huge reserves of moral strength to draw upon; while the
> man who even in everyday life has constantly to exert all
> his moral strength in order to curb his natural inclinations
> into a semblance of normal social behavior is very likely to
> break down completely in case of additional stress. . . . It
> is no paradox but plain common sense that we use two dif-
> ferent standards for judging the deeds of a man and the man
> himself.*[75] In any case, then, "plain common sense" obvi-

ously trusts the "instinctive" good deed no less than the categorical imperative.

The case of a child who has fallen into the water is often quoted as an example. We expect everyone to be prepared to jump in after the child "without thinking twice." A moment of thought would suggest the same course of action, but by then the child would have drowned. So we can say in favor of instinctive action that it is quicker off the mark than action guided by reason. But we could also quote the tragic case of the hero, who shoots without second thought out of a natural inclination to help a friend in danger, but overlooks a few details that would have shown him that in this particular case his shot will put the friend into even greater danger if not kill him.

Since man can find himself in a great many more different situations than were provided for in his instinctive behavior, he cannot avoid having recourse to reason at times to decide whether he may follow his instinctive natural inclination or not. And I believe man knows this, and that basically he does not evaluate an action according to whether or not it corresponds to natural inclination but according to whether reason came into it at all in the first place. This brings us to a—perhaps unexpected—technical problem. How does one tell whether a man has had recourse to reason? If one knows what the natural inclination is, and he acts against it, then one can be almost sure that he considered his course of action beforehand. But if he acts according to his natural inclination, then he may have had recourse to reason beforehand, or he may not. And since one simply cannot know for sure, a certain asymmetry necessarily creeps into the evaluation of action; we tend to favor those that overcome natural inclinations and to lump these natural inclinations together as the "beast within." This attitude is very odd, not to say suspicious. For it assumes that man is wrongly constructed—so wrongly that, in order to act well, he must constantly fight against his makeup. This does not make sense in biological or theological terms, since at least the natural endeavor to preserve the species must be good. So the problem of how nature and ethics go together is particularly acute in the field of reproductive behavior.

We may begin with the basic general assumption that in principle it is immoral for man simply to act without reflection, even if the outcome is good. That is why the example of the child who has fallen into the water is misleading, if not dangerous. For it merely shows that it *can* be good to follow natural inclinations; but it does not show that unreflected action is good as such. Here the distinction is confused by the haste with which the action should take place in this special situation. If one took the time to consider whether to jump in after the child or not, and then jumped, this would be entirely meritorious, although perhaps less effective. Precisely today, when man is always rushed in any case and often seduced into senseless hasty action, we must not discredit reflection merely because it takes time. Of course, no man can consider all the possible principles involved before each individual action. This is why we need guidelines, norms, that have come into being through the same consideration of principles. Actions that are performed against the natural inclination are only considered worth particular merit because they make it abundantly clear that the person had recourse to reason first, not simply because the action was counter to his natural inclination. It is no less meritorious if reason has commanded him to follow his natural inclination. Instinctive action is morally neutral; what is of value is the decision made by reason or conscience, by the final authority whose decisions each man must follow without fail. And this is by no means a new insight. "For whatsoever is not of faith is sin," says Paul (Rom. 14:23). Evidently Paul is not concerned whether objectively seen the action was right or wrong.

So it is no excuse to call on the aggressive drive or other drives. We must not make them into demons, nor must we ignore them if they have been proved to exist. If they should actually prove themselves liable to do good, then it is the man who fails to do this good, who withholds or even cuts off this opportunity from others, who is acting immorally.

2. Ethology

Ethology and ethics

The scientific term for behavior research is "ethology" in Anglo-American parlance. The word derives from the Greek ἔθος, which denotes custom or usage. Our words "ethics" and "ethos" derive from the Greek ἦθος, meaning "good custom." So the scientific terms ethology and ethics sound more similar phonetically than they are in meaning. Ethology is not the doctrine of ethics. Yet the findings of behavior research overlap into the field of ethics, in the form of subsidiary quantities. This is very easy to show in the field of reproduction. For the preservation of the human species is both an ethical and a biological good for which we must strive. It is ensured by biological mechanisms and human laws. On a purely biological plane, all that serves to preserve the species has a positive value. But we cannot simply transpose this to the ethical plane, as the following simple reasoning will show.

For many species of animal, a considerable measure of intraspecific aggression, i.e., aggression directed against conspecifics (members of one's own species), is very advantageous; in very simple terms it leads to the extension of the species over all available and suitable living spaces, including the less good "second- and third-rate" ones, and it favors the fittest at the cost of the less fit. The fitter individual is the greatest opponent of the one who is merely fit. Let us assume that this also applied to the ancestor of man and that we are now living in an environment that demands far less aggression toward our fellow men than we produce. Then the balance between the natural characteristics of man and the demands of the environment in which he lives is upset, perhaps so much so that it is a threat to the survival of the species "man."

Now man has the ability—and perhaps even the duty—to regulate such imbalances. On principle this can be done in two ways: Either he himself changes or he changes the environment. Indeed, in most fields man acts rather ruthlessly toward his environment in order to satisfy his own needs (for comfort, better food, more rapid transportation, more leisure, etc.). In purely biological terms, he could take the simplest way to ensure the survival of his species. So biologically it would be legitimate to consider whether suitable changes to the environment could not create a situation in which man can once again make use of as much aggression against his fellow men as he has at his disposal. It is indeed possible that man owes his higher evolution to precisely such a violent rivalry between groups of pre-men or primitive men. But we must also take into account that on the biological plane the relative number of offspring counts, but not each single individual, and the individual counts the less the younger it is. The moment we consider the preservation of each individual human life as a necessary ethical good, we have raised a demand that is not very common on the biological plane. And this demand excludes certain corrective measures that seem inherently suitable for re-establishing the disturbed balance between man and his environment.

Yet we will prefer those corrective measures that seem most in harmony with the nature of man and the laws of nature in general, if we consider the laws of nature as part of the revelation of the will of the Creator. We cannot discover the corporal nature of man solely from observations of man. For one thing, it would require experiments that are not allowed to be performed on man, and for which other, more suitable creatures must therefore serve as guinea pigs. Second, man has a long phylogenetic history that—like all history—has left traces in its current end product. Its origins can only be shown by a comparison of many other creatures, which could enable us to reconstruct the phylogenetic development of man.

According to Teilhard de Chardin, the true nature of man is not to be found in his animal past but in his spiritual future. However much we may agree with this, we cannot accept the possible inference that we should accordingly concentrate on the spiritual future of man and leave his animal past to the past. For this past is still very demonstrably present. So, for instance, in spite of all deliberate decisions to have a child, however responsibly they may be expressed and freely decided, there is a very close correlation in both man and animals between frequency of conception and seasons or temperatures of the environment; this can be shown by statistics published in 1966 by the U. S. Department of Health, Education, and Welfare. In West Germany, Sweden, and England the maximum frequency of conception occurs from May to July, the minimum between November and February. Other minor factors also play a role here, as the following may show. On November 9, 1965 there was a power failure in New York lasting one night; there were no lights, no movies, no television, no theater. For a short period, nine months later, the clinics noted a rise in births of 33 to 35 percent. In December 1966 a great flood shut many Venetians in their houses; just nine months later, in the first half of August 1967, 45 percent more babies were born in Venice than usual. From January 26 to 31, 1967, a heavy snowstorm in Chicago paralyzed shops and traffic. Nine months later the normal birth count rose by 30 to 40 percent. In the small mountain town of Somerset, Kentucky, the community aerial for television reception for the seven thousand inhabitants was switched off for a month owing to a legal dispute; nine months later, in January 1969, the number of babies born in the hospital reportedly rose to three times the normal count.

It is not just excusable but even called for today to speculate on the appetite for news. Newspapers, radio, television, and the underlying appetite for novelty, for interesting news from the whole world, are extremely necessary, among other things because they report the news from those distant parts to which we have more or less deliberately extended our influence. Not to see, not to find out what we are achieving (with the decrees that are issued, the medicines that are brought on the market, the aid to development that goes out to other parts of the world) is to reduce our sense of responsibility. The dangerous outcome of this became clearest during the Second World War. In his diary of the years 1946–49, Max Frisch describes the "difference which consists in whether I drop bombs on such and such a model, which lies there under the chasing clouds, half pathetic, half boring and paltry, or whether I too stand down there, open my pocket knife, and go up to a man, a single man, whose face I shall see. . . . I cannot believe myself capable of the latter. As for the former, and here lies the difference, I am not at all sure."

Like long-range weapons that can aim outside our field of vision, every action or effect that goes outside the direct range of our conceptual world must be compensated for by reports back; for these reports bridge the spatial gap between us and the events and give us the possibility of control and responsible behavior. That is to say, we must apply our technical progress equally on all fields; narrowness is dangerous here too. Compensatory measures are now required in many fields. The criterion is obviously always whether a natural equilibrium can be maintained or re-established. In any case, there is always more than one factor to take into account. We must think in systems. Ethics also demands this; ethics is not keyed to the individual alone, but also to the preservation and functioning of society. So the limits to the free play of the personality are the legitimate interests of the community. When ethics gives guidelines for behavior, they will be dependent on the current state of knowledge of the complex connections between the well-being of the individual and that of society. As our knowledge of the laws of nature grows, so too does the number of ways of eliminating disturbances in the corporate life of individuals and of finding a way out when legitimate interests come into conflict. For example, it is biologically advantageous that individuals age and die. An immortal living being is certainly no contradiction in terms, for the most simple living things, those that are in many ways closest to the primitive state, are still potentially immortal today. True, they perish in great numbers owing to outside influences of the most varied kinds, but not through age. But if we want a rapid evolution toward ever more advantageous forms of life, then each population must bring its capacity for reproduction and means of varying its heritage into play as fully as possible, i.e., bear as many offspring as possible, all slightly different from one another, tested under real-life conditions. If, however, there are only a certain number of possible places to live, they must not remain permanently occupied by existing individuals, for then there would be no room for new developments. Necessary as it is for the individual to assert himself and remain alive, it is equally necessary at some point to withdraw from circulation a model that has already been tested, so that the population can survive in the competition with neighboring populations. Since the same rules apply to the automobile industry, this vocabulary is quite apposite.

Ethology and medicine

If a biologically predetermined, natural behavior exists for man, then anyone who wants to alter or influence human behavior must know it. This is best shown by a comparison with medicine, which also attempts to influence the biological functions of man. In both cases it is a question of removing deviations from the norm. Where this norm comes from, how the medical man knows the constitution of a healthy man, and what therefore counts as diseased, or how one can tell what behavior is right and what therefore is wrong or in need of correction, shall remain out of the discussion here. We must only remember that the norm is not merely a question of the majority, that is to say, of what could if need be described as "normal." Even if 90 percent of mankind suffered from diabetes, we would not say that they were "healthy" diabetics. Moral theology has made occasional attempts to substantiate the idea that monogamy is the norm for mankind by arguing that it predominates among most peoples and that there is a "trend toward monogamy," as Thielicke puts it, in the history of mankind. Quite apart from whether or not such statements are true, they cannot be used to set up an ethical norm. We could apply the same method to show that most people lie, that closer and closer contacts between more and more people produce a "trend toward lying"; then we would have to declare that lying is an ethical norm.

Accordingly, we will assume that the medical man knows what a healthy person is. So illnesses are deviations from this norm, and it is necessary to redress them. The most ancient method of doing so is by exorcism: "Thou shalt become healthy." Exorcism and faith healing are still practiced today, but they are not very reliable cures. Causal analyses of diseased states that allow the doctor to recognize foci of infection and organic malfunctionings and to treat them specifically have a much better success rate. Naturally, an exact knowledge of the functional connections also enables the doctor to make a healthy person ill or a sick person even more so. Ethically the method is neutral; it can be used for good or evil.

Similarly, we will assume that it is known how a man should rightly behave. Most deviations from this standard, experience has shown, occur in the realm of social behavior. The method that is still most widely used today to correct or prevent such deviations consists in the adjuration "Thou shalt love thy neighbor as thyself." Again, the results of this method leave much to be desired and tend rather to encourage an attempt to make an exact causal analysis of the disturbed system and its functional structure here too. At best, the outcome will once again be a neutral scheme of possible treatments, which will also enable one to elicit other things besides the valid norm. For the sake of experiments and in order to discover generally valid laws, researchers also study animal behavior in comparison to that of man. They can even test methods of influence on suitable animals, not because man "is nothing but an animal," but because he has some verifiable features in common with animals. Medical men successfully experiment with medicines on mice, without thereby asserting that man is a rodent. Furthermore, neither the medical men nor the behavior researchers can transfer their finding on one animal species to another animal species or to man. All they can transfer is working hypotheses, certain predictions; and these always have to be checked again. Similarly, experiments on animals only allow the researcher to predict the probable effect of new medicines on man; and the predictions can sometimes be wrong in spite of the most stringent test conditions.

How to make predictions that will be as accurate as possible is a question of method that will be discussed in the following chapter.

3. How Can We Discover a Law of Nature?

This is a question of method, and one that is very topical in many of the sciences today. It arises whenever a scientific statement becomes doubtful. The source of these doubts is not so important. If one "has a kind of feeling" that a statement is wrong, one can always check how it came to be made at all. This also means checking on the fundamental facts and the way the statement was deduced from these facts. But one can also examine the question of method for its own sake and find out what statements a new methodic process would produce. The method is tested as to the truth of its finding. Truth in this sense is the agreement between different statements or, for example, between logic and facts. We do not want to stray into philosophy, however, but simply to discuss facts of nature. In this context, "nature" is first and foremost the part or aspect of creation that is accessible to the working methods of natural science. Later, when we are discussing man, we will also take into account those parts of human nature that are not accessible to the methods of natural science, but are accessible to our own immediate experience. Natural science is an empirical science; the truth of its findings are determined by verification. According to Weizsäcker, this results in propositions that, admittedly, are unproven axioms, but that are generally accepted as true. A biological statement is true if it is applicable to the living thing, if it is in conformity with its nature. The statement must indeed conform with the nature of the living thing; it would obviously be non-sense to assert that a statement was true but did not agree with nature because the living things were wrong.

There are, however, various scientific methods of testing one and the same fact. Moreover, there are statements about man that stem from different sciences and were therefore discovered by different methods. Since mistakes can creep into every scientific working process, it may happen that such statements are irreconcilable with one another. This has one great advantage. It is the only way of calling attention to the fact that one of the statements may be wrong. Accordingly, both statements will have to be verified as to method, and in the end we may legitimately hope to have advanced a step farther in our knowledge. When methods are not questioned we are in the realm of ideology.

It is characteristic of behavior research that it does not confine itself to studying certain parts of living things, such as hormones or sensory organs, or certain biological abilities, such as hibernation or cell division. Rather it attempts to find out how the different animal species, as they exist today, do in fact exist. It examines the living animal, if possible in its natural habitat. It asks what the consequences are in terms of the continuance of the species, if the individuals defend territories, live in well-organized states, have innate responses to certain environmental stimuli, acquire personal experiences, and in given cases transmit them to others, etc. Behavior research tries to explain why some closely related animal species have considerable differences in behavior—why, for instance, some animal species severely wound or even kill one another in intraspecific fights, while others do not in spite of possessing dangerous weapons. This also requires a study of history; the researcher must know why the individual behavior patterns of fighting, courtship, etc., have changed in the course of phylogeny, and how they develop during the growth to maturity of the individuals. All these factors force the researcher away from the isolated detail and toward systematic thought. For example, he could ask what would happen if chimpanzees were forced to live on a treeless seashore, or just why it seems such a ridiculous idea for a cow to lie in wait in front of a rabbit burrow, catch a rabbit, and then devour it. It has been demonstrated again and again that different species of living things exploit entirely different living conditions and that they are equipped to do so in very specific ways, like the fish for swimming, the bird for flying, or the mole for burrowing in the ground. But it is also clear that identical abilities are developed independently of one another and existing coincidences can disappear again. The penguin is a bird, but it cannot fly; instead, it can swim as well as the whale—and yet neither is a fish. Birds, insects, and bats can fly, but they have developed this ability independently from one another.

So there are two fundamentally different methods of comparison: the *comparison of relationships* and the *comparison of abilities*. The first examines how the same organ can produce different things (for instance, a front leg can become a bird's wing or a bird's wing can become a flipper, in the case of the penguin). The comparison of abilities examines the coincidence that different organs can produce (for instance, a wing can come from a front leg among birds and bats, or from a dorsal skin projection among insects). As far as the method is concerned, characteristic behavior patterns can be treated in the same way as organs, for it has been shown that although their form is largely traditional, it also depends on the function of the behavior pattern in question and gradually changes if the behavior pattern changes its function.

If we want to know how a certain organ or behavior pattern has arrived at its present form in the course of phylogeny, we must look at its forerunners, which means that we must adhere strictly to the same organ or the same behavior pattern. It is no use comparing insect wings in order to understand where the bird wing comes from. But a comparison between bird and insect wings does help us to understand what is essential to the function of a wing. Obviously this is not so much a question of whether the wing is made of bones and feathers or of chitin. Since this methodic approach is very important, we will clarify it by yet another technical example. One and the same automobile factory can develop as different models as private automobiles, trucks, and buses; in the same way, the "mammal" factory can develop moles, gazelles, and squirrels. That these very different models all come from the same factory is not apparent at a glance; but it can be determined by a close examination of their structure. On the other hand, very different factories produce almost identical types of vehicles, such as buses; similarly, very different classes of animals have produced living things able to fly. Although they often look rather similar from the outside, a careful analysis of their construction will show that these largely analogous models come from different factories. So if we want to know what is characteristic of the principle of the bus, the best way to find out is to compare buses from different factories. Then we will find differences typical of the different factories that are obviously inessential (such as the method of wheel suspension, whether the engine is in front or behind, or which way the windshield wipers work); we will also find analogies that exist in spite of the different methods of construction typical of each factory, and that are therefore essential to the construction of such a thing as a bus at all.

In the same way, the anatomist compares organs that are largely analogous but that have evolved quite independently, like the eye of the vertebrates and the eye of the octopus. Externally they are extraordinarily similar, yet they prove to be two quite separate "inventions." The octopus eye developed as a skin depression, and the sensory processes of the retina are directed toward the eye lens; by contrast, the eye of the vertebrate is a projection of the brain, and the light-sensitive cells point away from the lens, i.e., the

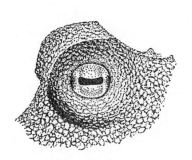

Two cases where almost identical organs of sight came about in the animal kingdom. Left, the eye of the octopus; right, the eye of a mammal (goat).

retina is inverted. The details of the structure are unimportant to the function; what is important are the component parts typical of the lens eye, such as lens, iris, vitreous humor, and retina.

The behavior researcher compares animal abilities in the same way, for instance reproduction or fighting, or the different types of animal society, such as permanent pair-bonds or compact larger groups. And if we want to know what is essential to pair-bonding, then we will have to compare animals that are as different as possible, that have "invented" monogamy independently from one another. This method will yield the natural laws that the lens eye obeys as well as the natural laws of pair-bonding, or marriage. It is only when one has perceived these laws that one can attempt to apply them and make them prevail by the methods peculiar to man.

II

4. Relative Masculinity and Femininity

Every living cell is potentially male and female and can react as a male or a female according to the predominant influences. The incidence of a particular sex can be determined by the genes, which are often situated in the so-called sex chromosomes; but it can also depend on external influences. In the first case we say that the development of male or female tendencies is genetically determined, and in the second that it is determined by modification. A cell becomes male or female according to which of these two tendencies predominates in its development. It is important to note here that this predominance is only in comparison with another cell in which the opposite tendency predominates. Even among very simple organisms such as algae, which have threadlike rows of cells one behind the other, one can observe that during copulation the cells of one thread act as males with regard to the cells of a second thread, but as females with regard to the cells of a third thread. The mark of male behavior here is that the cell actively crawls or swims over to the other; the female cell remains passive. So sexual differentiation is not absolute; there must be differences in the "strength" of the sex within each male or female, so that a cell that is normally female can behave like a male with regard to a more strongly differentiated female cell. This has now been proved true for many species, although the necessary tests are usually extremely complicated; in some cases it required almost ten years of work with pure-bred pedigrees.

There is one unicellular animal species in which one can tell at a glance the sex and the strength of each individual cell's development. This is a little flagellate, related to the *Polymastigina* and called *Trichonympha*, which lives in the

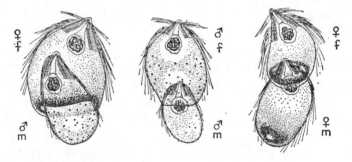

Each individual of the flagellate *Trichonympha* either has a stronger female (♀) or a stronger male (♂) differentiation, but can react both as a female (f) and as a male (m). So a male animal can play the role of female (center, ♂ f) toward a stronger male, and a female animal can play the role of male toward a more female animal (right, ♀ m). Left, "normal" mating between individuals whose sex is clearly differentiated.

intestines of the wood-eating American cockroach. As with many unicellulars, the individuals fuse entirely in the sexual act. In this case the male individual follows the female and penetrates her from behind through a special zone of plasma. This process resembles closely the penetration of a thread of semen into an animal egg. A typical *Trichonympha* female is recognizable by the number of little dark pigment spots arranged in a dense ring on her rear cell section. The male, by contrast, has only a few of these little dots distributed freely over the entire body of the cell. But there are all manner of transitions between the two extremes, and one can determine how strongly developed the female tendency of such a unicellular individual is by the number of dark dots. During a typical copulation, an individual with only a few dots penetrates one with a dense ring of dots, as shown in the illustration; so it is playing the part of the male. But it will be forced into the female role if it meets up with an individual with even fewer dots on its plasma, who will in turn take over the male role.

In the same way, a rather weakly developed female can act as a male when faced by a strongly developed animal. It can even happen that three individuals copulate with one another, the middle one penetrating the first one as a male, while at the same time serving as female for the third one.[15]

This kind of relative sexuality does not occur only among lower plants (algae, fungi) and unicellular animals, but also among fairly highly developed animals. Among segmented worms, to which our earthworm also belongs, the large related class of marine segmented bristleworms (*Polychaeta*) includes the species *Ophryotrocha puerilis*. These animals gradually grow from the larval stage into ever longer worms. The longer the worm is, the more segments it has, and any worm with more than twenty segments to its body is a female. The familiar experiment of cutting one of these animals down to five or ten front segments turns the animal into a male until it again develops the number of segments typical of a female. But the experiment works only if one feeds the animals badly at the same time; and, if one continues to do so, the worms will remain male, even if they have already grown too long for males. This worm demonstrates a typical instance of protandria or "provisional masculinity"; at first the individuals are male and then they become female. The experiment shows something else too: If one keeps two fully grown females together in a culture bowl, one of them will soon become male and fertilize the eggs of its partner. This transformation is effected by a substance emanating from the eggs that are still in the body of the female. The animal with the most eggs will assert its influence and thereby force the other to act as the male. After the eggs are liberated it can, of course, now occur that the other animal will produce more eggs more quickly; then they will exchange roles. This is possible because, in each segment, the animals form indifferent sex cells, which can become eggs or sperms depending on the external circumstances influencing them.[41]

Zoology textbooks also mention the worm *Bonellia viridis,* which lives hidden in rock crevices in the Mediterranean and North Atlantic. The fertilized eggs produce free-swimming larvae that are still of indifferent sex. The larvae grow up, settle somewhere, and become females with a thick body several centimeters long and a proboscis almost a meter long with which the animals search for food in the vicinity. If one of the free-swimming larvae comes upon the proboscis of a female, it will settle there too, and in the course of four days it will turn into a male; then it separates from the proboscis again and wanders into the sexual canals of the female where it remains and—often together with other males—proceeds to fertilize her. It develops into a male so rapidly because the animals scarcely need to grow during this process—the males only reach a size of about one millimeter. The process of larvae that are not yet sexually determined turning into males through influences emanating from a female is actually quite widespread among invertebrates. Among one species of wood louse, the sawbug *Ione,* which is a parasite living in pairs on the gills of a ghost shrimp (*Callianassa*), the larva becomes a female if it settles directly on a host gill. But the next larva to settle on this female becomes a male; if, however, it is removed and put on the next gill, it too will become a female. Other wood lice have only old females and young males, because each individual is a male when young and later turns female. Similarly, the offspring of the small slipper-limpet *Crepidula* is male while it is still living alone. When it reaches a certain size it settles somewhere and changes into a female. The young animal settles on a conspecific that has already settled, and so we find rows of up to twelve animals sitting one on top of the other. The last arrivals are always male and remain so for a very long time, since the female animals sitting underneath them emanate an influence—presumably some substance—that keeps the young animals in the male state for the long period.[41]

So the final development into male or female is determined by outside influences among these lower animals too. However, the sexual differentiation affects many organs of the body, so that in the end the animal cannot revert in the same way as the *Ophryotrocha* could. Besides bodily structure, the physiological processes of the body and its behavior are also affected by the development of one or the other sex. Of these, the body structure is of course the most rigid, while behavior is the most variable factor. It can happen that even among animals who are indubitably male or female according to their bodily structure, each individual can still display the behavior of both sexes. Even birds, who have no penis and only copulate by pressing the rims of their cloacae firmly against each other, can still copulate inversely, i.e., the female can hop on the male, behave like a male, and copulate. In this case it is possible for a bird to actually fertilize another, as happens among pigeons.

On closer examination, it will become apparent that even among mammals, male and female behavior is often not as precisely demarcated and distributed among different individuals as is normally thought. We tend to connect very definite roles with the concepts of "male" and "female," not only in the act of mating but in every facet of social life. Often we take the idea of roles from our own cultural sphere and transfer it to the animal world without realizing it. In extreme cases this leads to talking about perversities among animals, simply because the observed behavior would be called perverse if it occurred among humans.

The Bighorn sheep (*Ovis canadensis*) offer a good example of how relative male and female behavior can be among mammals. The sheep live in the Rocky Mountains either in small or fairly large herds. The most experienced members lead the herd to the feeding places known to be most favorable in the respective season; these sites can often be separated by up to twenty miles, so that no individual would find them by itself. For this reason alone it is more profitable for the sheep to assemble in herds.

Outside the rutting season, the animals live in herds consisting of males only or of females with their young and a few smaller males. What is curious about these animals is that between the extremes of rams over eight years old and lambs less than a year old one finds every possible transition in age, but no other differences whatsoever. There is no clear distinction of sex; the bodily form, the structure of

Age groups of male mountain sheep, from left to right: 8–16, 6–8, 3–6, 2½, 1½ years of age; far right, a fully grown female with the weakest horns.

the horns, and the color of the coat are the same for both sexes. Since the males become bigger and heavier, the typical female is absent from this pattern. Geist has examined the social behavior of mountain sheep in depth[35] and found that even the males often cannot recognize a female as such. In addition, the females are only of interest to the males in the rutting season.

The social life of these mountain sheep demonstrates a large number of clearly distinct behavioral patterns, such as presentation of horns, pawing with the forelegs, mounting, butting, battle leaps, pursual, sniffing, and baring the lips (*Flehmen*). So the more one is inclined to class behavior patterns according to sexual roles, the more one will be astonished to find that *both* sexes play two roles, either that of the male or that of the young male. Outside the rutting season the females behave like young males, during the rutting season like aggressive older males. The female is in heat only two days a year and will let herself be mounted only if she is defeated by a stronger ram. Subordinate rams behave in the same way. This means that male animals behave aggressively toward subordinate animals, but behave like a female in heat toward their superiors. Females in heat attack rams, females not in heat retreat from attacking rams. Young rams and females in heat automatically prefer the proximity of strong rams with powerful horns. So, day in, day out, the high-ranking rams always have animals around them who behave like females in heat, either because they really are, or because they are inferior males. (If the high-ranking male simply fought them with all his strength, he would also drive away all the females in heat around him and would lose the chance to reproduce.) The strong ram must tolerate this behavior of females in heat, so the lower-ranking rams have a chance of remaining unmolested by their much stronger rivals by camouflaging themselves with the behavior of females in heat. This very aggressive behavior incites high-ranking rams to mount them, which explains why rams also mount lower-ranking members of the same sex. Since young animals and females who are not in heat evade male attacks, one finds herds of female animals and young ones who remain apart from the group of males outside the rutting season. The aggressive behavior is always present, however, in the group of males, above all among low-ranking males; as we have seen, the high-ranking males are obliged to tolerate this. So the group of males offers the rams an opportunity for aggressive and sexual activity. Females who are not in heat avoid both. But when in heat they seek out the groups of rams of their own accord.

So these mountain sheep treat conspecifics differently according to their grade, which is dependent not on sex but on size and ranking order. There is a line of development leading from the lamb to the high-ranking ram, and the female animals (♀) behave exactly as though they were in fact males (♂) whose development was retarded. Since they alternate between being in heat and not in heat, they also alternate between the behavior of a male and that of a young animal several times in the course of their life. This can be shown schematically:

Typical behavior

EVASION	ATTACK	MOUNTING
♂ — lamb ⟶	low-ranking ♂ ⟶	high-ranking ♂
♀ — lamb		

↓

not in heat ♀ ↔ in heat ♀

We can say that the only fully developed mountain sheep are the powerful rams, for they alone, within five to seven years after attaining sexual maturity, reach the final stage of fully mature physical structure and behavior possible to this species. Even when they are sexually mature, the females remain at an early stage of development, corresponding to that of the young ram.

There are examples showing that behavior patterns typical of one sex can also appear as a kind of transitional stage at certain moments in the youth or later development of the other sex among many species of animal. Careful observation will show that this can take different forms even among closely related animals. Half-grown male bull-finches, for instance, display purely female behavior up to the first winter; they make nest-building motions (although the adult male bullfinch does not take part in building the nest) and even utter mating calls. But female bullfinches of the same age do not behave like males. By contrast, both sexes of young tree sparrows display male and female be-havior; one can recognize the males only from their juvenile song. But young tropical finches never exhibit the behavior of the other sex.

In the social behavior of mountain sheep, female be-havior evidently counts as of low rank, male as of high rank. This is not only so among sheep. Among tropical cichlids of species that have clearly differentiated sexual behavior, if one keeps only individuals of the same sex together—females only, for instance—one will always ob-serve that one of the animals, usually the strongest, will act like a male, dig a spawning hole, display, and try to entice the other females there. On the other hand, if one keeps only males together, one of them will soon occupy a spawning territory and attack the others violently. One of the at-tacked can then assume the female role, follow the dis-playing animal to his spawning hole, and even make spawning motions there. In the case of a rather unusual cichlid, *Tilapia macrochir*, whose males deposit the sperm wrapped up as though in a parcel (spermatophore) when the female has liberated her eggs,[121] two males were ob-served "spawning" with each other, one wearing the male display dress, the other in female dress. Naturally neither of the two spawned, but both deposited their spermatophores.

It is fairly common in the animal kingdom for female sexual behavior to occur only in connection with submission, as with mountain sheep. Of course this is not apparent until one has come to know the animals well and has let both sexes live together at will. It is fairly rare today for us to allow our domestic animals to mate freely; usually man intervenes to control mating, in extreme cases by means of artificial insemination. Some breeds of domestic animal, such as highly bred dogs and horses, are incapable of copulating at all without the helping hand of man. But the owner also keeps a watchful eye on less highly bred horses, often enclosing the mares in a paddock by themselves and only bringing them a selected stallion at certain times. Unpleasant incidents can occur during this kind of "free herd-copulation," because the mare of highest rank takes over the role of stallion and attacks the new, genuine stallion without mercy or keeps all "his" mares from him. Among monkeys kept in captivity, if the only old male is absent due to death or accident, a fully grown female can take his place; this occurs particularly among macaque monkeys. Even if there is a lower-ranking male in the group dominated by this female, he will not often manage to mate with the female of higher rank than himself, so that she remains without progeny for the time being.

The fact that subordinate animals often play the role of female can sometimes lead to curious behavior. Among cichlids, we have often seen the loser give up his poster-colored display dress (which can happen in the space of a few seconds thanks to the physiological color changes peculiar to these fish) after a violent conflict between two males. Yet he does not follow this by trying to escape from the aquarium; rather he swims after the victor. This would seem the silliest thing he could do, since he risked a new thrashing. In fact it is the best thing he could do; for to pursue the territory owner without threatening him is typical female behavior; at most it incites the victor to court and lead the loser to his nest.

Naturally, subordinate females also play the female role,

often in very intensive fashion. This is why a male hama-dryas baboon always achieves success if he violently attacks and bites a female who strays from the band. Afterward he simply turns around and goes back, and the rep-rimanded female follows him closely "at heel." Here again one could ask why she did not make a wide berth around the "angry" male after his attack or even try to flee from him. In fact, in such cases the aggression of the highest-ranking animal can promote the cohesion of the group, even when it is not directed against outsiders but against members of the group.

The same, incidentally, applies to the parent-child bond. Young ducklings who follow their mother cannot be pre-vented from doing so by punishment disincentives—they will only follow all the more eagerly. Admittedly this is an experimental situation and the punishment is not meted out by the mother. But similar factors seem to me to play a role in the weaning efforts of monkey mothers; they actually turn aggressive toward their young, but they have little success at first and are only successful later because the young monkey eventually joins up with other members of the group, particularly with its contemporaries.

We can see how closely related aggression, ranking be-havior, and sexual behavior are by observing how easily one can turn into the other. The "furious" copulation of various mammals, for instance sea elephants, baboons, macaques, pit-tailed macaques, and chimpanzees, is well known. In each case an enraged male mounts any member of the same species in sight at the time and makes copu-latory motions or actually copulates with it. The animals also do this if man puts them into a state of furious ex-citement, for example, if a man shows a caged monkey a delicacy but does not give it to him. Chimpanzees react by storming around the cage in a fury, with erect penis. Rage copulations do not occur if the animals are put in a state of fear. So aggression can easily turn into mating behavior among males. By contrast, females in a sexual mood take cover in "coyness" toward the male; they wait or come back if the male does not follow and incite him to pursue and mount them by repeatedly fleeing a short distance away. We will discuss in detail on pp. 206f. how subordinate males often act out female mating behavior in face of a higher-ranking conspecific.

5. Behavior Precedes Body Structure

It is easier to reply to the question why male sexual behavior tends more toward aggression, whereas female sexual behavior is more closely bound up with submission or flight if one rephrases it as follows: What has male sexual behavior to do with aggression, female sexual behavior with flight? "Aggression" derives from the Latin verb *aggredior*, which in English means to go up to, to approach, to attack. Among very simple organisms, which are bisexual but whose sex cannot be determined externally, it is the individual who moves toward another to copulate with it who is considered male. We have mentioned the flagellate algae as an example of this (see p. 24). On this level, then, it is all simply a question of definition. We call the more aggressive individual the male. But higher organisms no longer consist merely of one cell, which is also the gamete, but have a body that is clearly separated from the gametes. In the context of reproduction, this body can help to bring the gametes as close together as possible.

Sponges and many molluscs draw in the sperms with the currents of water; so the eggs remain "in place," i.e., in the mother animal, while the sperm have to travel. The sperm will be more likely to reach their destination if the animal does not simply liberate them anywhere but brings them close to the egg cells, which are either within the mother animal or liberated too. In the latter case eggs and sperm must be ejected at the same time; this is achieved by a synchronization of the sexual animals that involves their hormones, senses, and locomotive abilities.

The marine ragworm (*Nereis*) rises to the surface of the North Sea in the nights around April 15. Then the worms assemble and eject eggs and sperms en masse. At this time their eyes, antennae, and other sensory organs also grow much larger. After this reproductive journey, they die. By contrast, the palolo worm (*Eunice*), a bristleworm living in coral-reef hollows of the tropical seas, ties off the rear half of its body where the male or female sexual products are located. This rear end leaves the front of the body, swims to the surface of the water to meet other such independent body halves and to empty out its sexual products, and then dies. The remaining front half, however, regenerates a new rear end. This process is synchronized according to the phases of the moon (during these predictable lunar phases the Samoans collect great quantities of the swarming segments of worm; they regard them as a delicacy). The main segment of the worm with head and brain takes no part whatsoever in sexual life. The tied-off rear end of a closely related worm (*Autolytus*) does not die off but regenerates a new head, thus becoming an independent new individual. So nature has many different ways of bringing the gametes together. And anyone interested in the natural laws of "copulation" and "reproduction" in general must have some knowledge of these processes. Since there are something over a million animal species in creation, of which only 6 percent are vertebrates, the so-called lower animals must also be taken into account.

Water is a fairly good method of transport for sperms, but many are still lost, and if different species of animals liberate eggs at the same time, too many sperms will meet up with the wrong eggs. So even marine animals have "invented" copulation, which later became very important for terrestrial animals. In copulation, the actual act of mating or coition, the sperms are once again brought to the egg cells: The entire male animal seeks out a female and deposits the sperms on her, externally or by introducing them into her body. The male marine horse-hair worm (*Gordius aquaticus*, found in European streams) deposits the sperm beside the female genital aperture and in the course of two days the sperm wander into her sexual passages of their own accord. The dog leech (*Erpobdella*) deposits the sperm, packed in spermatophores, anywhere on its partner. A fluid from the packet of sperm eats its way through skin and muscles into the cavity of the body, where the sperm then swirl around. Some reach the eggs, but most are eaten up beforehand by resistance cells as though they were invading viruses. Among velvet worms (*Peripatus*), who are land dwellers, the male crawls onto the female without any preliminaries and attaches a spermatophore anywhere. The resistance cells of the female eat a hole into her body and into the wall of the spermatophores below the place where they are attached, so that again the sperm can swim around in the blood of the female until they reach the ovaries where they fertilize the eggs. In spite of their curious form of copulation, these animals are by no means primitive; for instance, the young develop inside the female, are nourished by the mother through the placenta and finally, fairly large and well-developed by now, are born alive.

Bedbugs (*Cimex*) copulate in a similar fashion. The male pierces a hole into the female's back by means of a spike situated in front of his penis and ejaculates the sperm into the hole. Many other flat bugs do the same—although the females have well-developed sexual organs which, however, they never use for copulation. Instead, the females have a special tissue on the part of their body where the male is most likely to pierce; this tissue absorbs the sperm and then conducts them on into the bloodstream. In fact one bug, called *Xylocoris*, finally evolved a new aperture, of complex structure, on the female's back, into which the male copulates.[14]

The ancestors of these animals once mated "normally," using the appropriate female sexual aperture. Then a sexual aberration occurred among some species that would have had to be termed unnatural at first, with regard to the existing copulatory organs of the two partners. In this case, however, evolution did not eradicate the aberration; on the contrary, it became normalized. Even the animal's bodily structure adapted itself to "extragenital copulation." Comparative studies of variously specialized species now enable us to reconstruct this piece of phylogenetic evolution without too much trouble. If anything was unnatural here, it was our habit of thinking in static norms. *One simply cannot deduce, on the basis of body structure and the forms of organs, binding norms for the future behavior patterns for which these organs are used;* nor, therefore, for example, can one assert that ventroventral copulation is the only form of copulation natural to man *on the basis of the site of the organs.* (Incidentally, the ability of sperm ejected into the female's abdominal cavity outside her sexual passages to find their way to the eggs and to fertilize them has not disappeared even among the most highly developed animals. For instance, this "intraperitoneal insemination" can occur among hens, rabbits, and cattle.)

6. The Development of Genital Organs

The example of bugs taught us that changes in behavior can entail changes in body structure. This is not only so for bugs. Normally we imagine that copulation occurs when the male introduces a penis into the sexual aperture of the female. But totally different kinds of copulation and genital organs also occur. Whether one calls it mating or not when the male deposits a packet of sperm on the outside of the female is a question of definition. This is in fact a borderline case; for although it is very common in the animal kingdom to deposit spermatophores, the accompanying circumstances can be very different. Among beetlemites (*Oribatei*) and certain springtails (*Collembola*), the males deposit large quantities of stemmed spermatophores anywhere on the ground, with no relation to the female, so that they look like fungoid growths. If the female comes upon one of these "gardens of love" she will pick a few spermatophores with her cloacal aperture. Even when they meet, males and females make no sign of recognition. But with another kind of springtail (*Dicyrtomina*), the male at least takes cognizance of the female. He deposits his drops of stemmed sperm around the female like a stockade, so that she is bound to happen upon one of them when she moves. The male bristly millipede (*Pselaphognate-Polyxenoidea*), one of the smallest groups of millipedes, deposits its sperm drops without coming into contact with the female; but he spins "guidelines" of threads that catch the attention of any female in the vicinity and lead her to the sperm drops. The fifty-legged centipede (*Lithobius*), the bristletail (*Machilidae*), and the silverfish (*Lepisma*) have evolved very enterprising "web games" that help guide the female to the spermatophore—they are in no way less complex than the foreplay to pairing and copulating of higher animals.[98]

Among vertebrates, the males of our native newts also deposit spermatophores in front of the females in their pools in springtime. Then they entice the females to crawl over the spermatophores by waggling their tail, thereby directing a scent, and at the same time walking slowly backward. Scorpions grasp their female by the pincers, deposit a spermatophore on the ground and then, moving backward, pull the female over it so that she can pick up the spermatophore with her cloacal aperture. In this form of copulation, the sexual apertures of the animals do not come into contact; yet the sperm reach the eggs by way of the female's sexual passages.

There are other methods too. The males of the small, blind garden centipede *Scutigerella* also deposit a stemmed drop of sperm. The female, who encounters it at some stage, bites the drop off its stem, but instead of swallowing the sperm, she stores it in special cheek pouches. Then, when she lays eggs, she takes each individual egg into her mouth and smears it with a small portion of semen. The females of the small, segmented marine tarpon (*Megalops*) bite off the sperm-bearing segments of the males who swarm around them, and devour them; the sperm penetrate through the gut, reach the body cavity, and then swim over to the eggs and fertilize them. To ask whether or not this can be called copulation is not as important as to realize that many paths can lead to fertilization and that in each case definite behavioral traits determine the direction in which organs and physiological processes will evolve in order to make fertilization possible. This is so even if the female is "snappish" and eats parts of the male. Among vertebrates, a number of cichlids (e.g., *Haplochromis*) have evolved a method of oral insemination similar to that of the *Scutigerella* I described. The females take the eggs into their mouth to hatch them before the males come to inseminate them. Now, the males have colorful egg "dummies" on the pelvic fins, and the females try to take these "painted" eggs into their mouth too. At the same moment, the male ejaculates and the female, trying vainly to get at the egg snares, instead receives the sperm in her mouth; the sperm joins the eggs in her mouth cavity and subsequently inseminates them. Here too I have been able to show by comparative studies how a "behavioral anomaly" is not corrected in nature but compensated by the modification of other behavior patterns and organs; it becomes a new norm.[120, 125]

In every case where the sexual partners come into direct contact during copulation, which parts of their body will turn into copulating organs depends entirely on the partners' relative positions and on their behavior. Cuttlefish and octopuses mate with the partners facing one another; the mouth areas of the *sepia* touch but the octopuses sit far apart. In both cases, the male deposites a spermatophore directly on the tentacle (to the left of his abdomen) that has been specially modified for this, and then uses this same tentacle to introduce it into the female cloacal aperture. The males of most spiders ejaculate a drop of sperm onto a small web especially constructed for this purpose. Then they take the sperm into a leg converted into a copulating organ—the so-called "pedipalp" or mandible antenna—seek out a female, and pump the sperm into her cloacal aperture with the pedipalp. So in effect they copulate "with their hands." Among fish, the sexual partners of egg-laying toothed carps (*Cyprinidae*) synchronize very carefully and then eject eggs and sperm at the same time. During this process the female rolls up the front part of her anal fin into a cone and puts it around the anal fin of the male; the eggs and sperm are kept together in this channel. In a related group of toothed carps (*Poecilidae*), which give birth to live young, the males probably rolled up the anal fin originally too. The males of species still in existence today have anal fins that are fairly specialized in this direction. Their few remaining finrays are folded against one another during the mating time, and this produces a groove just in front of the sexual aperture on which a ventral fin can lie like a lid. The whole serves as a copulating organ, whose tip is introduced into the female sexual aperture. The copulating organ of the Southeast Asian toothed carp (*Phallostethidae*) is made up of parts of the thorax and shoulder girdles and the first pair of ribs. The males of the shark and rock have formed copulating organs out of the rear part of the pairs of ventral fins, and some species of grope (*Scorpaenidae*) and *Brotulidae* have a "penis," i.e., a fleshy extension of the genital papilla, which they use for copulation.

Quite independently from one another, very different groups of animals have evolved a penis of the kind we find so normal as the male organ of copulation. For instance, while the dog leech I described deposits sperm packets on the outside of the female, the medicinal leech (*Hirudo*) has a penis for copulating with the female; during copulation, the couple lies abdomen against abdomen. The whirl-worm has a penis, and so do snails, who are hybrids. Some mites deposit spermatophores; others transfer them to the female sexual aperture with their mandible antennae. Others again have a penis. The mite *Pyemotis*, which feeds on caterpillars, gives birth to live young who are already sexually mature. The young males remain attached to the mother after birth, sting her, suck out some of her body juices, and then wait for a young female. They take no notice of other brothers who are born, but if a sister should appear in the genital duct, one of the brothers will grab her, drag her out, and copulate immediately.[52] Among spiders, the harvestman (*Opiliones*) has a penis, and ventro-ventral copulation is typical of some species. A very complex penis structure and a similarly complicated female genital organ is often so characteristic of higher insects that taxonomists use these organs to differentiate the species. In the great fish kingdom, there are also a few species with penis (see above); among amphibians there is at the most one case, namely the African tree toad (*Nectophrynoïdes*). These are the only amphibian toads to bring fully formed young into the world; but no one has seen them mate yet. Reptiles, lizards, snakes, tortoises, and crocodiles usually have a fairly specialized penis. An exception is the famous tuatara (*Sphenodon*), a member of a very ancient order of reptiles. During copulation, tuatarae press the rims of their cloaca firmly against each other. Most birds copulate in the same way, for only very few (e.g., the ostrich and the goose) have a penis. Male mammals all have a penis, although its form and structure can vary a great deal.

This list suffices to make it clear that the penis was very often "invented" as an organ of copulation in the animal kingdom, even among higher vertebrates. The copulating organs of tortoises, crocodiles, and mammals have one common origin; those of lizards and snakes have another. The latter have a double penis, made up of two halves that act separately and are inverted for copulation like the finger of a glove. In terms of the methods of copulation described above, all this shows that the male organ of copulation is also a subsequently evolved, auxiliary structure, which appeared on those animals whose behavior during the act of mating called for it. Again, body structure follows in the wake of behavior. Accordingly, the homogenous term "penis" refers at most to a same function in each case; in fact, the organ of copulation evolved out of quite different existing bodily organs and in entirely different ways. This is why it can also have various secondary functions. Among some flatworms, the penis comes out of the oral aperture, is equipped with spikes and poison glands and, besides copulation, is also used to catch prey (e.g., among the *Prorhynchus*). Some types of flatworm introduce the penis into the female sexual aperture, others sting the female with it anywhere on her body. This method has also been evolved by several other species in the animal kingdom.

The naïve notion that animal behavior conforms to the organs the respective animals evolve must therefore be corrected as follows: the evolution of organs conforms to *existing behavior*. This is just as easy to show for many other organs besides the sexual ones. Hence we can deduce the following very important general law: *Behavior patterns are the pacemakers of evolution.*

The relative strength and rank of the two sexes have played an important part in determining the mating position that was adopted. The superior pursuer mounted his partner from behind. The differing copulating positions of many lower animals have not yet been studied in terms of relative rank, but such studies would no doubt teach us a great deal more. Many female insects sit on the male during copulation. As far as mammals and men are concerned, they do not copulate in a certain way because they have a penis, but they have a penis because the mating behavior of their penisless ancestors foretold the evolution of such an organ. By virtue of this, the male genital organ has taken over all the functions involving the behavior that gave rise to the evolution of this organ. This is why the penis of some flatworms is used for catching prey. What functions the penis of mammals and men can fulfill besides copulation will be discussed in the following chapter. Here we need only point out that it is wrong to assert, as people sometimes do, that only man mates in the ventro-ventral position with the partners facing each other. In fact this position already occurs among lower animals, such as leeches, harvestmen, centipedes, North Sea shrimps, and common crabs; among fish such as the ray, among mammals such as the whale, and among monkeys such as dwarf chimpanzees or bonobos (*Pan* [*Satyricus*] *paniscus*). However, it is very likely that man is the only one to use this mating position—which was no doubt made possible to him for other biological reasons—in order to strengthen the profound personal relationship between the sexes.

7. Apparent Homosexual Behavior

In the context of ranking order, sexual behavior patterns are often independent of the sex of the participants. It can sometimes happen that female animals will mount each other, just as males do. But the concept of homosexuality is misplaced in this case, although it is often used for it—perhaps because the observer is not fully aware of the circumstances that have led to such behavior. We should only speak of homosexuality if an individual clearly prefers conspecifics of the same sex within a sexual context. The word "prefers" is important here, for it presumes that conspecifics of the opposite sex would be just as accessible to the individual. If this is not the case, we could be dealing with a so-called blocked drive, which is worked off on the wrong object for lack of anything better. Here too the precise choice of word is important: If no conspecific of different sex is available, the observed homosexual activity *can* be an ersatz satisfaction of a drive—but it can also be genuine homosexuality. Under these circumstances, it is difficult, if at all possible, to decide. It is equally difficult to interpret an individual case of apparent "homosexual" behavior exactly. Once again it could simply be a question of rank demonstration. Here, as in every realm, to use a concept carelessly only creates confusion. In the framework of our theme, we are not concerned with the interpretation of the behavior patterns we have just discussed; rather it is a question of describing regularly recurrent types of behavior.

From what we have already said it becomes clear that

when male baboons mount each other, this need not be homosexual behavior but could also be a demonstration of

"Playful" mounting between young hamadryas baboons.

rank. The same applies to female baboons who mount each other. When a subordinate male assumes the role of a female in face of the victor, because this role is also a sign

Copulation of the hamadryas baboon and (right) a superior baboon mounting an adult subordinate one as a gesture of dominance.

of submission, we are dealing once again with a demonstration of rank and not with homosexuality. The examples of relative sexuality described earlier are not instances of homosexuality either.

Similarly, a high-ranking female hamadryas baboon mounts a lower-ranking female.

Apparent homosexual behavior can also occur when the active individual cannot distinguish male from female, either because of special contingencies or on principle. That animals can make mistakes, even in questions of sex, will surprise no one. There are in fact cases where the sexes really are indistinguishable. This may seem nonsensical if one starts from the assumption that it is essential for an animal to find its sexual partner and to be able to distinguish it from a conspecific, at least during the mating season and for those animals who copulate, i.e., actually seek out a partner rather than simply liberate their sexual products together in a great swarm. Among the already mentioned flat bugs, the species *Afrocimex* proves that there are other possibilities too. These animals have evolved a form of extragenital copulation in which the male bores a hole through the back of the female with his genital apparatus and deposits the sperm there. He also treats all other males in the same way, i.e., the males copulate in this way with all members of the same species. Their ancestors could at least feel or tell by the genitals whether their partner was male or female at the beginning of copulation. But today these bugs bypass the female genitals during copulation and this obviates the possibility of control. Now if the male produces enough sperm, it may happen that he simply distributes them among all the available members of his own species—the *Hesperoctenes* species even distributes them among the larvae of both sexes. This means that the wastage is greater, but it also means that the females get as many sperm as they require to fertilize their eggs. But it seems that this is still not the whole story. Just like the females, the males too have a special body tissue under their back, which absorbs the sperm and conducts them on into the body.[14] Naturally, the sperm never reach ovaries in the body of the male but are distributed throughout, even in the legs and head. Presumably this copulation among males is not simply a breakdown in nature but has some special value. Further investigation is necessary here too.

Bugs are only one example of how extravagant organisms are with their sperm. Egg cells are carefully stored, not because they correspond to a higher level of being but simply as a matter of economy, for the egg cells are often full of nourishing substances for the embryo; these substances must eventually be mustered by the mother's body and "cost" more than the plain gamete. Sperm, by contrast, have no "material value" worth mentioning. Our native red stag uses ejaculated fluid (which almost certainly contains a large number of sperm) in order to mark out his territory. He spurts it on his coat and antlers with erect penis and then smears streaks onto twigs and branches as scent marks![11] The North American wapiti or elk (*Cervus canadensis*) also uses sperm for marking. If two territorial neighbors do this, it is, of course, not homosexual behavior.

No more can one call the curious behavior of the sperm of South American marsupials such as the opossum homosexual: The sperm of these animals lay themselves one against the other in pairs as though they wanted to copulate before they are brought into the female sexual passages. The biological significance of this mating of sperm is not known.

8. The Phallus as a Sign of Rank and Threat

Besides copulation, the mammal penis is also used for urinating, and urine in turn quite frequently serves to mark out a territory. In the case of social animals, the marking out of territory is always the affair of the highest-ranking animal. We can determine their rank by the degree of frequency with which, for instance, olingos (*Bassarycion*) mark out their habitats at certain points. If one removes the highest-ranking animal, the next will move into his place and also take over his typical frequency of marking. But animals do not only mark out territory; a stallion, for example, marks the pile of droppings of a mare, and some species mark the subordinate member of the same species or the female they are courting directly. The Asian marten (*Nyctereutes*) sprays his female with his urine, and wild rabbits, porpoises, scaly anteaters (*Manis*), the large Patagonian Cavy (*Dolichotis*), the acouchy (*Myoprocta*), and the North American porcupine (*Erethizon*) spurt a powerful spray of urine onto their partner with erect penis. In given cases the partner shoots back, so that a brief urine-spraying duel can develop.

The fact that the penis is erect for this suggests a common behavioral root for urine marking and copulation; for marking, the urine is usually ejaculated sporadically too, while for simple urinating it flows regularly. Marking paths with urine is known among half monkeys, such as slim lorises (*Loris*), slow lorises (*Nycticebus*) and lemurs; the mon-

A young squirrel monkey presents its genitals in order
to impress.

goose lemur also marks his female with urine. These animals are predominantly scent-oriented and most of them are
nocturnal. But the higher monkeys are diurnal and largely
orient themselves with their eyes. This is why the erect
penis becomes a direct signal rather than the scent marks
emanating from it. We can follow the transition very well
in the case of South American squirrel monkeys (*Saimiri*).
These monkeys impress one another by straddling their
hind legs and displaying their erect genitalia. This gesture
serves to threaten individuals foreign to the group—including their own mirror images—and as the most important
demonstration of rank within the group.[90] Occasionally a
little drop of urine is also emitted in the process, but it is
not significant. The same display of the genitals also occurs
among capuchin monkeys (*Cebus*). Urine emission disappears entirely among the even more highly developed old
world monkeys in this situation, but the penis is very clearly
displayed. Since these monkeys—unlike many lemurs—no
longer follow scent traces in fixed territories but often
wander about freely in nomadic fashion, they use genital
display as a demonstration toward others of the current

Doguera baboon "on guard."

boundaries of the group. The males openly sit "on guard," often turning their back to the group. The penis is extended far out, and this alone makes it very conspicuous, as with savannah baboons (*Papio*), whose penis is scarcely visible when drawn in. The genitals of African monkeys of the genus *Cercopithecus* have become extremely colorful for this signal function: the penis can turn bright red, the scrotum a luminous blue. The color combination can vary from species to species and it is one of the brightest body colors found among mammals. This use of the genitals is not directly related to the sexual drive. It can occur independently of sexual behavior patterns and is occasionally to be seen among, for instance, young squirrel monkeys a few days old in the appropriate social situation.

We also find an emphatic exhibition of the male genitals without sexual connotations among humans. Greek hoplites and Etruscan warriors wore greaves, helmets, and breastplates, but left their genitals uncovered. When they had slain an enemy, they cut off his penis. Haberland still found this custom, which used to be widespread, in southern Ethiopia a few years ago.[39]

The penis as trophy of victory was soon replaced by images. Even today almost all the tribes of southern Ethiopia wear a simple phallic ornament made of light shining

Phallic brow ornament made of metal worn by a southern Ethiopian as insignia of rank.

metal on their brow; it is called "Kalatsha" and is thought the most important of ritual objects. Originally it was a sign that the wearer had killed an adult male opponent and was now allowed to start a family. Most of the Galla tribes adopted it as an insignia of rank that only high priests and holders of special honors were allowed to wear. The king of the great southern Ethiopian kingdom, Kaffa, used to wear on his brow a three-part phallus, which was at first interpreted as a crown. Divinities of very high rank, such as Ammun Rê in Egypt, Tlaloc in Mexico, and Shiva in India are also represented with erect phallus.

Besides being displayed on a man or even on his hut as an insignia of rank, we find the phallus on the phallic figures that are described as ithyphallic (i.e., with erect phallus). The most familiar are probably the ithyphallic stone hermes that Herodotus described as an ancient tradition. One still finds figures of the same type, worked in wood, on the Sunda Islands today. From exact details of the sites of the finds and from reports by the respective peoples or their priests, as well as from the prayers of consecration and supplication connected with the erection and veneration of such figures, the following amazing coincidences with the monkeys "on guard" have emerged:

1. These figures are guards. They stand at the entrance of villages, houses, and temples as well as on graves and property boundaries.
2. They always stand with their back to the guarded object and display their genitals to the outside.
3. Often the phallus is painted in conspicuous colors, for instance red.
4. These guards protect against demons of various kinds, against earthly and supernatural enemies, and against the spirits of the dead, i.e., always against beings whom man treats as members of his own kind. On wooden figures of this sort, which are still made in southern Bali, the threatening phallus is accompanied by a clearly defined threatening expression.

In no case I know of are these guards aimed against predators' vermin. Instead they are opposed to those spirits and demons whom man holds responsible for the appearance of vermin and animals that damage crops, which is why they also stand on fields. In Bali, ithyphallic straw figures were placed on the rice fields. But the further the old function of the phallus as sign of rank and threat fell into disuse, the more these guards against threats to fertility were made into direct promoters of fertility and symbols of fertility, especially since the threatening organ is also a reproductive organ and this reproductive function is familiar to man.

Left: straw guardian the height of a man from a rice field near Sanur. Center: wood-carving of a guard ("Mo-emmedi"), height 44 cm.; both made in Bali in 1968. Right: wooden house guard ("Siraha"), height 150 cm., from Nias.

The phallic signal acquired this significance from the observer. The same applies to the very simplified guard figures on which arms and legs, and eventually even the rump and head, were often left out, so that the phallus alone remained as a "mushroom stone." Sometimes, secondary human outlines were added on the shaft, and this is the origin of the naked stone figures with "hat."

The more abstract shapes are allowed to become, the more objects we will find that seem to resemble them for various reasons and also have a phallic effect. Menhirs, monoliths, obelisks, Etruscan tombstones, Islamic prayer towers, and southern German bulbous spires have all been

Left: Korean "stone god," height 150 cm.; Right: stone
sculpture from Guatemala, height 31 cm.

interpreted as phallic. Recent tests and spontaneous oral
accounts showed that many men see lipsticks as phallic
symbols; accordingly, lipstick advertisements have deliberately been rendered more sexual. Even psychoanalysts are
in danger of overlooking the fact that the phallus has two
meanings—which are biologically related but can be separated: Primarily the phallus is a symbol of power; it only
became a symbol of fertility secondarily, on the roundabout
route of its possible associations in the human mind. So it
would be one-sided to relate the phallus only to the sexual
realm. Many exhibitionists are disturbed not in their sexual
life but in their integration into society; they do not want
to incite their opponent to sexual activity but to frighten
him.[81]

We do not know how far the conspicuous penis guards
of primitive peoples who go naked (e.g., in New Guinea
and the Congo) also serve as a symbol of rank or defense
against spirits. What *is* known is that in Indonesia the phallus is used to drive away evil spirits; island dwellers who

believe that wind and waterspouts are provoked by evil spirits take their bared phallus in their hand and point it in the relevant direction to drive away the evil spirit.[101]

There are countless other details that could be recorded on this theme; I have noted some of them in other books.[122, 124] Here I am only concerned with showing how a comparison of the behavior of as many species as possible can also throw light on the darker sides of human behavior.

9. Social Stress

Whenever the problem of overpopulation is raised, the question of food also moves into the foreground. This is justified insofar as the food supply sets a definite limit to population. There have been extensive calculations concerning this limit, and efforts—usually based on theoretic considerations—are being made to find out just how far the limit can be stretched if all the food reserves known to man are exploited. In addition, attempts to raise the yield of grain and other crops are being made as are efforts to make seaweed, plankton, and other unusual plants palatable to man. This too can stretch the limit but it postpones the problem rather than solving it. Perhaps we can afford to do so if we hope to acquire enough knowledge during this period of respite to be able to find a real, final solution to the problem of overpopulation.

But we cannot afford to overlook the fact that the density of population also has another limit, and one that is perhaps lower than the "starvation line." Men are not machines that can be crowded together as closely as the electricity supply permits—always taking care, here too, to dissipate the work heat. Unlike machines, men get on one another's nerves, not only when a density that entails food problems has been reached, but much sooner. This is another of the many things man has in common with animals.

Many people are, no doubt, familiar with the very different effects of full and empty buses. In an empty bus, the few passengers distribute themselves in an entirely "un-forced" way, sometimes leaving a whole row of seats free, look quite at ease on the whole, and react to one another or the conductor in a fairly friendly fashion. In a crowded bus, free seats are, of course, limited, and the passengers look much less comfortable and react in a much more ir-ritable way. Many try to ignore their closest neighbors as far as possible, as though the only resort were to take as little notice as possible of the fact that the neighbor has already moved much too close for comfort. And yet it would be very easy to supply all these passengers with sand-wiches on a longer journey. One could transport more pas-sengers in airplanes if the passengers allowed themselves to be herded together more densely. The first class is not more expensive because there is more to eat but primarily because everyone has more room. So we do not pay only for food but also for the distance between us and our neigh-bor. The same applies to the constant demand for living space. The higher the pressure of the population density, the more "money power" will have to be spent on keeping one's neighbor at a distance.

Hutt and Vaizey have made careful studies of the effects of overcrowding in playrooms on children between the ages of three and eight.[46] Each child was observed in three playgroups of different sizes, with up to five playmates, with six to ten, or with more than ten other children. The playroom was always the same size, nine meters by six meters. The tests showed that the number of social con-tacts between the children decreased the more densely the room was "populated," although this was when there were in fact the most opportunities for social contacts. So the children avoided one another. When there were more than eleven children, quarreling increased noticeably, as, inci-dentally, did the abuse and destruction of toys, which is interpreted as an open expression of aggressive tendencies worked off on the toy instead of the neighbor. This indicated that man has certain regulating mechanisms that are dependent on population density and influence his behavior. It is striking that children with brain damage are much more likely to react aggressively under the same conditions, and they have a clear advantage if they play together with normal children in an overcrowded room.

In a quite general context, people feel distinctly uncomfortable when they cannot keep the desired distance from their neighbors. What is this sense of discomfort? Various kinds of experiments on social animals in recent years have suggested the kinds of factors that could be responsible. At least the tests showed which organic functions are altered by population density. There are far more of these than one might have supposed. The organic changes also show what aspects of behavior, hormones, growth, maturation, etc., are interdependent and consequently also affected in extreme situations. But it is not even necessary to wait for extremes; all these functions are always affected to some degree, no matter under which conditions the living thing happens to live at the moment, whether alone, with a few of its own kind, or with very many. Since we have no reason to assume that man can escape these effects, we should ask ourselves how far our present behavior is dependent on such environmental influences, rather than proceed from potential future conditions.

Tests on various living things, plants as well as animals, have shown that under natural conditions the size of a population regulates itself automatically. "Automatically" here means with the assistance of predators, infections, lack of food, etc., i.e., by methods that man likes to describe as "cruel." It is known, for example, that in the so-called "mouse years," when mice multiply at an unusually high rate, mouse-eaters also bring forth more young, so that the mice are under greater enemy pressure. Where man sees to the mass increase of an individual species, as in the great pine plantations, there is great danger that the corresponding enemies, here the pine-eaters, will soon gain the upper hand. Predators and parasites could be included in the general concept of "enemy" here. But these enemies do not gain unlimited power either, since they themselves begin to perish when their victims decrease in number.

No living thing can multiply to an unlimited extent. Each great tit must find an insect approximately every two and a half seconds, even in winter, to cover its food requirements. So in places where there are few insects, correspondingly few great tits can survive. Many animals mark out territories for themselves and defend them against their own kind; thus they create a "garden" for themselves from which they can draw their food supply.

This has been well documented for the willow ptarmigan (*Lagopus lagopus*) of Scotland.[28] From autumn to the following summer, the cocks defend territories in which each cock tolerates only one hen. These territories are situated in areas of heathland, for the ptarmigans eat the berries and shoots of the plants there. If one removes the territory owners, for instance by shooting them, they are soon replaced by animals who were previously outside the heathland. So there are "reserve cocks." But not in summer. Individuals who have no territory have no chance of surviving until the next autumn or of reproducing. The only thing, of course, that prevents them from so doing, is the lucky owners of territory. So they are by no means sick or ailing individuals who could not defend a territory in any case or who are on the mortality list. On the other hand, the yield per unit area does in fact influence the size of a territory. When some areas of heath were made to yield more by the use of artificial manure, the willow ptarmigan cocks were satisfied with smaller territories, which meant that more cocks could settle on the same area and begin to breed. So the food supply does not directly affect the population density in this case; indeed, it would be impractical if all the animals who could not eat their fill simply died. As long as all the ptarmigans have to fight for the little food available, they will at least all receive a little; but perhaps they would all get too little, and then none would survive in the end. So it is more advantageous to the species to ensure the support of the territory owners by a system of territories and to sacrifice only those individuals who have no "real estate" to support them. Admittedly this often seems cruel, because each individual "egoistically" sees to its own needs and—from the human point of view, of course—is therefore responsible for the death of inferior rivals.

But this social behavior is important to the preservation of the species. And it sets limits to the population density. One cannot make an unlimited number of ptarmigans breed, even on extremely well-fertilized areas of heath. Even in the Land of Cockaigne, not as many common or brown rats would reach adulthood as there is room for. This was tested by making an abundant food and water supply available to a group of brown rats living in a large enclosure. Although eventually one could have expected a population of five thousand young rats, the group did not reach a size of more than 150. Another example: If two pairs of chaffinches are kept in a cage, only one will breed in spite of good feeding. The reasons for such "population regulations" were studied on various animal species in recent years. What the animals suffer from, although they have enough to eat, is called stress. The factors that produce stress are described by some researchers as stressors. In general, stress is characterized by the fact that it can be elicited by many different causes, for instance cold, loss of blood, infection, overpopulation, etc. This suggests that stress is a generalized, unspecific reaction on the part of the organism. If we limit our considerations of stress to the reaction provoked by members of the same species—although it could equally well be provoked by something else—we can speak of "social stress." It has been found that all stress is characterized by the fact that the suprarenal gland cortex produces more hormones than usual, which means that there are fewer growth, thyroid, and sex hormones in the body than in the normal state. The effects of this on population increase have been chiefly tested on mice, rats, rabbits, and tree shrews, because these animals can be kept in captivity and bred so easily.

The tree shrew (*Tupaia*) is a very interesting animal from Southeast Asia, whom we shall come back to in another context (see p. 162). It has proved a very good test subject for the problem under discussion here since it allows one to determine the effects of stress externally. Accordingly one can test the same individuals in different situations. For the other species we have mentioned, we only know of inner signs of stress so far; so one has to kill the individuals and examine their organs, which means that each animal can only be tested once. But every disturbance to the tree shrew makes its tail hairs stand on end, so that the tail becomes conspicuously bushy (normally these hairs lie flat so that the tail looks smooth and slender). D. von Holst worked out elaborate tests[44] that demonstrated that the bristling of the tail hair is evidence of a general excitement typical of stress that can be elicited by any kind of disturbance such as sudden noise, the sight of an unknown object, battle with its own species, capture by the test organizer, etc. Each tree shrew bristles its tail hairs for a certain percentage of the twelve-hour day, and this value remains equal for months, as long as the animal lives in the respective situation. Every change in its environment leads to a new "bristling value" of the tail hair, which again remains constant for the duration of the new situation. If an animal is placed in a cage with an unknown conspecific of the same sex, a short battle will ensue, ending with the submission of one of the animals. From then on the two rivals behave almost the same, but their tail-bristling values differ considerably: The victor almost never bristles his tail, while the loser bristles his almost all day but stops if the victor is removed from the cage.

Von Holst has been able to discover the following connections by dint of careful comparative studies: Young animals who have a high tail-bristling value evidently grow more slowly than their brothers or sisters in an undisturbed environment. Even with adult animals, the body weight varies with the tail-bristling value; if this value rises by about 60 percent, the animal can lose a third of its weight within a few days. Adults regain their original weight again when the disturbance ceases; but young animals, whose growth beyond puberty was inhibited by disturbance, never reach the typical adult body weight and remain lighter. Maximal excitement (indicated by continual bristling) always leads to the death of the respective animal, sometimes even in the space of a few hours.

With young male tree shrews whose tail hair stands on end for more than 40 percent of twelve hours, the testicles do not, as they normally would, pass through the inguinal canal into the scrotum but remain in the body. Moreover, the scrotum skin does not turn dark. If the animals are removed from the environment disturbing them, it will take about a week before the scrotum changes color and the testicles enter the scrotum through the abdominal wall. With adult males who bristle their tail hair more than 70 percent of the time, the testicles move back into the abdominal cavity. The scrotum regresses, loses its dark color, and is hardly visible after about two weeks. The weight of the testicles decreases and sperm production ceases. Things only return to normal when the situation of stress ceases.

Female tree shrews living under conditions where their tail hairs stand on end for half the day do not produce offspring; when the bristling value drops, they bear offspring again. However, if the female has suffered this disturbance for many months, the progeny of the next three litters can still die of starvation because the mother will still not have produced enough milk for them. Even when she eventually produces the normal amount of milk, the progeny of the next litters will starve, and this is because the female "forgets" the feeding times. Not until the fifth or even later litter will the young animals be reared normally. So social stress can have quite considerable after-effects, even if it appears on the surface to have been overcome.

Even lesser situations of stress, which only elicit a tail-bristling value of 20 percent of the normal timespan of twelve hours, are sufficient to prevent the rearing of offspring. The females give birth normally, have enough milk for the young, and suckle them too. Yet, within a few hours of the birth, any animal from the group, sometimes the mother herself, will go into the nest, take out a young one and, undeterred by its furious noise and desperate struggles, partially or wholly devour it. This cannibalism stops as soon as the tail-bristling value falls below 20 percent. The reason is not some mysterious maternal instinct to spare the offspring from growing up in a bad world, but more probably the deficiency of a gland secretion. Adults have a gland in the region of the thorax between the forelegs with whose secretion the mothers mark the young shortly after birth, by rubbing the gland against them. This scent mark keeps all members of the species, including complete strangers, away from the young. Situations of stress, when the sympathetic nervous system of the animal becomes excessively active, produce a number of effects besides tail-bristling; one of these is the absence of the gland secretion. So the young are not marked and other adult tree shrews are not prevented from devouring them.

Female tree shrews exhibit yet another behavioral change under moderate social stress: They try to "mate" with members of their group in male fashion. They pursue an individual, lick his genital region, mount him, massage his flanks with their forelegs, and perform thrusting movements with their thorax. This behavior dies down with the disappearance of the stress.

All these effects of social stress can be explained in terms of the well-known collaboration between the central nervous system and the hormone system. But this is not so important here. What we must note is the variety of effects social environment has on the social behavior of animals, above all on the processes related to population or birth control.

If tree shrews live too densely, they can keep the population count constant; but, strictly speaking, this is not always achieved by birth control. For offspring are in fact born, even though they are then devoured—because of excessive population density—or starve to death. What can, however, be described as birth control is the so-called "Bruce effect" found among many animal species. The Bruce effect is the termination of a pregnancy that has already begun. The fertilized eggs of the embryos that have developed in the uterus of the mother are destroyed, and this can still happen in the last days before birth. Over half the pregnancies of wild rabbits in New Zealand are terminated in this way. Normally the young are born after eighteen to thirty days of pregnancy and weigh forty or forty-five grams; but they can still be resorbed in the womb after twenty days. When this happens the mother's body hardly loses any nutritive substances—much less, at any rate, than it would in a miscarriage. The more densely the rabbits have to live, the more young rabbits never see the light of day. Young females resorb more embryos than old ones. And if the highest-ranking females in a rabbit population have six or seven litters a year, and the lower-ranking ones less, this too is due in part to social stress that naturally affects younger, low-ranking animals more seriously.

The tests of Parkes and Bruce[88] have shown that the population density of mice and some other rodents can be regulated a step earlier, by means of the so-called "pregnancy block." In the first four days after mating, female mice react very sensitively to foreign males, i.e., to males other than the one with whom they have mated. If one removes this male and puts another male in with the mated female, she will not become pregnant. But by the fifth day after conception this effect appears only in some females, and by the sixth day it disappears entirely; if one does not replace the male until then, the female will become pregnant in the normal way. Similarly, female mice still become pregnant if they are completely isolated from males, even if this is done immediately after they have mated. So the male is no longer necessary after mating to bring about pregnancy. Yet his presence does have some effect, for if one does not replace the male, but instead adds a strange male to the pair, the female will become pregnant normally again. This means that although neither of the males mates with the female now, the male who originally mated with her can remove the effects of the strange male by his presence alone.

But how does the female mouse recognize "her" mate? This is not a difficult question to answer: by smell, for mice largely orient themselves by their nose. Indeed, there is no need to introduce a strange male to the mated female; it is enough for the female to smell him, the best means being by placing the droppings from the cage of any male into the female's cage. And this male need not even be sexually active; he could even be a eunuch. The operative scent is contained in the male's urine. It is probably a mixed substance, whose composition varies from male to male. The female must be able to smell the substance; female mice whose organ of smell has been removed do not react to strange males. Moreover, the female has to be exposed to the scent for quite a time. Sometimes twelve hours are enough; but the reaction gradually increases in strength in the course of two days. This is why one can prevent a pregnancy block by separating the "right" male from the female for only twenty-four hours and then putting him back again; even if a strange male or his smell has been acting on the female during the whole of this time, she will still become pregnant.

The gradual buildup of the female's reaction suggests that hormones play a part here. Also, it has been found that the foreign smell—which the female must, of course, recognize as foreign—that is carried via the hypothalamus (a region of the midbrain) and the pituitary gland (hypophysis) prevents the release of hormones necessary for the fertilized egg to embed itself in the uterine mucous membrane of the female. So one can remove the pregnancy-blocking effect of the foreign smell by giving the female the appropriate hormones. But normally, when a female has mated, the smell of a strange male will mean that eggs that are already inseminated do not become embedded but are ejected from the womb.

Here we must stress that this is not the only effect of olfactory stimuli to affect the reproduction of mice. By virtue of their sense of smell, the animals can distinguish castrated from noncastrated members of the species, and females in heat from those who are not; very often experience plays a part here, so that very young, virgin animals are not yet able to make these distinctions or so that particular smells that the animals came to know in their youth are preferred later. Moveover, mice in exclusively female groups stop being periodically in heat, but if they are joined by a male, or even the smell of a male, almost all females will immediately start a cycle again. Each of these effects is being studied individually with increasing precision. So far, we have only a hazy notion of how it all works and interconnects in the normal life of wild mice, uninfluenced by experiments. Nor can we expect a regulation of the population density of mice accompanied by the nervous and hormonal reactions we have described except in extreme cases.

Yet it is important to know about these effects of social situations on the creation of new life.

Tree shrews eat their newborn young, rabbits resorb the half-formed embryos, mice do not even allow the fertilized eggs to become embedded. What all these cases have in common is that new individuals who already exist are annihilated again. In other realms of nature, the offspring are not treated with kid gloves either. While the South Sea albatross brings up one young bird every two years, the Central European goldcrest has two clutches of ten eggs each year, i.e., twenty young. Yet, as far as we know, neither species is increasing or decreasing. In consequence, as with all animals, each parent pair must in the course of its life be rearing exactly two young, who will take the place of the parent animals when they die. All offspring beyond this die, one way or another, depending on the species. Apparently the carp lays one million eggs, but most of the young are devoured by predators while still at the larva stage. Similarly, more than a quarter of all young rooks that hatch perish in the nest for unknown reasons. It is easy to understand why many animal species ensure themselves against inevitable but also quite unpredictable accidents by overproduction of progeny; for floods can destroy nests, periods of bad weather can make it more difficult to find food so that many young starve, diseases can break out, etc. Some species seem to make provision for such eventualities: The common buzzard brings more young into the world than it can later feed, so that a few, usually the weaker ones, always die. But if there is an unusually large number of mice in one year, the buzzard can exploit this by rearing a corresponding number of progeny; so he does not miss his opportunity. The "nestlings" can, therefore, act as reserve young, useful to the species either when food conditions are particularly favorable or if the other young birds should die. In addition this means that if there are too many young, natural selection will choose in favor of the fittest. What is less easy to understand is the behavior of the sea eagle, who lays two eggs and hatches them but never brings up more than one nestling, namely the one to hatch first. The eggs are laid at an interval of three or four days, and accordingly the young hatch at an interval of three or four days. As soon as the second chick hatches, the older one sits on it, not by mistake or out of clumsiness but quite deliberately. Even if one rescues the smaller chick and feeds it, the elder one will come up at once and crawl around continuously until it is again sitting on the smaller chick, who is thus cut off from the food and smothered, i.e., actually murdered.[74] We cannot as yet tell exactly why the sea eagle does not abandon the idea of laying a second egg from the start, although there are a number of possible reasons that have not yet been fully investigated. What is certain is that almost all animal species produce a marked excess of offspring, which is very quickly reduced again. Although the losses are quite considerable, we can usually understand why so many young animals have to be sacrificed.

It is not clear, however, why the production of young is cut short, so to speak, in the cases of the tree shrew, rabbits, and mice that we have described. No doubt, if the young are devoured or destroyed in the womb, there is no great material loss and the building material stays "in the family." But an inquirer into the natural laws governing the transmission of life would surely be perplexed by the fact that these offspring are destroyed without much inhibition, yet copulation still takes place.

10. Regression

Psychologists are well aware of the occurrence of reversions to childish behavior among humans. These states appear quite commonly as reactions to stress, difficulties in life, and failures in general. One such reaction is bed-wetting. These temporary or permanent returns to earlier behavior are called regressions.[21] But the individual never reverts entirely to an infantile stage and all its behavior patterns, only to some aspects of it. A quite general deduction we can make from regressions is that infantile behavior patterns still exist in adults; normally they are not in evidence, yet they have by no means been eradicated in the course of a subject's life. This is also shown by the fact that certain brain diseases can cause behavior patterns typical of infants to reappear. Here, however, they are caused by an organic illness, in which case they are not called regressions but are pathological disinhibition phenomena related to the breakdown of certain parts of the brain or brain functions. By contrast regressions are not so obviously pathological.

Experienced animal observers have long since noticed that regressions occur not only among humans but also among warm-blooded animals. Presumably regressions are common among cold-blooded animals too, and even among invertebrate lower animals. But in order to uncover such behavior one must know the animals in question very well. We usually only know domestic animals, who are almost exclusively warm-blooded, so well.

Regressions very often seem quite normal on the surface; in fact, the further one analyzes the total behavior of the respective species, the more normal it will appear. Why do regressions exist? What good do they do the animal? The best way to find an answer to this question is to try to determine the age from which regressions actually appear. Surely it is not quite suddenly, overnight. For they are not new patterns of behavior but have been there for a long time, living underground, so to speak, only to break through again at some later date. It would only be expected then that childish behavior patterns would appear more frequently during childhood, less frequently later, and then ever more rarely without ever quite disappearing. Although no systematic tests have been evolved to date, enough cases have become known in the course of time to confirm this view.

Young kangaroos always flee into the mother's pouch at first; but the older they are the less often they will do so. In situations of danger, however, even sexually mature animals will still flee to the mother and hide at least their

Left: newborn kangaroo at the mother's teat (pouch not shown). Right: A fully grown giant kangaroo may still flee to its mother's pouch in cases of danger.

head in the pouch. Baboon babies cling to the mother almost continually and ride on her back; older offspring flee to the mother when they are threatened and cling tightly to her; and if he is scared, even a grown male baboon will rush up to another friendly baboon and clutch hold of him.

Regressions among adults are known to have been elicited by massive provocation in some cases. For instance, tree sparrows who have flown slap into a windowpane and are stunned or very dazed can sit around for hours, sometimes for days, without a sound and "gape" at the human with open beak; this enables one to provide them with food. When their condition improves, the gaping behavior disappears.[97] Childish patterns of behavior are not directed only at man. Adult male robins and linnets have been observed feeding another male who had a broken leg; normally two males will fight each other, as these males had done too before one of them had an accident. A fully grown frigate bird and a gannet were found in a large breeding colony of sea birds, each with only one wing, together with a large but blind white pelican. They were all several years old. None of these birds could catch its own food, so they must have been fed by other members of the colony for years.[1, 71] In the Bronx Zoo some years ago an accident cut off the beak of a female jay in such a way that the animal could not eat by herself. She begged just like a nestling for two years, even turning to members of different species in her cage, and was fed by a small capped jay throughout this time.

In all these cases the individual who still begged like a child, although adult, had suffered bodily harm. It had had a shock, or met with an accident, and was about as helpless compared to its normal contemporaries as a nestling is compared to adults. But forms of behavior that could be described as regressions can also appear when nothing has befallen the individual directly but something has altered in its environment.

Young storks who are almost fledged wander about their nest flapping their wings, but they stop this as soon as the parent birds return. The behavior typical of older birds is evidently inhibited then and gives way to more juvenile behavior when the superior parents are present. This is particularly striking with some small birds who have been brought up by a human whom they now look upon as their parent. At first the hungry nestlings simply gape with open beak and beg at their foster parent just as though he were their real parent. Later they manage to eat by themselves, picking food from the ground. Gaping and picking are two quite distinct behavior patterns at this stage, and picking is the later one to develop. Normally the gaping behavior is inhibited or blocked by the picking so that it disappears as soon as the animals can pick properly. What is interesting here is the transitional stage, i.e., the phase in the juvenile bird's development when picking is just beginning. At that point, so long as they are left to themselves, the juvenile birds may be able to pick up food quite well and so be able to get enough to eat. But if their human foster parent is in the vicinity, they gape and beg at him again. Even if he does not react, they will continue to gape. A bird of this kind, that has already fed itself for days in the absence of its foster parent, would rather starve than feed itself when the foster parent returns. Lorenz, Meyer-Holzapfel, and other ethologists have observed this repeatedly.

Within an animal society with members of different rank, regressions occur most often among inferior animals. This becomes very clear when one individual suddenly falls in ranking order. An adult hound can suddenly display the typical behavior of a whelp toward a superior rival, throwing himself on his back, whining, and urinating a little. As we all know, from the moment of sexual maturity a normal hound urinates against trees and posts with his back leg raised.

Other examples of adults exhibiting childish behavior in

the face of higher-ranking members of their species will be discussed later (see p. 131). Since this childish behavior makes the higher-ranking members of the species feel they are being approached as parents, any potential aggression they might feel is subdued. So regressions can protect an individual from attack. They are widespread among social animals and have an important function: to deflect social threats. When they achieve this they are, of course, not pathological phenomena. Exhibited by a child, regression has the function of eliciting brood-tending activities without which the child could not thrive. Regression protects juveniles who act thus, although not as frequently as before, from stronger members of the group, because the brood-tending attitude it elicits inhibits aggression. In this context of inhibiting aggression, the same actions can survive in adults too, although springing from an entirely different motive, as shown on p. 133. For instance, begging between the partners of a pair can be a form of greeting or a behavior pattern that strengthens the pair-bond. Such regressions mean that the animal is resorting to signals from childhood in the interests of communication in newly developed social behavior patterns. Seen in this light, these behavior patterns have also been termed "symbolic actions." How have they acquired the connotation of pathological? Probably because they are seen most often where they occur most often. And this is in abnormal situations of captivity when an inferior animal cannot avoid higher-ranking members of the group; so he remains entrenched in conciliatory childish behavior. In brief, then: When such behavior is expressed occasionally it is quite normal; when it becomes a permanent behavior pattern we may be dealing with an unnatural situation and the individual himself is not necessarily abnormal.

11. Psychic Castration

When higher-ranking animals, such as stork parents, inhibit the adult behavior patterns of young animals, these behavior patterns may still have matured in the juvenile animal before they actually appear. At least this is so if the young stay with their parents. But if one isolates the young, these behavior patterns could appear comparatively earlier. Then we can describe the young animals reared separately from their parents not as early developers but as uninhibited. Indeed, examples are known that could be explained in this way. However, there are other possible explanations too.

Inversely, one can also postpone the appearance of adult behavior in the young animal by prolonging parental care. Young butcher birds gape at their foster parent for up to six months beyond the normal time if he continues to provide them with food. An even more striking example: In a colony of cattle egrets in captivity provided with ample food, Otto Koenig has produced phenomena that he describes half in earnest half in jest as "spoiled hippies" (*Wohlstandsverwahrlosung*).[59] Even on attaining sexual maturity, the young egrets still gape at their parents and beg for food (and are still fed, for begging young egrets are very insistent and the parents must feed them if they want peace). It can even happen that the young egrets beg their parents for food and then pass it on to their own young! Meanwhile the whole family continues to sleep in the eyrie. By the next spring the young egrets want to brood too, in the same place where they grew up themselves, and they build their nest on top of that of their parents. The young egret will choose as his partner an animal as familiar to him as possible, i.e., one with whom he has always been together, and this will be either one of his sisters or his mother. But the father has no intention of giving up his rights, and the son can only play husband as long as his stronger father is absent from the nest. So these egrets do not learn all the things a young heron normally learns when he has separated from his parents and has to "stand on his own feet."

The case of cattle egrets is particularly striking because they generally mature very early, much earlier than other herons. Under normal conditions they are capable of brooding quite independently by the time they are a year old; other herons can brood only after two years. But in this caged colony they never became self-sufficient. Nevertheless there were no fights, for the cattle egret is the most social of herons and never quarrels with good friends. All the members of this colony knew one another well, however, since they could not possibly escape from one another. So it was possible to create a compact group that displayed a number of characteristics we already know of from animals who normally live in similarly compact troops. Here the colony was held together artificially, externally by the enclosure and also by the large supply of food. In the wild, however, it costs considerable time to find food for three or four large young cattle egrets. The parents have to stay away from the eyrie for increasingly long periods of time, and the young gradually begin to seek their own prey during the period of waiting.

One other feature is worth note. A normal heron displays several very striking color markings in the pairing season: The bill, which is normally yellow, becomes glowing orange at the tip and red at the root, and the skin of the nose is often a bright blue-red. The legs are also red. But in the parent-child group in the eyrie, some of the young retained their everyday coloring. This allows us to conclude that they never attained the state of excitement normally related to the beginning of the reproductive period, a failure which may be connected with hormonal disturbances characteristic of situations of stress.

During our discussion of symptoms of stress we mentioned that lower-ranking animals could be "repressed" by a group of higher-ranking animals of the same sex and then remain in a state corresponding to that of juveniles who have not yet reached sexual maturity. This could also be regarded as regression, yet it is not so much a display of typical childish behavior as it is the absence of normal adult behavior. With male tree shrews, sexual behavior disappears entirely under these conditions, the testicles move back into the body cavity, and sperm production ceases. And young stags who are already sexually mature but have high-ranking old males above them in the herd do not manage to mate nor do they show any inclination to do so. Similarly, in bands of hamadryas baboons, only the highest-ranking male is sexually active. But among stags, a one-year-old brocket begins to rut and be fertile as soon as the older rivals have been eliminated.

This effect of repressing sexual behavior is not limited to male animals; it can be even more in evidence among the females, especially when they have a regular reproductive cycle. It is known that if the females of various species of monkey are put into a strange band of monkeys, they will not come in heat for a fairly long time, in given cases not until they have reacquired a fixed position in the ranking order. One can observe the same phenomenon among even the lowest vertebrates, fish, when the said species lives in compact social bands. This is the case with the *Tropheus* cichlid from Lake Tanganyika (see p. 199): Here too the females stop spawning regularly if they are put in an unknown shoal and kept there.

This phenomenon, namely that animals who have sometimes already been sexually active are forced back by social circumstances into a state corresponding to that of an animal who has not yet reached sexual maturity, has been called "psychic castration." The expression is not a very happy one since it is misleading. Castration is an operation that cannot be revoked. Here, by contrast, sexual activity is only repressed; it returns as soon as the animal is freed from the situation in question.

Sexual repression in younger social animals results in the stronger and therefore higher-ranking animals becoming more likely to bear offspring. We have already described the case of rabbits, where the lower-ranking and younger females often resorb the embryo again. A more familiar example is that of animals living in packs where only the highest-ranking male copulates with the females, so that in effect he becomes the father of most of the offspring. Here it makes no difference if other males are excluded from reproduction; but if females are excluded, the number of offspring will drop. Perhaps this is why females are less prone to psychic castration than males.

It is not hard to understand this in biological terms, for barren females bring no advantage to most species; they are wasted, in a sense. This does not apply where there is a division of labor, as in insect states where barren females, the workers, do most of the work. Their gonads are kept inactive by certain substances emanating from the queen; so this is a kind of social castration too, but one that is reversible to a degree. For if the queen dies, the gonads of some workers can begin to function again. In insect states, however, the exclusion of female animals, which entails the absence of offspring, is offset by an incredibly high production of offspring by the queen, who can lay as many eggs on her own as all the other female workers could together.

The loss of offspring due to other forms of specialization on the part of the female animals is made up in this fashion. But it is only possible if the differently specialized individuals are kept firmly together in a functional community. This is rarely the case in the animal kingdom, so that it is also rare for nature to permit females to have no offspring.

It is a different matter for males. Often their time is not nearly fully occupied by the business of reproduction; moreover, they supply and make available their necessary contribution, the sperm, in excessive amounts. So it would do no harm if many of the males were excluded from reproduction. But would it be useful? Where is the advantage of high-ranking males keeping their lower-ranking rivals from reproducing? Might there not easily be, among these subordinate individuals, some who have a combination of genes that would benefit the species? This benefit could only be proved in terms of biological fitness. And that is tested not by means of a gene card but by the success that an individual achieves in its life. Of course, genes are not the only factor that contributes to success, but they do play a decisive part. If anything can be proved to have stood the test, then it is the genes of those individuals who have "made it" in life, who have survived all the perils of enemy attack, starvation, competition, etc. And it is quite reasonable to assume that to multiply this heritage that has been tested as far as possible in the "trial by fire" of life, even at the price of other, as yet untried, combinations of genes, must be advantageous to the species. Psychic castration can, therefore, bring advantages, but this is not to say that there cannot also be disadvantages attached to it, which may even predominate in certain circumstances. Indeed, the existence of a "council of elders" among baboons shows that the baboons have overcome the system of giving a monopoly of reproduction to the most successful individuals (see pp. 191f.). One disadvantage of psychic castration is that it sometimes leads to a superior member of the species being overprivileged; but this implies that only one of the participants is already at a disadvantage. Indeed, it would be a rather arbitrary display of emotion were we to consider the following with either satisfaction or horror:

Paper wasps of the *Polistes* species form nesting societies in which several sexually mature females build their nests one beside the other. But these females who live together do not all have the same rank; there is a ranking order. This order is built up on the special behavior patterns exhibited in the meeting of two animals, i.e., whenever they feed each other reciprocally (which will be discussed in more detail on p. 153). One of the wasps raises itself up, quivers its antennae at the other, and chews the other's head and thorax. Meanwhile the other wasp cowers and does not move at all or only moves in a very inhibited manner. The wasps whom such encounters prove to be the high-ranking ones now devote themselves exclusively to laying eggs. The lower-ranking individuals only lay a few or no eggs; instead they see to providing food and to the construction of the nest, which they moisten in hot weather. The behavior patterns that the high-ranking wasp exhibits toward the others probably stem from combative behavior. In serious cases—for example, if a strange wasp comes to the nest—this behavior also involves embracing the other wasp with the legs and stinging it. The reason why subordinate wasps lay hardly any eggs is that their gonads are rendered inactive by social repression. Now the same can also happen to the highest-ranking wasp, whom we can call the queen here. For there is a very closely related species, the parasite paper wasp (*Sulcopolistes*), whose females visit a paper wasp's nest and conquer it.[99] The parasite paper wasps begin by defending themselves against the attacks of the nest-owners by slowly embracing one after another, stroking them with their antennae, sitting on them about-face, bending with the abdomen, and dabbing at the neck and waist of their victim with their darting sting. Hereupon, the host wasp stays as quiet as after an encounter with its own high-ranking queen. The queen herself is subdued by the parasite wasp in the same manner. And the effect on her is also to block the activity of her ovaries. She stops laying and reverts to the life of a worker—"reverts" because she had originally built up the nest alone and had reared daughters who then lived with her as subordinate females. But the parasite paper wasp does not go through a worker's existence first; she conquers a paper wasp's nest and has her eggs hatched by her paper wasp hosts and their former queen. This form of social parasitism is very common among social insects.

III

12. Mating, Reproduction, Pair-Bonding, and Brood-Tending

Is it true that animals and humans mate in order to reproduce? Or that parents stay together because this facilitates brood-tending? We can determine whether these statements are in fact laws of nature by observing nature. A survey of conditions among very primitive living things tells us about primeval conditions.

Mating among unicellular animals takes two different forms. Either the copulating partners fuse, or they lay themselves one against the other, exchange parts of the cell nucleus, and then separate again. The biological significance of this process is that the genes, which are always slightly different between individuals, are mixed anew, producing new variations. These slightly divergent variants form the basis for further developments. The same applies in the reproductive behavior of higher animals who recombine their genes. With unicellulars, however, it is to be noted that mating has nothing to do with reproduction; on the contrary, when the partners have fused there are only half as many individuals left as before. When unicellulars reproduce, it is without sexual activity, by division into two (fission). We also find reproduction without sexual activity among fairly highly developed animals, who do not simply divide into two. This is called parthenogenesis (i.e., development of ovum without fertilization into new individual). New offspring develop from the ova of the female without the intervention of a male. Many polyps and various small crustacea such as the water flea (*Daphnia*) reproduce in this manner. So mating and reproduction can co-exist without any necessary connection. The animals we have just named reproduce without mating as long as the environment is favorable; then they produce as many offspring as they can as fast as they can, to make use of the good nutritional possibilities. Reproduction becomes sexual when living conditions deteriorate, for instance when the available space is exhausted. When unicellular animals or crustacea mate, reproduction ceases for a considerable period of time. That is to say, in this case mating and reproduction, each serve a different function: reproduction serves the extension and survival of the species, while mating serves to increase the number of variations within the species and provides the basis for the development of new types and even of new species.

Sexual reproduction is not always tied to mating among vertebrates either. The male water newt deposits a packet of sperm on the lake or pond bottom and the female comes and picks it up with her cloaca. Other examples of sexual activity without contact between the partners are listed on pp. 35ff. On p. 226 we show, conversely, how mating is not necessarily linked to sexual reproduction. So mating and sexual reproduction are also independent in a number of cases. Many species of fish who discharge eggs and sperm anywhere and abandon them to their fate nevertheless live in permanent monogamy; examples are many well-known butterfly fish (*Chaetodon*) of the tropical seas, familiar to all aquarium owners. Since, on the other hand, all animals that mate are certainly not all monogamous, monogamy and mating are also independent. Moreover, both can occur independently of brood-tending. We already find brood-tending among the lower animals that bear offspring anonymously, without contact between the parents. Various starfish tend their brood on the body of the mother; in the case of *Lepasterias*, the offspring develop in the mother's body, as with many shellfish. *Stygiomedusa*, a colored deep-sea jellyfish, gives birth to live offspring ten centimeters long. But the monogamous butterfly fish do not concern themselves with the eggs or larvae they hatch, and some birds who no longer tend their brood, because they have become brood parasites, nevertheless live monogamously, like the African didric cuckoo (*Chrysococcyx caprius*), the cuckoo weaver (*Anomalospiza imberbis*[34]), and probably the black-headed duck (*Heternonetta atricapilla*[119]).

What use, then, is monogamy is these cases? It achieves the same end as the fusion for life of the sexual partners among many lower animals (e.g., the double animal—*Diplozoon*—among sucker worms, and the blood fluke—*Schistosomum*—that causes bilharziasis). In fact, it still occurs among vertebrates, for example deep-sea anglers (*Ceratias*). It means that the sexual partners do not have to search for each other again and again. Any search entails the risk of error, and if animals of different species mistakenly fuse their gametes, they produce hybrids who can be sterile or otherwise affected. More important is the fact that closely related species in particular, who could still bear fertile offspring with one another, are specialized in different ways, with respect to nutrition, habitat, or some other part of their environment. This different specialization allows them to make better use of existing conditions and prevents intraspecific competition. In very simple terms, a species of animal that eats grass can only tolerate a limited number of individuals on a particular pasture ground; should a related species appear that ate leaves from trees, its members could safely co-exist on the pasture since they did not compete with the grass-eaters. But it is important for the grass-eaters to recognize the leaf-eaters, for otherwise they would waste efforts to chase them away as supernumerary grass-eaters.

So each species must distinguish itself externally by recognition signals.

Such signals are also necessary in sexual reproduction, for if hybrids appear, the species will lose its specialization again. The animals must, therefore, be able to recognize a conspecific sexual partner. Here it is enough if one sex is different from species to species, so that the other sex can choose according to the differences. Among many animals, the female is occupied with brood-tending, so she would put herself and her offspring in great danger if she had bright markings. In these cases the males are more striking, and wear a display dress, differing for every species, while it is the female who chooses. The most attractive example of this phenomenon is in the emphasis on contrast among closely related species inhabiting neighboring territories. In places where the species occur side by side and there is a risk of mistaken identity, the recognition signals, songs, or markings contrast more strongly than at the other ends of the area of distribution where only one species occurs. Living things that do not choose and largely leave the meeting of the gametes to chance, suffer from continual hybridization, which spoils any chance of different specializations and the formation of different species. (This is typical of plants, which cannot seek out a sexual partner; although the plant kingdom is much more ancient than the animal kingdom, there are about five times as many species of animal as plant species today.[78]) The display dress, which often differs so much from species to species, prevents mistakes in the choice of sexual partner. The more often an individual reproduces, the more often it will have to choose, and the more risk it runs of making a mistake, especially if the partners only meet briefly, copulate, and then go their way again. The longer they stay together, the easier it is for them to notice and correct an initial mistake. If they stay together permanently, they avoid the need for a new choice and the ensuing risk of error.

Comparisons between certain groups of animals have shown that permanently monogamous animals are indeed protected at least as well if not better from choosing the wrong mate than those of their relatives who do not form lasting pair-bonds. This applies even when the latter have evolved extremely conspicuous display dresses, differing according to species, as recognition signals. It is very clear in the case of tropical cichlids and birds of paradise,[78] and it explains why the male and female of non-pair-bonding species have strikingly differentiated colors and clearly distinct display dresses, while the monogamous species do not as a rule. *Monogamy replaces display dress.* It prevents mistakes in mating and the ensuing waste of time and gametes; that is to say, it preserves the characteristics of the species. This is true of monogamy whether or not the parent animals tend their brood. So monogamy is functionally independent of brood-tending; but it can also serve the interests of brood-tending. One could describe the physical fusion of sexual partners as "physical marriage." But in a genuine, permanent marriage, the individuals remain mobile independently of each other; in a sense they grow together in their behavior while recognizing each other as individuals. A transitional step between the two forms is "local marriage" (*Ortsehe*). Here the partners attach themselves to the same locality or nest but not directly to each other. The Californian blind goby (*Typhlogobius californiensis*) spends its whole life in pairs in the channels a burrowing shrimp digs in the seabed; the male or female of the fish will drive off all rivals of the same sex but tolerate any partner of the opposite sex who has chosen the same habitat. One can replace either the male or the female by another at will. Similarly, the stork is more attached to its eyrie than to its partner: the male stork and female stork are "married" not to each other but each to the nest[38]; they are faithful to a place but not to a partner.

Because mating, reproduction, and pair-bonding have entirely different functions and are largely independent from one another in nature does not, of course, mean that they cannot also be related to one another. The more highly developed animals have combined mating and reproduction and made pair-bonding subserve brood-tending. Eventually, brood-tending and mating are made to promote the interests of pair-bonding, as will be shown in later chapters.

13. Permanent Monogamy

We can distinguish between several different forms of marriage, depending on the number of participants. We speak of single marriage (monogamy) when there are only two partners, and multiple marriage (polygamy) between either one male and several females (polygyny) or between one female and several males (polyandry). Depending on the length of the bond, we also distinguish between seasonal marriages, which can last at most the length of a reproductive season, and permanent marriages that last longer, in extreme cases a whole lifetime. Polygamy in the strict sense of the word means simultaneous bonds with several partners; the male has a harem rather than allying himself with different females one after the other. For polygamous animals, the number of offspring in a population depends on the number of sexually mature females; but with monogamous animals it is the number of firmly paired couples that counts. Over and above such side effects, the various forms of marriage must also be considered as adaptations to particular modes of life. We will not go into this further here; I only want to point out that even within the most closely related species (tropical cichlids, for instance) there are quite different marital forms. If we retrace phylogenetic evolution, we will find that certain conditions lead to a conversion from monogamy to harem marriage and finally to nonmarriage (agamy).

So permanent monogamy is not necessarily a final stage

of development. Polygamy can be structured in a more complex way and can be more highly developed; and, in addition, it can be more beneficial to the care and well-being of the offspring. Investigations into the natural connections between marital forms and modes of life under certain environmental conditions have only just started. We know that in some way each affects the other. We also know that marital form is genetically determined among animals. It would appear to be less so for man, just as man is not genetically committed to a particular environment. From this we may conclude that the different marital forms of different peoples are adapted to their different modes of life and that a marital form that once predominated can give way to another if living conditions demand it. Again, monogamy will not necessarily be the final stage of a line of development. In any case, we would have to start by clarifying the connections between mode of life and type of marriage before demanding from any people that it should change its current form of marriage.

Permanent monogamy is widespread among animals. Examples are cichlids, butterfly fish, small birds, ravens, pigeons, geese, parrots, moles, jackals, dwarf antelopes, whales, marmosets, and gibbons, to mention only a few groups of quite different animals. In each case there are also closely related species who live in polygamy or without pair-bonding (in agamy). So monogamy is not typical of man alone. And the well-known moral theologian who asserted that permanent monogamy, among graylag geese, for instance, belongs to a group of phenomena found among highly developed animals in whom we see incipient manlike traits[22] was being rather careless. Animals who are monogamous in the strictest sense of the word are those who still remain firmly attached to their sexual partner when their gonads are in a state of rest—for instance, in winter—and sexual activity stops entirely. For man, the gonads can usually only become inactive in very old age. So permanent monogamy in this sense of the word is demonstrable for animals, but not for man, where it can only appear vestigially. In extreme cases monogamy among animals can last well into old age, when they are no longer capable of reproducing. It may also happen that one partner dies and the other mates again with a much younger new partner, or that one partner becomes seriously ill. The old or sick animal stops all courtship and sexual activity and the young or healthy partner is often overwhelmed with sexual offers from other members of its species who have not yet mated. Nevertheless it quite often adheres to its mate, which shows clearly that the pair-bond is not based on the sexual activity between the partners. We know examples of this: Bourke's parrots (*Neophema bourkii*), violet-eared waxbills, (*Granatina granatina*), and the bullfinch (*Pyrrhula pyrrhula*). Of course, firm monogamy with a partner who is too old or sick prevents the healthy partner from reproducing too. This shows that pair-bonding is independent of reproduction and can even come into conflict with it. One can forcibly separate such pairs, and sometimes the healthy partner will then mate again. But there are also cases, for instance among the graylag geese, in which the remaining partner stayed alone, hardly ate, and finally died. So it seems that even among animals the pair-bond can endure beyond death. But normally it does not do so, and instead of further abstract discussion we shall now give a few examples describing the usual biological procedure.

Two typical permanently monogamous animals native to Europe are the bearded tit (*Panurus biarmicus*)[58] and the tree sparrow. The bearded tit occurs from southern Europe to Asia, and in the belt of Lake Neusiedl in Austria. Even in its juvenile dress it mates. The partners spend their whole life in very close permanent monogamy and can only be separated by force. The color of the plumage is different for the two sexes, but this is only apparent after the juvenile molts, long after the animals have paired. The young animals soon recognize the sex of their partner by its beak, which is orange-yellow for the young male, but blackish for the female. This color marking appears soon after the young leave the nest. At first they live in flocks of their own age group. At night they sleep close together with plumage fluffed in spheroid shape, but they are rather quarrelsome in daytime. The males in particular hack, peck, and pluck their flight companions at every opportunity. But soon each young bearded tit concentrates his devilry on a certain female; and if she tolerates it willingly, the issue is decided in a very short time: Two or three days later the two sleep closely clumped together at night and not each with its brothers and sisters as before. During cleaning and drinking, foraging, bathing, and sleeping, the one will hardly leave the side of the other, and they continually preen each other's ruffled feathers. If one flies a grass blade farther away, the other will land beside it a moment later. If one loses sight of the other, it will call loudly till they have found each other again. Soon the pair separates from the others and the flight communities break up.

The juvenile full molter begins about two months later, and from now on the pair does not stick together quite so closely. Of course they do not separate, but at least there are no more quarrels if they meet another member of the same species. The pair recognize each other by their voice and the call-bond is enough for them now, so that they can tolerate a separation of a few meters. But the marital partners sleep close together throughout their life. If one dies, the other will fly around excitedly, searching and constantly calling; it will then sit around miserably, but it will become extremely agitated the moment it hears the call of another bearded tit or a sudden rustling in the bulrushes, as though hoping that at last its partner was about to land beside it.[58] Eventually a second marriage can take place, but this bond will not be so firm and can only take place between widowed partners. A partnerless old bird will find no contact with the young flocks formed of sibling communities. The continual quarreling and pecking prevents it from communicating and soon drives it away again. The quarrelsomeness of the young bird, which rises to full strength during puberty, makes it impossible for an old bird to marry a teen-ager. But in flights of adults there is neither courtship nor jealousy. Even widowed birds can make contacts and find new partners here.

So the expression "lifelong monogamy" can easily be misleading. Firstly, of course, the pair-bond does not last a lifetime in the literal sense of the word, for life has already begun in the egg; yet a pair-bond can come into being surprisingly early, although a part of life will already have passed. And often the span from life to death is not very long either. Indeed, it is almost certain that only animals of about the same age mate (as we shall explain in detail on p. 116). Yet it is very rare for both partners to reach a fairly old age; the hawk snatches one, the cat devours the other. This is why one can only find out how permanently monogamous such animals are designed to be by extensive observations or by "protective imprisonment" in aviaries.

The pairs of the Eurasian tree sparrow (*Passer montanus*) are also "lifelong" partners as a rule and have three broods a year. However, it is seldom that a pair is lucky enough to rear young birds together for two consecutive years. Normally one of the two will lose its life one way or another, and the survivor has to mate again. The partners are faithful to each other, particularly the females, who refuse the advances of every other male even when their own partner is ill or wounded. The males, by contrast, although they do not leave their female either, will sometimes take care of widowed neighbors. For widows blatantly prefer males whom they already know to total strangers. "So it can happen that a male has to mate with three females, to build three nests for the next brood, to brood on one clutch already, and yet feed young chicks in three other nests. Such a bird will not have a moment of rest all day long."[20]

Frau Deckert has described the following rather animated episode in the life history of a male tree sparrow whom she ringed with green and therefore called "Green" (the other individuals are also called after the color of their ring[20]). He was ringed as a brooding bird in 1956, and the same year he probably reared three broods in the same nest and probably with the same female. In 1957, "Green" brooded again, in the same cavity under a tiled roof, and also adopted the widow of a neighbor, whose nest lay at a distance of two meters from his own. Principally he helped the widow to build her nest, but only reared the offspring of his first wife, for the widow had none. But both females reared their second brood with the assistance of "Green." Then they both disappeared. In July "Green" courted again and mated with a neighboring widow called "Left Black," who had a hollow twenty meters away but left it to move into "Green's" hollow. They both built the nest, but this female was already beginning to molt and produced no brood. Nevertheless the new pair stayed together till "Left Black" was suddenly missing in October. "Green" now mated with the next nearest neighbor, who was at least three years old, a widow for the fifth time, called "Red," and whose hollow lay forty meters away. At the same time, "Red" also had another wooer and until she decided in favor of "Green" she carried feathers into her old nest with the help of the other male, and into "Green's" nest with the help of "Green." Then she and "Green" spent the nights together in his nest all winter long. In spring 1958, "Red" chose another abandoned nest halfway between her old nest and "Green's" hollow. There they reared three broods together successfully and remained together until February 1959 when "Red" became the prey of a sparrow-hawk. By March "Green" had a new female, with whom he reared and fed another three broods.

Tree sparrows very quickly notice the absence of a father in a neighboring family, and then take care of the widowed female together with her nest cavity and her chicks. The female reacts first by defending her nest against the new male, and for days she drives him away from it with loud clamor; on the other hand, she does allow herself to be mated by this male—for her next brood. This is because all courting males behave like young birds, even, of course, when wooing a female who has never mated. The male sits with ruffled feathers and slightly lowered wings and warbles. During intensive courtship this turns into a hoarse, polyphonic call that cannot be distinguished from the note of the seven-to-fifteen-day-old nestling. If the female comes closer, he ruffles his feathers even further, makes hesitant bows, often still quivers his wings, accompanies the female if she flies off, and remains ruffled in flight. By contrast, when the pair has come to an understanding, the female usually follows the male when they take trips together and comes up close to him when they are roosting. They also find the nest material together. From April on one can see the pair copulate frequently; but they stay firmly together beforehand too when they are not copulating and also remain together outside the brooding period. The partners can recognize each other individually, even by voice alone. And later, long after they have mated, the male still puffs up his feathers occasionally and utters the nestling call. So these rituals very probably have a pair-bonding function; no pair comes into being without them.

Copulation occurs most frequently during the egg-laying period, but occasionally also in the first quarter of the brooding period, and then again shortly before the chicks of the first or second brood are fledged. The male hops up on the female two to seven times in succession while rapidly repeating a characteristic tender "vluug" sound several times. Both sexes utter this sound, the male more frequently than the female, when they fly away from the nest, when they land in the cavity, when they relieve one another in brooding or brood-tending, when they bring nesting material, etc. It is a greeting call, which occurs only in the reproductive period, and which marital partners address exclusively to each other, never to strangers or neighbors. This call can be described as a "tender greeting" that is exchanged between the actively reproductive partners of a pair as soon as they relate specifically to each other, which is, of course, especially during copulation.

14. Ambiguous Social Signals

The examples we have just quoted show that some social signals are not clearly explicit. Even with the guillemot (*Uria aalge*), mating and greeting calls are the same; the partners of the pair greet each other at the nest with the same barking call that the male uses during mating. The mating call is slightly higher pitched than the greeting or contact bark, but there are fluid transitions between the two.[116]

If we want to translate such calls into "human" terms, we will have to watch very carefully to see what their true meaning is. Perhaps, as with the "vluug" of the sparrow, the bark of the guillemot is never anything but a greeting, and the male is simply greeting his female during mating. But the young of the bearded tit have a very quiet nest-begging call, which later turns into the light "dididididi . . ." with which the male entices his female into a thickly matted bulrush and indicates that this is where they will build. Do both calls simply mean "here is the nest"? The young bearded tits call "shr shr" as soon as they have left the nest so as to let their parents know where they are and that they are hungry. The male in the dense bulrush also calls "shr shr shr . . . ," whereupon the female comes up very close to him. Does "shr" simply mean "come up close to me"?

Very many of these calls occur in two situations. Are we giving them the right name if we look for what both situations have in common, or is it more accurate to class them according to their specific meaning? This is very difficult to decide.

If several related species of bird have a certain call that only the young utter when they are hungry and that causes the parents to feed them, then we can speak of begging calls. If this call is also used by adult males of one of the species to entice a female, then one must conclude that for this species the begging call has been emancipated. Whether it has then faded into the generalized meaning of "come!" or whether it means "come and feed me" in both cases, and the female merely finds no one to be fed by her in the second case, could be decided by careful observation of all the reactions; in some cases this can be done by imitating the one call in the other situation and similar experiments. We shall come back to this problem later. Here we only want to confirm that the same calls that the young address to their parents also occur between adults. This does not only apply to calls, i.e., acoustic signals. Among nearly all species of pigeon the males entice their partner to the nest by means of special movements. These movements are identical to those that the young bird uses for begging. This becomes particularly striking among pigeon species where the begging behavior of the young birds is clearly distinguishable according to species and the same differences appear in the nest-enticing behavior of the males. In our language, enticing to the nest by the young birds would mean "come here and feed me"; enticing to the nest by the males would mean "come here." So the meaning of the signal has been extended. Now this assertion would presume that the food-begging of the young is in fact the earlier signal. Among pigeons, this is difficult to decide because we always find both meanings in the enticement behavior. But if one compares birds in a wider context, it becomes very clear that the begging of young birds is indeed earlier, for it is far more widespread and always made up of the same elements. This begging only occurs with a different sense for the adult animal among comparatively few species, and then it is usually to entice a sexual partner.

The less probable a posture or locomotive process, the easier it will be to recognize it again. This is very important when there is a suspicion that one and the same posture or movement occurs in two quite different situations. If a bird opens its beak wide, this does not mean much at first, because it does so for yawning, threatening, begging, and perhaps other situations too. What else should it do with its beak but open it? But if a young tropical finch bends forward and down with open beak toward its parents, and turns its head away from the axis of its body, twisting its neck so that it is looking up at its parent from the side, and then makes curious pivoting motions of the head, this is such an extraordinary manner of begging that it alone will show that the bird belongs to the group of tropical finches (see p. 194). Now if a male fire-tail finch (*Staganopleura guttata*) displays in this way in front of an approaching female, we can be quite sure that in this case the childish begging movement has returned in the pair-bond situation and that we really are in presence of the same behavior pattern and not a superficial resemblance.

It is necessary to point this out because anyone who is extremely familiar with a group of animals can recognize simple behavior patterns from small and unobtrusive features; often, however, he omits these details from a more general description for the sake of simplicity, which then makes the layman suspect that he has made his assertions quite arbitrarily. It is no use for the expert to say superciliously that disbelievers can check the facts for themselves; usually they cannot do so because rearing these animals is far too complicated, nor can one expect a layman to observe every one of the animals about whom he wants more information. It is better for the layman to assume that the

Like the diamond finch nestling begging for food (top),
the adult male twists his head with a stem of grass in his
beak when he displays in front of the female.

assertions of the experts are presumably well founded and
that he may therefore believe them. Misinterpretation and
suspicion can only be avoided by exact description. The behavior patterns analyzed in the preceding chapters have
been studied and described with sufficient care for us to
venture more far-reaching comparisons. Where there are
still doubts, they have been noted separately.

15. Measurable Advantages of Monogamy

Pair-bonding is often exploited for brood-tending among higher animals. It seems self-evident that two parent animals can feed and protect their offspring better than one simply because they can share the various tasks. However, seasonal monogamy would be sufficient for this. But we can also show that permanent monogamy leads to better brood-tending results. This is because it gives the animals a chance to acquire experience and this experience will influence their later behavior, as can be proved for animals whose previous history is known. For instance, if one treats American ringdoves (*Streptopelia risoria*) with hormones and keeps the animals in pairs, some twenty-seven out of forty will brood. The reason why thirty percent of doves do not brood, although all the preconditions for it have been fulfilled, lies with the partner, as can be proved by observation of the doves in two consecutive, experimentally produced brood cycles.[10] For the second cycle, each animal is given a new partner. But two groups are formed: In the one, each animal is given a partner who has reacted in just the same way as itself in the first experiment (positively or negatively—i.e., has brooded or not brooded); in the other group each animal is given a partner who has reacted differently—i.e., this group consists only of pairs in which one partner has brooded, the other not. Result: In the first group, one out of nine animals reacted differently from the first time; in the second group it was every fourth. The clear

difference shows that the animals really do adjust their behavior under the influence of the behavior of their partner,
and—this is important—to not brood in certain cases,
whereas they would have brooded with a suitable partner,
conditions otherwise being the same (as they had proved in
the first brood cycle).

If this is so, it must be advantageous if partners who
suit stay together, instead of risking a less suitable partner
next time, always assuming that we are dealing with animals who live long enough to survive several periods of
reproduction.

This too can be proved. True, only one species of animal
has been studied in enough detail in this respect, namely
the kittiwake (*Rissa tridactyla*). A colony of this northern
species of gull was observed for twelve years by J. Coulson,[16] who found that sixty-four percent of females brooded
with the same partner as in the previous year. And only
one-third of the animals who changed partners had been
forced to do so because their previous partner had died. In
other cases the partner was still alive and even lived in the
same colony. Then it became evident that for an over-
whelming number of animals who had changed partners,
the previous brood had been a failure. This is not to say
that the animals decided to separate because of the failure;
what is far more likely is that the failure of the brood and
the separation had the same cause: The animals were not
suited.

Pairs who were successful and stayed together began to
lay and to brood three to seven days earlier in the next
season than other animals of the same age who had
changed partners. So older animals usually brooded earlier
than young ones. Females who change partners lay fewer
eggs in the following year and have less success with their
brood—i.e., a lower percentage of eggs develops into
fledglings. Animals who changed partners twice in two
consecutive years, thus having three different partners in

three successive years, were more affected than those who had only changed since the previous time. This demonstrates that reciprocal habituation to a new partner is not the only factor responsible for the lower success rate; for all animals who had changed partner since the previous season would have to adjust to the new partner, whether or not they had also changed partner the year before this. The disturbing after-effects of a change of partner only disappear gradually and can still be traced at least two brood cycles later. Whether the partner had died or had not returned for some other reason does not matter; the adverse effect is the same. So what we are simply calling "adverse effect" depends only on the fact of the change of partner, not on its causes. Naturally it is made up of many different reactions by the partners affecting quite different facets of brooding behavior, as the tests described in the chapter on social stress indicated (see pp. 65f.).

From observations of the kittiwake it has become quite clear that the permanent monogamy of successful partners is advantageous among these animals—i.e., it produces the greatest number of offspring. Yet it is also advantageous to change partners if a pair has no brooding success; for then there is a chance that each will find a suitable partner next time. In this case, the brood success is still less than for a long-paired couple, but notably greater than with an unsuited pair.

With the tree shrew (*Tupaia*) too, harmony between the partners of a pair plays a considerable role in the success of reproduction. Even small remnants of aggression between male and female mean that the female will always eat her young (see p. 66). This is not so for all kinds of animals, but it occurs in some cases. And if harmonious relations between partners can become so important that it is clearly worthwhile not to change partners if an animal is currently living in harmony, then it is only to be expected that there are also special biological developments that facilitate the coming and staying together of the partners of a pair. This is indeed the case, and I will list a few of them here, although only in terms of the connection with permanent pair-bonding and not of the effects on brood success.

16. Pair Formation

The bearded tit is a striking example of how early the animals mate. Early marriage is fairly frequent among birds, but it raises some special problems.

The bullfinch (*Pyrrhula pyrrhula*) lives in permanent monogamy. The beginning of a bullfinch friendship, however, does not lead one to expect this. The unmated bullfinch female flies up to a male, dips her upper body down low, ruffles her ventral feathers, and threatens the male with wide-open beak and hoarse calls of "chooah." At first the male retreats from this stormy wooing, and if he is already paired or otherwise uninterested, actually flies off. And he is right to do so, for the female becomes increasingly furious and pursues her partner wildly; if they are in a cage she will chase him around until he subsides bewildered in a corner. But if the male bullfinch is in fact interested in the female, he soon dares to defy the female's threats. The more self-assured he is and the less he allows himself to be intimidated, the more quickly her aggressive behavior breaks down. Her threats decrease more and more and finally he dares to hop up to her and to touch her beak with his for a split second; then he turns away very markedly and hops slightly to one side. If his partner is in agreement with him, she will soon flirt back in the same way; now they both hop up to each other with ruffled ventral feathers and tail held sideways, touch beaks briefly, turn away and repeat this pattern again and again.

The goldfinch, siskin, serin, and linnet beak-flirt in a similar way and also utter notes of tenderness. The male siskin, goldfinch, and serin go up to their partner during the beak-flirtation ceremony and slowly grasp her beak in their open beak. Now this looks very much like feeding. And feeding is indeed its origin. Even with the bullfinch, the male soon starts to feed the female from his crop when they have both firmly decided on each other. In the meantime the female makes childish begging movements like a dependent young bird. She even makes herself as small as possible, looks up at her partner from below, and gapes at him. In the short pauses while he regurgitates new food from his crop, the female begs, oscillating her body and flapping her wings like a young bird, but without the latter's begging sounds.

Partner feeding becomes necessary during the brooding time. Normally a bullfinch clutch consists of five eggs. When the female has laid the fourth egg she broods for thirteen days. During this time she is fed exclusively by her mate, who appears near the nest with full crop at regular intervals and entices her to come to him; he never feeds her in the nest itself. Partner feeding is the prerogative of the higher-ranking animal, who is normally the male. In exceptional cases, if the male is ailing or temporarily weakened in the molting season, the roles can be reversed and females can feed their males.

So, as these very exact studies by Nicolai[84] show, feeding the young has become partner feeding for the bullfinch while the female broods. In addition, tenderness feeding has come into being outside this period; this has evolved into a beak flirtation without the transmission of food, which serves the partners as greeting.

It is curious that even seven-week-old young birds beak-flirt with one another; this always occurs between nestlings from the same nest, since they already know one another well individually. They affiance themselves with one of their brothers or sisters while still in their juvenile plumage, but do not distinguish according to sex, which is not yet recognizable at this age. So just as many same-sex as opposite-sex pairs are formed. All these young birds exhibit only female behavior and even invite their partner to copulate with them; yet they never achieve copulation, since all the young males also behave in this way. In the course of their life, then, all bullfinches at first behave in typical young bird fashion, i.e., gape and beg the parents for food; later they all behave like females, i.e., make nest-building motions and invite others to mate. Only adult males exhibit typical male behavior, feeding their partner and mating with her. In terms of their partner, females employ elements from their juvenile behavior throughout their life, while males only do so when they are ill. So nestling, female, and male behavior follow in the above sequence. And at each higher stage of development, the animals still dispose of the characteristic behavior repertory of the previous stage, as we saw with the mountain sheep (see p. 28). In a mythical story of the creation of the bullfinch or mountain sheep, the male would probably be created last and not, as in Genesis, the female.

The sibling pairs of bullfinches cling together just as firmly as the adult pairs, but not as long. After some three months, in about August, juvenile molting begins, and with this sexual differences appear, both in plumage markings and in behavior. Now the males begin to feed their partner, but still display in the female mating posture, which in fact still occurs among their fully colored brothers too. These sibling marriages are dissolved by the end of the year, those between members of the same sex sooner than those between opposite sexes, and now each bird seeks out an unrelated partner of the opposite sex. During the period of transition the animals can have double "engagements," one still with a brother or sister and one with the future marriage partner. When the gonads begin to function, the early bonds are finally dissolved, and the former partners of a same-sex marriage now fight each other with particular violence. Marriage between brothers and sisters would, of course, lead to inbreeding, so it must be avoided or dissolved.

Normal as it may seem to us at first glance that a bird such as the bullfinch, who lives in permanent monogamy, should form a firm pair-bond while still young, its biological significance is still not clear. Could the birds not wait a few months and then pair properly, instead of forming a provisional marriage first that has to be dissolved later and replaced by the final marriage? We do not know whether, if one removed the opportunity for sibling bonds, these individuals would later have difficulty in their relations with their marriage partner. It seems very possible, and certainly requires study.

We could of course assume that this very early juvenile pair-bond is a by-product of social behavior, probably connected with the later permanent marriage, but biologically unimportant in itself. Then it would be an amusing incident, hardly worth bothering about. But one cannot dismiss an as yet unexplained phenomenon as unimportant, thereby saving oneself the trouble of further research, if the phenomenon becomes too frequent. Early pair-bonding exists among very different birds, and some birds take quite considerable trouble to effect it; so it must have some value.

There is a very striking example among tropical finches (see p. 194) such as the African violet-eared waxbill (*Granatina granatina*), which also lives in firm pairs. Adult males are a lovely chestnut brown on their back, the females somewhat lighter. Both sexes have a blue band around their brow above the reddish beak and a large round area of color on the cheeks, which is deep violet for males, a lighter violet for females. In addition, the male has a black spot on his throat. The scarcely fledged young bird, who leaves the nest at the age of nineteen days, has a gray beak and is dark grayish brown on top, brownish orange underneath. At first the young bird is still fed by the parents, until the age of about thirty-five days. A few weeks later the young birds molt into their adult dress; they reach full maturity in the ensuing dry season, which lasts some months in Africa, so that they are ready to reproduce at the beginning of the next rainy season. They do not wait until then before seeking their mate, however, but begin before they are thirty-five days old, i.e., while they are still being fed by their parents. In this case, however (unlike with the bullfinch), the formation of same-sex pairs is prevented; for, from the twenty-first day and in the course of about a week, markings of different colors for the two sexes are very rapidly added to the simple juvenile plumage. In this period the animals molt in precisely those areas of their cheeks, upper beak, and throat where the characteristic sexual markings are located; by the time they are thirty-five days old they already display the typical sexual markings on their head, while retaining their juvenile dress on the remainder of their body, and are already firmly paired off. This early molting on the decisive parts of the head ensures pair-bonding with the opposite sex.[85]

The isolated early molting of individual parts of the plumage certainly acts in the interests of early pair-formation and gives us an idea how important this juvenile pair-bonding is (so important, in fact, that a special molter is inserted!). This would not be nearly so striking if the animals had simply shifted the over-all molter into adult dress forward to this time. It would surely have achieved the same result, and in addition it would have been simpler merely to alter the molting date rather than upset the whole molting plan. So why do they do this? Why do they retain their juvenile dress? Presumably, says Nicolai,[85] it has something to do with the fact that quite a few of the firmly paired animals are widowed in the course of a reproductive season, as we have shown with the tree sparrow (see p. 97). From the onset of the first rains, two, three, and even four broods follow one upon the other. The young birds from the first brood would already look like adults if they molted immediately, while the real adults were still busy with the second brood. And an old bird who had lost his partner around this time would be tempted by the large supply of young birds ready to form pairs and might choose one of them as a replacement. But the young bird would not be capable of reproduction yet. So the old bird, if he happened upon an immature "teen-ager," would have to let his reproductive talents go to waste. This can be avoided if teen-agers are recognizable as such, i.e., still wear juvenile dress. The young birds themselves probably place a different value on these markings, since they pair off with each other; but only in cases of necessity do adults resort to a young bird who is not yet fully colored.

These examples show how many different aspects must be considered and how much one must know of the living habits of a species before the fundamentally quite simple questions on which the attentive observer will stumble can be answered. We still need to know much more about these birds before we can determine the biological significance of their early pair-bonding. The same applies to the following species, on whose life in the wild we know even less than we do about the violet-eared waxbill.

Indeed, the violet-eared waxbill is not the only bird to have an isolated early molter on the parts of its plumage that are important for sexual recognition. Its closest relative, the purple grenadier (*G. ianthinogaster*), also lives in pairs and molts in the same way. We find the same in quite different groups of birds, for instance Australian black honey-eaters (*Myzomela nigrita*). Among Asian timalias, the Pekin robin and the silver-eared robin (*Leiothrix lutea* and *Leiothrix argentauris*) molt on their throat and breast while they are still being fed by the parents; they also form early pair-bonds and are monogamous. In the woodpecker family, the tiny, soft-tailed piculets commonly found throughout Africa, South America, and Asia (genus *Picumnus, Sasia*) molt the specifically sexual markings on their head in the same way as the waxbills, as soon as they become independent, but do not molt the rest of their juvenile dress until they are about a year old.

It would seem only natural to assume that it is always important to prevent the pairing of individuals of very dissimilar ages. The bullfinch (see p. 95) achieves this thanks to the extreme quarrelsomeness of the young animals just able to mate, against which adults are powerless. Yet we must check these working hypotheses thoroughly, even if they sound very plausible. This takes a great deal of time and good knowledge of animals. The only method to achieve it is for nature-lovers or bird-watchers, or whatever the researchers who largely work without instruments are often rather disrespectfully called, to observe patiently in the field.

17. Pair-Bonding

It is not only in connection with the coming together of partners that remarkable biological processes take place; the same applies later too, between the partners who stay together. They include certain ceremonies that each individual performs only with its mate or with a closely related member of the family, but not with unknown members of the species.

One such striking ceremony is duet songs, which are typical of monogamous birds whose sex cannot be distinguished externally. In the simplest and probably most primary cases both individuals give voice to the same notes or phrases, echoing each other or singing together in unison. In more specialized cases the partners in their duet utter different phrases or parts of phrases, which can be combined in various ways. This occurs among very different groups of birds—pairs of cranes, screaming sea-eagles, little grebes, and others. Some African shrikes have arrived at an extreme form, for instance the tropical boubous (*Laniarus aethiopicus*), where every pair has its own repertory of several fairly long phrases, which each partner can sing alone but which the pair normally sings with carefully divided roles. As far as we know at present, the duet also contributes toward the spatial coherence of the partners, since each can hear where the other is even when they are hidden in dense undergrowth.

These duets have been evolved quite individually by vari-

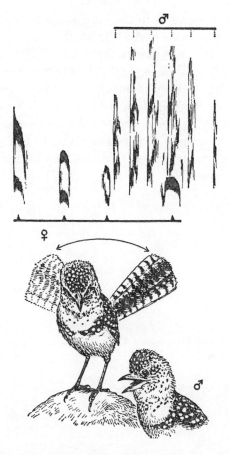

Greeting ceremony of d'Arnaud's barbet (*Trachyphonus d'arnaudii*). Top: sound spectrogram of the duet. The tail-wagging female constantly repeats four notes, the male always adds his hoarse call in the same place; it is shown by the six vertical strokes in the spectrogram.

ous other birds besides songbirds (among whom the shrikes belong), for instance by some of the barbets related to the woodpecker. In recent times the African d'Arnaud's barbet (*Trachyphonus d'arnaudii*) has been studied very carefully. Here the male inserts a hoarse "shrée" call at certain definite intervals in the repeated sequence of the female's calls; this note derives from the nestlings' begging call. The female accompanies the whole duet with conspicuous tail-wagging. We also find duet songs among the highest monkeys, namely the siamang (*Hylobates syndactylus*), a monogamous large gibbon from Sumatra. Research into the origin of these duets and the influence they exert on pair-bonding has only just begun. We shall discuss other behavior patterns typical of the partners of a pair in the following chapters.

18. The Derivation of Billing

Although it is difficult to discern any definite origins in simple motor patterns, we are not entirely helpless in this matter. For instance, it is worth trying to trace their evolution. What use it is if this attempt succeeds will be shown by the following examples, the first of which is the masked lovebird (*Agapornis personata*).[111]

The lovebirds from the African steppes are also called "inseparables," an indication of how closely the pair clings

A budgerigar feeding its young in the nest.

together. The partners can be observed feeding each other throughout the year. Usually the male feeds the female; the reverse is rare. Feeding between partners is important to the survival of the female during the brooding time, for she broods alone, sitting in her nest the whole time and being fed exclusively by the male.

Outside the brooding time, the female eats independently. And yet the male still keeps feeding her. In this phase, feeding has the function of a contact gesture and obviously serves pair-bonding (like allopreening, see p. 145). Partner feeding also occurs in the foreplay to copulation. But here only small bits of food are regurgitated, whereas genuine feeding usually involves large portions.

Partner feeding works only if the other bird is ready to take the food at precisely the same moment. If, for instance, the female looks away even for a moment, the male cannot feed her, so he swallows the food and then has to regurgitate it afresh; probably he can only balance the food in the right position on the tip of the tongue for a second or two. During the transmission of food only the tips of the birds' beaks come into contact, and the food is pushed across with the tongue. The female holds her head erect while the male twists his a little, so that their beaks cross transversely. This is exactly the same position as for feeding

Beak contact as greeting between paired masked lovebirds.

thc young, and no doubt feeding between adults is derived from brood-tending behavior. It can happen because the female begs or because the male offers food of his own accord. But the female's begging posture is not entirely the same as the begging position of young birds. When young birds beg, they crouch down, directly facing the parent, who, incidentally, is always the father if they are fledged, because by then the mother takes no more notice of them. Begging young birds stretch their head forward and ruffle their feathers; the wings are raised, and they sometimes make flapping, balancing movements. When an adult female begs, she draws her head back a little and turns it in a half-sideways or sideways position to her partner; it may be that the female does not adopt the normal childish posture because she holds the whip hand in the pair and is now superimposing begging on rank position.

When the male initiates the feeding, he begins to regurgitate the contents of his crop, bends down toward the female, and briefly touches her beak with his, sometimes also pulling the upper part of her beak to him. This brief beak contact, during which the partners turn their heads toward each other for a split second and interlock the tips of their beaks like two links in a chain while inclining their heads at different levels, also occurs on many occasions outside the feeding ceremony, usually while the animals are sitting next to each other or allopreening. In this case it is occurring in a quite neutral situation. We only find billing between partners, not between flock members who are on less familiar terms with one another. Whenever members of the flock come close enough to a pair to disturb it, so that the pair clearly feels importuned, the partners throw brief glances at the disturbers and make rapid preening and evasive movements; and, billing increases, as it does if strangers are introduced into the aviary, or if changes are effected in the environment, or after a great outside danger has passed.

Billing also increases during pair formation and during

greeting if the partners have been separated for some length of time. Quarrels between partners always end with billing; in the middle of a violent beak duel or during a short pause for breath, one bird, usually the male, will suddenly incline his head for billing; the partner immediately agrees, and the quarrel is over. Even if one of the pair has a quarrel with a third bird, the other partner immediately comes up and rams the first on the flank so violently and for so long that it finally turns around for billing; the "arriving" partner shows no interest whatsoever in the object of the quarrel! The appeasing or pair-bond strengthening function of billing is just as evident here as in the relaxed neutral situation we described earlier. Again the beak contact can last a certain time; the tongue may be stuck out a little and the animals may utter noises similar to the nestling sound and make sporadic movements of the head, which we normally see only with young birds. These additional elements are good bases for the conclusion that billing is a part of feeding, or perhaps an extremely abbreviated version of feeding. However, Stamm, to whom we owe these detailed observations,[111] drew the following conclusion: Since the mechanism of the beak does not permit all that many modes of action, although the beak does serve many purposes (eating, cleaning, preening, pecking, fighting), these various behavior modes must necessarily involve such similar movements that one could just as well say that billing derived from allopreening. Admittedly, one must be cautious in interpreting these behavior patterns; nevertheless Stamm is overlooking a whole series of common features here that point clearly to the derivation of billing from feeding. For instance, allopreening is not addressed to the beak of the other, nor does the partner turn its beak toward the other if it wants to be preened; similarly, the sounds and movements of the tongue and head found in billing do not occur during allopreening. This case can show all the details to which one must pay attention. Perhaps one or another reader will still have lingering doubts. Such doubts can, in part at least, be removed by comparative observations of other birds, on whom one can retrace the derivation more fully, while yet passing through the same transitional steps. The common raven may serve as an example.

The role that the common raven (*Corvus corax*) played in myths and legends as the bird of Wotan suggests that even our ancestors were good observers and had noticed the following: Ravens in general and the common raven in particular are more alert and eager to learn and, if brought up by human hand, more affectionate than most other birds. Indeed, the behavior of the common raven is only tied to instinct to an astonishingly low degree, so that the bird has quite a lot in common with mammals like brown rats or primates who "specialize in nonspecialization." The expressive and social behavior of this most imposing of ravens was recently analyzed in detail by Gwinner.[36] In contrast to jackdaws and rooks, who breed in colonies, the raven is only sociable in youth. At first the fledged young stay with the parents for a remarkable length of time, almost five months, in fact. Then they join into flocks with other groups of brothers and sisters; here they form pairs, who separate from the flock at the beginning of the third year of their life, establish fixed territories, and then remain together for the rest of their lives.

As we said, ravens have less rigid behavior patterns than many other birds, and accordingly we find that behavioral elements from brood-tending or pair-bonding occur in other situations here too. The partners of a pair are not very different in rank, and although the female invitation to copulation is most likely to involve the drive to flee, it also occurs in the male foreplay to copulation, if the courted female has not exhibited it first. The wings are spread out to the side, the folded tail quivers horizontally, and the neck is stretched out horizontally forward. This posture coincides with the extreme submission posture of common ravens, when it occurs together with the sounds uttered by begging young birds. Among jackdaws, this female invitation to copulation is entirely freed from its sexual connotations and has become the usual form of greeting of female to male.

This childish begging behavior, during which ravens squat down, flap their wings, and utter begging sounds, can also occur independently from hunger and no matter whether or not the partner has food to offer; then it serves to appease the partner. The appeasing animal can open its beak wide and, like a young bird begging for food, bring it as close as possible to its partner. Instead of attacking or pecking, the latter then abandons its threatening posture; sometimes it may insert its beak in the wide-open beak of its mate and even make thrusting movements with it as though feeding, although it is not in fact transmitting anything at all. Animals who wish to approach a higher-ranking member of their group also display this begging behavior, often making themselves small and thin at the same time, by sleeking their small feathers, drawing their head in between the shoulders, and bending their legs. In addition, begging behavior always occurs in a pair when the male is feeding the female.

As with the lovebirds we described, the female common raven broods alone and is fed by the male throughout this time; and he will feed her better, the more firmly she sits on the clutch. During this time the male "must" feed his female. But he also does it throughout the year, although not always as frequently. Toward spring, pair-feeding and incipient courtship display increase continually, to reach their highpoint during the nest-building time. Now the female who is fed begs like a young bird and also takes the food like a young bird with her beak twisted in a longitudinal axis of ninety degrees against the feeder's beak. The male, who brings his female small, tasty morsels outside the brooding time too, feeds her continually now. First the food is carefully prepared or fetched ready-prepared from

Common raven feeding its young (left) and greeting by
billing (right).

its hiding place; the male stows it in his beak or throat
pouch, approaches his partner with splayed steps, often
flapping his wings too, and—to the accompaniment of feeding noises—offers her the food. The position of the beak and
the soft feeding noise "gro" clearly indicate that this pair-
feeding derives from feeding the young. When feeding its
young, the beak of the old bird is turned at an angle of
ninety degrees against that of the gaping young bird so
that the food can be plunged very deep into its throat. This
is no longer important during pair-feeding, yet the position
remains the same.

The soft "gro" sound with which the old raven summons
its young to open their beak and with which the male
raven summons his incubating female to take food is not
the same only in pair-feeding but occurs throughout the life
of raven pairs whenever they make contact with each other.
Young birds also say "gro" during their first attempts at
walking, but only if the parents are present; and they will
utter it more loudly and more rapidly the less steady they
are on their feet. So "gro" is not only a feeding sound but
also a contact or greeting sound.

Since there are so many similarities between pair-feeding
and feeding the young, we may ask whether perhaps among
these birds both have the same motivation and are de-

pendent on the same mood. In fact, with the raven in particular there are indications that pair-feeding and feeding the young belong to different moods. Ravens have an extremely varied repertory of usable sounds, consisting of elements they know from birth to which are added sounds they have learned. Like many other songbirds, ravens learn best from those beings to whom they are bound by the strongest individual ties; normally, of course, these are the parents, and especially the father. The bullfinch, for instance, has created traditions of song, songs transmitted from father to son. Gwinner reared a raven, and in the first years he often lured him to the netting of the aviary for feeding with the word *"komm"* (come). The raven spontaneously took over *"komm"* himself for the situation of pair-feeding and later invited his female to accept tasty titbits by saying *"komm."* We do not want to discuss here what an extraordinary achievement in abstraction it is (although there are parallel cases, in particular among ravens) for the bird to bring this sound into relation with the food-transmittal situation and then to utter it again when he was no longer being fed himself but instead had assumed the role of provider of food. What is more important in our context is that the same raven, when he became a father, always used the normal "gro" feeding sound when feeding his young. *This shows that feeding the young and feeding the partner were two different things for him,* although he used largely identical behavior for both.

But ravens can do more than this. Some pairs can change the pair-feeding ceremony, quite by themselves and to different degrees according to the pair. Gwinner observed several pairs among whom, after a period of married life, the food given by the male to the female was pushed back and forward with the tongue from beak to beak several times, sometimes for more than thirty seconds, until the female took it. So the beak contact had to be extended for this whole period of time, and finally the pairs beak-flirted in the same way even without food. One pair went even further. It sat together with closely linked beaks for minutes on end, without making feeding noises or transmitting food. Another pair of ravens walked around in circles side by side with similarly linked beaks. That this behavior is really an altered form of brood-feeding can only be affirmed so surely because the process of transforming the ritual was observed extremely carefully in these cases. There was ample opportunity for comparative observations, for all the pairs repeatedly used the correct pair-feeding method besides this individual variant. Obviously we are not dealing with a process of maturation typical of the species and dependent on age either, for not all old birds changed the feeding ritual thus or in other similar ways. *Rather we are dealing with rituals "invented" by the birds.* And it is very likely that equally precise observations of other birds, especially parrots, will show us similar series of alterations in brood-tending behavior, which would not only help to remove any remaining doubts on the correctness of our interpretation of

Monk parrot feeding its young (left) and beak-greeting between the partners of a pair (right).

beak contacts and such, but might even bring to light hitherto unnoticed connections with other social greeting ceremonies.

The herring gull (*Larus argentatus*) is also monogamous.

The fate of several pairs was followed over a period of ten years, and this showed an easily overlooked preliminary stage of pair-feeding.

Even outside the nesting place and outside the brooding time, the partners of a pair remain together, in winter too. The pairs are formed in the so-called "clubs" of unpaired gulls, and it is the female who chooses. She pulls in her neck, sticks out her beak and lifts it a little, and then circles slowly around the object of her choice. The male may go off with her immediately or start by strutting about and attacking other males. Occasionally females choose a male who is already mated and try to intervene in an existing pair, which provokes violent aggressive and defensive behavior on the part of the original female. To the careful observer, the term "jealous behavior" seems almost self-evident as a description of her behavior, although one must note that it is not meant to suggest anything about the bird's possible feelings or the form of the behavior. The comparison with human behavior that the term "jealousy" suggests is only intended to make it easier to outline the situation and function of the actions.

If one partner of a pair of herring gulls dies, the other may pair again. The male herring gull also feeds his mate. He regurgitates a little food, which she swallows greedily. Normally she begs for it, particularly during the reproductive season.[114] Careful observation will allow one to discern the inception of pair-formation before mating and pair-feeding have begun. It can be seen by the fact that a gull allows another to take food away from it right in front of its face. It is well-known how incredibly food-jealous gulls in particular are. So pair-bonding begins with not begrudging food to another, which in a sense represents the lowest stage of pair-feeding.

We find the same phenomenon with a quite different group of animals, who are not vertebrates at all—namely, spiders. The few spiders who have any form of social life eat together, i.e., do not begrudge food to other members of their kind. On p. 159 we discuss the societies of these curious social spiders.

We will learn about other forms of social behavior with different functions later. Here we will begin by showing the behavior patterns of the young bird toward the parent animal; this behavior will assume an important part in the relations between adults. Begging and feeding can indeed serve to provide nourishment, for instance in the case of a brooding female, as happens with many if not most parrots. In the first days the male actually feeds the whole family in this way. He brings the female food, which she in turn regurgitates and passes on to the young nestlings. Pair-feeding can also acquire a quite different significance for the pair: wax-wings (*Bombycilla*) are paired from the moment the female takes a berry from the beak of the male who has offered it to her. Among terns (*Sterna*), the marriage contract is sealed as soon as the courting male has offered the female a fish. Actual food provision only plays a subordinate part here.

The courting female of robin redbreasts, whose behavior has been examined in great depth by Lack,[71] utters a shrill, monosyllabic call in front of the male, and then, when he approaches with food, dips her wings and quivers them. Meanwhile her call turns into a rapidly repeated note. Then she is finally fed by the male. It is impossible to distinguish the posture and notes of the female from those of a young robin that is being fed by its parents. But although the female begs quite persistently, and is repeatedly fed by the male, food and appetite only play a negligible role here. On several occasions Lack observed parent robins who wanted to feed their young but were disturbed by observers in the vicinity of their nest. Here the female would turn and beg at the male although her beak was already stuffed full of insects for her young. She was not begging for food but for "moral support," as we would say in human terms (for further examples see p. 189).

Feeding can disappear entirely too, and instead we can have billing or beak-flirtation. In general begging at the partner among adult birds corresponds to the food-begging of newly fledged young birds. Some elements can disappear or others be exaggerated, yet the resemblances are great enough to lead the observer to mistake one for the other at times. For instance, the young begging green-finches one hears in March are in fact courting females. The resemblances can also lead to mistakes by the birds themselves. Among wrens and seagulls, the father coming to the nest with food has been observed hesitating as to how he should respond to the begging of fairly well-developed young birds and then deciding to make an attempt at copulation. With the parasitic jaeger (*Stercorarius parasitusicus*), when a parent animal feeds a young one, the other parent may crouch beside the young bird and be fed too. Familiarity between the individuals seems to play a major role here: The female diamond dove (*Geopelia cuneata*), whose male entices her to his nest by childish behavior, treats this male in the same way as she would treat her young; she takes no notice of her actual young during this time, however, but only of the dove in the nest, whom she knows well.

This emancipation of childish behavior often becomes very apparent among monogamous animals, but it is not confined to them. Childish behavior can also be directed against unknown members of the species, whether the species in question lives in firm pairs or not. It can even evolve further into a social action that is executed in unison by a fairly large number of animals. The following examples will make this clear.

The gray jay (*Perisoreus canadensis*) native of North America lives in pairs; but in winter the jays gather at suitable feeding places in quite large groups. Weaker animals fluff up their feathers, raise their tails, and hop around, squeaking like young birds. In tense situations they quiver their wings and squeak like a young bird begging for food. In face of serious attack by a conspecific they lie down, stretch out their quivering wings on the ground, squeak softly, and stick their beak down into the snow. By doing this they display their black cap on their neck, which looks just like the black face of the nestling, whereas adults have a white face. So the aggressor is confronted with all the signals that characterize young birds. If he still attacked, he would no doubt also do so to his own young, thereby imperiling his own succession.[35]

We owe exact details on the behavior of the European bee-eater (*Merops apiaster*) to Mrs. L. Koenig,[56] who was the first to succeed in rearing these lovely animals in captivity. The bee-eaters breed in horizontal tunnels some meters deep, which they have dug themselves in clay walls. The sexes of these elegant birds are barely distinguishable, since each sex exhibits both male and female behavior toward its partner. These birds often exchange roles at short notice so that one cannot even distinguish male and female behavior patterns. Very often a male who is slightly sexually excited will perform the female mating invitation to his female. Yet only the male seems to feed the female, and always before copulation. He offers her food in the tip of his beak, she takes it, swallows it, and then adopts the invitation to mating position, with outstretched head and usually with eyes closed. The young birds are fed only by the parents at first; as soon as they come out of the brooding tunnel, other adults feed them too. The begging call of the newly fledged young bird is a strange, penetrating, slightly falling "eeeeeeeeeeeeeeeeeeeee" sound uttered with wide-open beak. This call serves the old bird as a show of submission when faced with threatening conspecifics. In addition, a bee-eater threatened by a conspecific can gape at it, without a sound, its body bent back. Then the aggressor grasps it by the beak, tugs and shakes it, but never starts the wild beak-snapping and wing-flapping of a violent fight as it would do if both animals were equally aggressive. Such fights can also take the form of real air battles. The defeated bird flees and is violently pursued by the victor and sometimes attacked again. But the weaker bird can from the start avoid a fight by resorting to the submission posture drawn from childish behavior.

Among Indian white-eyes (*Zosterops palpebrosa*) from the Ganges, partner feeding serves to deflect a threat. According to the observations of Kunkel,[65] these animals appear to live in rather loose pairs; at least they change partners fairly often. Attacks are fairly common even between partners who already know each other. Compared with that of many other small birds, the white-eye's pointed beak is a very dangerous weapon. Both sexes can divert an attack by their partner by offering it their fully raised feathers for preening (see p. 146). If the female opens her beak wide in front of the male, he will quickly introduce his own in it; sometimes this is preceded by obvious regurgitating movements. If she threatens him with closed beak "he touches the tip of her beak with his and lets the tip of his tongue enter her beak." This "tongue kiss" is never provoked by other than threatening behavior on the part of the female, and it serves to overcome her contact shyness. The actual feeding takes place in a moment. Hesitant females can thus be fed by several males. Here too feeding does not, therefore, serve to keep the partners together but is an almost anonymous form of appeasing a member of the species.

The bald ibis (*Geronticus*) greets members of the nesting colony with begging movements similar to those of the wood swallow, to whom we shall come back later (see p. 139).

Australian honey-eaters of the *Meliphaga* family use the wing-quivering of begging young birds in precopulatory courtship. The males quiver more violently than the females. But this behavior also serves as a greeting between pairs who meet at the boundary of their territory. They all quiver their wings for a few seconds and give half-suppressed calls like a begging young bird.[47] This gesture of peace never occurs between the partners of a pair, perhaps because the partners never stray more than a few meters away from each other; since they adhere together so closely they hardly need to greet each other. But among one species, the yellow-tufted honey-eater, *Meliphaga melanops*, begging behavior also occurs apart from its function of greeting, as a genuine social action in their communal group singing, in which up to twenty birds can take part. In its social function, wing-quivering is even more conspicuous than during begging (whence it originally derived), for young honey-eaters beg very "listlessly" and only quiver, with half-spread wings, in exceptional cases (for example, if they are very hungry). *So this childish behavior pattern is more strongly defined among adults than among the young birds themselves;* it has atrophied in the original function from which it derived —by comparison with the greedily begging young of other songbirds—but it is fully preserved in its derived social function and has even developed further.

This suggests that the derived behavior pattern has been emancipated. It becomes very clear in cases where brood-tending has quite disappeared, i.e., feeding the young no longer occurs, whereas partner feeding does. Examples are brood parasite birds, such as some cuckoos who lay their eggs in the nests of other birds and have their young hatched and brought up there.

The American yellow-billed cuckoo (*Coccyzus*) still broods itself and feeds both its young and its partner. The South African didric cuckoo (*Chrysococcyx caprius*), by contrast, does not brood nor does it feed its young, but it does feed its mate.[94] Here, although the cuckoo is non-brood-tending, its readiness to respond to begging in part-ner relationships has remained unimpaired. Thus it can even happen that an adult cuckoo will feed a young bird of its own species that it happens to come across. This has been observed with Klaas' cuckoo and the bronze cuckoo (*Chrysococcyx klaas* and *Chalcites lucidus*) as well as with the Burmese koel (*Eudynamis scolopacea*),[76] and it is probably not a remnant of brood-tending but rather a partner relationship extended to a young bird.

Instead of "courtship feeding" we should perhaps use the term "greeting feeding," for the male of the small Galapagos "tree finch" (*Camarhynchus parvalus*) and the American yellow-billed cuckoo (*Coccyzus americanus*) feed their females during copulation, and the Javan pheasant-coucal (*Centropus javanicus*) holds an insect during copulation and only gives it to the female afterward—and this can no longer be called courtship. Nor is beak contact absolutely essential to this partner feeding, and each male feeds his

The begging and presentation of fish in a feeding scene between parent and young bird recur in the same form as the prelude to copulation between the partners of a pair of wide-awake terns.

female in the same way as he would feed his young. The tern holds a fish sideways in his beak, and the partner grasps it at the other end and takes it. But even here there are the species' typical differences: The wide-awake tern (*Sterna fuscata*) regurgitates food and lets it drip into its partner's beak, while little terns (*Sterna albifrons*) may link their beaks for feeding and during copulation. The female gull-billed tern (*Gelochelidon nilotica*) may beg out of hunger; then she will allow herself to be fed by the male but not to be mounted by him; but she may also beg as an invitation to copulation, in which case she allows him to mount. In both cases her begging looks just like that of a young bird, but it has different "motives."[73]

Social feeding is important not only between the two partners of a pair. It also occurs in societies to which a fairly large number of adults belong. Again, however, its form is the same as for feeding the young.

19. Harems and Larger Groups

If we allowed it, our domestic fowl would live, like its wild forebears, in social groups with one cock at the head of about five hens. Naturally we scarcely ever see this now. If we forget about the very many different varieties we have bred and about the fat pullets in batteries or young cocks bred in incubators, and quite apart from attempts to blunt their beaks so that they cannot hack one another to bits (how many hens can be crowded into one square meter?)—can we still find cocks quarreling about their hens instead of farmers quarreling among themselves? Can any hens still manage to hatch their eggs out of sight of man? Since we keep our fowl under such extremely artificial conditions we are unable to appreciate the instructive structure of their society. The most we may see of it today is a hen with her chicks.

While the hens are brooding and then while they lead the chicks, they live apart from the other adults. Each hen marks out her own territory and defends it against neighbors; during this time the hens do not react to the enticements of a cock. The hen leads her chicks to water and to feeding places; she gathers them together and takes care that no strangers join them. Chicks who stray into the wrong family are pecked and driven off by the hen and her chicks. The hen is particularly watchful if she has to cross an open, unprotected place. If something arouses her suspicion, she will utter a warning call that sends her chicks into cover. She herself always stands in such a way that she can keep the danger in sight. If an enemy approaches, she attacks it violently. While the chicks are eating, the hen stands guard with raised tail and slightly dipped wings. It is rare for her to eat anything herself at this time, and, when she does, the chicks usually come up to her at once. She can also lure them to a tasty morsel directly, by pecking very markedly on the ground, lifting what she has found with her beak, letting it drop again, and then uttering the clucking call everyone knows. When the chicks are about a month old, the hen roosts on a tree with them at night, first flying on to a branch herself and then enticing the chicks to follow her.

This typical maternal behavior disappears as soon as the chicks become independent and leave the mother. Then she joins a cock again and behaves quite differently. Yet in a normal society one sees the behavior we have just described all the time—on the part not of the female but the cock. In fact there are cocks of different rank. The lowest-ranking ones wander around alone, have no territory, and try to rape hens who have strayed too far from their group. Slightly higher-ranking cocks try to establish territories of their own in the domains of high-ranking cocks, but abandon them again as soon as the latter threatens them. When they are about a year old, they gradually manage to assert themselves against the old cocks, which they achieve most easily outside the reproductive season. The high-ranking cocks have fixed territories, within which they dominate all the other cocks. They crow in order to affirm their territory, and do so fairly often, while lower-ranking cocks raise their voices considerably less. (After sunrise the highest-ranking cocks crow up to twenty-eight times in half an hour, the lower-ranking ones only about eight times, the lowest-ranking ones not at all. This is a social effect of rank organization, as shown by the fact that the crowing frequency of low-ranking cocks rises as soon as one removes the highest-ranking cocks.) The highest-ranking cocks always have hens about them. Each defends his hens against his neighbors. Gathering the hens together, he can lead them to feeding and watering places. He guides them very carefully over places without cover. He warns them of impending danger, and then, while the hens are seeking cover,

The cock guards and entices his hens just as the hen guards and entices her chicks.

keeps the object of danger in view. He attacks any cats prowling around. While the hens are eating, he stands guard with raised tail and slightly dipped wings. Only occasionally does he himself eat briefly, and usually a few hens run up to him then. He can also call the hens to him directly, by very conspicuously picking something up from the ground in his beak and dropping it again while calling "cluck cluck." In the evening he is the first to take to the trees, and then calls to the hens to join him.

These parallels in the behavior of the hen and the cock catch the eye at once.[79] But there are similar parallels in the behavior of chicks and hens. Just as the chicks flee to the mother if they are attacked by a strange hen, so the hens whom a wandering cock wants to overcome by force flee to "their" cock. The behavior pattern of the chicken-hen group is echoed in the hen-cock group. This means that the harem society of adults is structured according to the same pattern as that of the mother-child family. This is because the hens can change their social role according to whether they are "head of the family" in a crowd of chicks or members of the harem of a cock. As territory owner, the cock plays the same role toward his hens as the territory-owning hen does to her chicks.

The birds called wood swallows (*Artamus*), which occur in the Indo-Australian region, offer a particularly interesting example of social life. Immelmann recently very carefully

Food-begging, prelude to copulation, and social greeting look the same for the wood swallow too.

observed some species in Australia.[49] Wood swallows cling very closely together in pairs, probably throughout their life; but over and above this they also lead a very highly developed social life. They are extreme examples of contact animals. When they are at rest they always sit closely cuddled up to one another and preen one another's feathers. Several times a day, particularly in the evening, they fly up to great heights in groups and wheel around with loud calls. They do many everyday tasks together in groups, such as foraging, cleaning themselves, attacking other birds, roosting, and even rearing young. The pairs do not establish territorial boundaries to separate them from their neighbors, nor do they brood in colonies, but nest in intimate proximity; neighboring pairs visit one another's nests and later feed the nestlings in turn.

So nestlings and fledglings are provided with food by a number of old birds, and sometimes this continues even after they have become independent. On the other hand, these young birds often also feed their own brothers and sisters from the next brood and in addition take a part in feeding unknown young birds. This behavior survives their whole life long, for adult members of the species may also feed one another. Similarly the young nestlings and fledglings do not beg only at their parents but at all conspecifics, a characteristic they will retain throughout their life. In this way, even ailing individuals can be provided with food by other members of their species.

Young birds who beg spread their wings slightly and raise them a little; older birds raise them almost horizontally. In this position they slowly move the wings up and down, but much more slowly than the quivering movement of most songbirds; in addition, they slowly pivot their head back and forth around the vertical axis.

White-breasted wood swallows (*Artamus leucorhynchus*) also sit close beside their sexual partner before copulation and quiver animatedly with slightly raised and spread wings. This behavior can be repeated several times; in between the male can fly off, catch an insect, and feed it to the female, who once again quivers her wings. What is curious is that the male joins in this childish begging movement when he is feeding her, i.e., he also quivers his wings. Among the black-faced wood swallows, *Artamus cinerëus,* the partners sit far apart, with wings extended to their full width and slightly raised, the one that is turned away from the partner raised slightly higher than the adjacent one and with fanned tail. Both animals perform slow circling movements with their wings and tail, and then they mate.

Sometimes it takes several minutes for the second partner to begin its wing and tail movements. The speed and extension of the movements increase a little, and it is only a minute or two after both birds have reached full speed that they copulate.

This sequence of movement can also occur without being followed by copulation and even outside the brooding time. Then the "prelude to copulation" is solely in the service of the pair-bond. The pattern of movements is derived from brood-tending behavior. Among the white-breasted wood swallow it consists largely of a presentation of food overridden by long and intensive begging. Here, however, unlike during brood-feeding, the feeding partner also quivers its wings and "begs" with them. With the other species, the black-faced wood swallow, wing-quivering has turned into slow, circular movements like rowing, and the presentation of food by the male has almost disappeared in the prelude to mating. So the childish begging behavior has been transformed more thoroughly in the prelude to mating. This species also leads a more highly specialized social life.

We also see begging very frequently in other situations. If a wood swallow lands close beside a member of its kind, it often begs at it briefly, again with exactly the same movements with which a young bird begs. The already seated bird may respond with the same begging movements. Both may content themselves with slight wing-quivering, or they may perform the whole gamut of behavior up to the transmittal of food by the new arrival. Here begging serves as a social gesture of greeting, probably with an appeasing function.

Some courtship movements and nearly all the social behavior of the wood swallow thus derive from the behavior repertory of the young bird. They include not only begging motions but also the contact-call that has developed without gradations from the begging call. The female utters this noise shortly before copulation and during the preliminary feeding by the male; in addition, a bird landing near a conspecific uses it as greeting. Accordingly, the acoustic accompaniment to wing-begging has also developed

Social allopreening of masked lovebirds, a species of parakeet; and of pelicans.

from the young bird's begging, and one can justifiably assert that these animals have exploited childish begging for the pair-bonding ceremony, for the foreplay to copulation, and for general social greeting. The effect on the partner has remained the same too, for in all these situations the begging behavior can incite the partner to real feeding, although admittedly this is rare between adults. Instead it often provokes the partner to hop up to his mate or to allopreen, or even to execute the same begging behavior.

That is to say, adults react to the begging of other adults in more varied ways than to the begging of young animals. So they can discriminate between the two (perhaps simply because adults look different from young birds). This is an indication that begging behavior "means" different things in the relationship between the animals and is "understood" in different ways. Moreover, it occasions different physiological effects—it is "intended" differently according to whether a young bird or an adult is begging. Young birds beg when they are hungry. But the same behavior among adults is independent of the state of satiety of the birds: A newly arriving wood swallow can even beg at the present company by way of greeting if it is already holding food in its beak. This suggests, first, that begging behavior occurs among adults when they are neither hungry nor sexually excited, and that it therefore has a special social function. But at the same time it means that these animals perform social actions that cannot be attributed to any of the normally accepted drives, such as aggression, reproduction, flight, feeding, etc., and that social life therefore contains its own particular drives. Whether one should speak of social drives is disputable, and rightly so insofar as we do not know whether the various social actions of this kind all depend on one and the same drive or on several different social motivations. It is not surprising that these social motivations create no new behavior patterns but exploit already existing ones, for evolution always builds on what already exists.

If a behavior pattern acquires a new or additional biological function, it must always undergo a change in its inner motivation or acquire a new motivation of its own—this latter is also called emancipation. Without this "change of motivation" the behavior pattern could only be used in its original context. In such a case, only a hungry bird could greet its partner or invite it to mate if begging movements always remained motivated by hunger, as with the young bird. For the sake of simplicity we have up to here omitted detailed discussion of this question, but it applies to all cases of derived behavior patterns. If a begging movement can appease or deflect aggression it must be available to a satiated bird too; it cannot be motivated by hunger alone, for otherwise only the hungry could live together peacefully in an animal society.

20. Other Emancipated Brood-Tending Actions

There is no distinction left between begging and food-offering in the beak-flirting of ravens. Among Adélie penguins (*Pygoscelis adeliae*) too, the male holds the beak of the female in his own without giving her food. Among various kinds of cormorants the partners of a pair are in the habit of grasping each other by the beak and tugging and shaking each other back and forth. Sometimes this may look like a quarrel, but it too derives from brood-feeding. Young cormorants plunge their beak deep into the throat of the parent animal and fetch their food from there. The parent bird who is offering the food opens its beak wide, and this often displays in the interior of the beak strong color markings that serve the young bird as a feeding signal. Like others, this signal can also become emancipated and serve the bird again later in life. The female shag (*Phalacrocorax aristotelis*), for instance, entices a shy male by opening her beak wide,[1] thus showing its colored interior, which presumably has a calming and inviting effect because it is the food-presentation signal. But, like chameleons and many other lizards, birds also open their jaws for threatening, and this action may also display striking colors. One can tell from the response of the partner whether the gesture has a threatening and frightening effect or an enticing one, but little investigation has been done in this field.

Nest-building also belongs to brood-tending in the wider

sense of the word. Among some kinds of birds both sexes together build the nest; among others the females do it alone while the males provide the nesting material. A new courtship or greeting gesture has evolved from the presentation of nesting material, as it has from the presentation of food. The male can make simplified nest-building movements in the air in front of the female, with a blade of grass in his beak, even if he is no longer helping with nest-building. The emancipation of this action and its transfer to a new field of function is proven by the fact that, like the partner feeding of cuckoos, it survives even when the original meaning has disappeared. It can also be shown to be emancipated because the relation to the object in question has changed; for example, when a male robin feeds his young he holds several insects in his mouth, but when he feeds his female as a form of greeting he only holds one insect.[71] The male crimson finch (*Neochmia*) holds stiff green blades of grass in his mouth for courtship; his ancestors built their nests from these blades; today, however, crimson finches build their nests out of half-moldy soft blades of grass and have only retained their former preferred object for courtship, which has become emancipated from the old nest-building behavior.[48]

In some cases it is not clear whether or not a behavior pattern that is important in the relations between the partners derives from brood-tending behavior, even if it still occurs there too. The reverse process, namely a shift from pair-bond behavior to parent-child behavior, is also possible.

Everyone must have seen birds allopreening, for instance among pigeons, parrots, herons, and ravens. Of course this does not occur among all species of birds, and there are occasions in which some do it while fairly closely related species do not. It is typical of penguins, albatrosses, storm petrels, cormorants, storks and maraboos, horned screamers, rails, pigeons, parrots, owls, mouse-birds, toucans and, finally, many songbirds. In all it is known of forty-one bird families. In some cases the partners preen each other alternately; in others they do it at the same time. The allopreening looks fairly similar, even when the birds' beaks are as dissimilar as those of parrots and pelicans. The flanks are very rarely allopreened, the breast and back somewhat more often, the various parts of the head always, particularly the back of the head, the throat, and the area around the eyes. These are, admittedly, areas that the birds cannot reach themselves with their beaks, yet there is no reason to assume that species that are not allopreened there suffer any disadvantage because of it. Even species that do allopreen often only do so for a short span of the brooding period; so this behavior is not essential to the care of their feathers. What is its use then? Harrison, who has deeply concerned himself with this, found that the following factors favored the occurrence of allopreening[40]:

1. Confined space, either because of the peculiarities of the nesting place or because the animals move awkwardly on land and therefore use less space than is available.
2. Prolonged separation of partners.
3. Companionship, in the flock or in a large brooding colony, and also in prolonged pair-bonds between two animals.

Confined space, frequent encounters, and unfamiliarity after separation, which can even lead to slight estrangement, are all factors that heighten aggressiveness. And allopreening is indeed closely related to aggressive behavior; sometimes an initial attack ends in allopreening, which then serves as *ersatz* and appeasement. Similarly, the invitation to allopreening is connected with the drive to flight, appeasement, and evasion. Presentation of the raised head or throat feathers, often with the eyes half closed, acts as such an invitation. This gesture cannot only appease aggression but it also reduces the partner's tendency to flight.

Among some species at least (for instance, penguins or relatives of the stormy petrels), allopreening is also very noticeable between parents and their young. But it is doubtful whether allopreening is an emancipated form of brood-tending behavior; in fact, it is not even certain whether it is an independent behavior pattern at all or whether perhaps it is only an action that occurs in conflicts—to express it in human terms. We know that allopreening may occur as an act of confusion or "displacement," but not whether it is ever done deliberately or even what its purpose is.

Actions that occur in its place are also important in the context of the social meaning of allopreening. Among boobies, for instance, there is one species, the brown booby (*Sula leucogaster*), which does not allopreen at all; it is very rare for the red-footed booby (*Sula sula*) to do so, but it is an everyday occurrence for others. Now in those situations where these other species allopreen, the red-footed and the brown boobies offer their partner a twig for building the nest. These little gifts brought back by the returning bird are necessary to the harmonious relations between the partners, as they are among other birds. Eibl-Eibesfeldt has demonstrated this very well: He took a bunch of seaweed (its gift) away from a flightless cormorant (*Nannopterum harrisi*) on the way to his nest; on his arrival empty-handed the bird was immediately driven away by his partner.[28] The invitation to allopreening cannot, of course, be removed from the animal in the same way, but by comparing the situations, particularly among closely related species, we may conclude that this gesture has the same appeasing effect.

21. Termites to Chimpanzees—No Change

The examples we have quoted so far of socially important behavior borrowed from childish behavior referred to birds. For a long time now birds have been the animals on whom most research has been done, and ornithology has always played a leading role in behavior research. Primarily this is because so many bird-lovers never tire of watching their protégés and have thus gained a very wide knowledge of their way of life. Another reason is that in the course of the evolution of vertebrates, from fish through batrachia, reptiles, and birds to mammals and monkeys, behavior has become increasingly more varied and differentiated. Meanwhile fairly long, rigidly established behavioral sequences disintegrated into ever smaller elements that became usable again, both individually and in continually new combinations. Naturally, this often makes it hard to recognize the elements. Among the lowest vertebrates, fish, it is still quite simple. Either they mate or they do not mate; their behavior is characteristic of a particular situation. Among higher mammals, however, the attribution of identical behavioral elements is often extremely difficult. Is pawing the ground with the front legs the beginning of flight, or of digging, or an attempt to cover something with sand, or simply "nervousness"? If all four legs paw in the sequence in which they are moved for running, one could say that pawing was an attempt to flee that had been inhibited for some reason. But if only one leg moves, we have too few points of reference to tell from which behavior pattern the action might derive. In this line of development birds occupy a position where series of movements evidently already serve new functions; and yet these series still represent sufficiently large chunks of former, even longer sequences of movements for one to identify them and affirm with some certainty that a greeting ceremony derives from the begging of the nestling.

This is only a very general argument to explain why people noticed this emancipation of behavioral elements among birds so soon. Naturally we find behavioral patterns of unknown origins among birds too, just as the emancipation of brood-tending behavior also occurs in other classes of animals. It is necessary to show this by examples too; otherwise the reader might get the impression that we were indeed dealing with a natural law, but one that only applied to the bird kingdom.

Among the very varied species of the cichlid family there are, as we mentioned earlier, some that form pairs who adhere firmly together for a long time. The Indian orange chromide (*Etroplus maculatus*) is one of them. The eggs are attached to stones, and both parents guard and fan the eggs until the young hatch, usually after three days. The parents carry in their mouth the freshly hatched larvae to a prepared sand-pit and continue to guard them there for another five or six days. Sometimes larvae are moved to a new sand-pit during this time. Some nine days after hatching, the young begin to swim freely, leave the pit, and follow their parents in a dense swarm. The parents continue to watch over the swarm of young, using their mouths to bring truants back to the swarm, drive off enemies, and move slowly enough all the time for the young to be able to easily keep up with them. The family remains together in this way for another twenty-five days; then the parents' interest in their by now fairly independent young wanes;

they separate from them and can now begin to prepare for a new brood.

From the first day on one can see the free-swimming young, who are some seven millimeters long at first, foraging for food. If the supply becomes short, the swarm will distribute itself over a larger area; if there is ample food, the young stay close by the parents. But in any case they return to them constantly from the first day on, for each young fish swims back to one of the parent animals about once every ten minutes and eats a bite of body mucus from its flank. The orange chromide belongs in fact to those fish who feed their young with an excretion from their own body. In the appropriate phase of the brooding cycle, the mucous cells in the membrane of the parents

The young of the Indian orange chromide eat from the body mucus of the parent. This movement becomes a form of greeting behavior between the partners of a pair.

multiply by more than thirty percent. They are essential to the survival of the young. Young fish who are deprived of them show a very high mortality rate and the survivors remain very backward in physical development and growth.[118] The same applies, incidentally, to a South American cichlid, the famous "discus" fish (*Symphysodon*). It too feeds its young with body mucus in the early days. Since this mucous secretion is stimulated by prolactin,[6] one could even call them "mammal fish," for prolactin is the hormone that stimulates the milk glands of mammals and the secretion of crop milk among pigeons. Milk and crop milk are well-known as essential nourishment for the very young, such as pigeon nestlings.

Whereas with the "discus," the frequency with which the young visit their parents decreases with age, it clearly increases with the orange chromide. When the young are over a month old they snap a bite from their parents every three minutes. Even when the family has dissolved, one still occasionally sees the young, and, more rarely, adults, swimming up to a larger member of their species and snapping at its flank. The partners of a pair do this continually, and in fact this is the only situation in which an orange chromide addresses such behavior to an equal-sized conspecific. So this behavior of the young animals who take something essential to their nourishment from the body of their parents also plays an important part in the pair-bond, both in the time when the pair forms and later during "married life."

We can also find permanent social groups outside the realm of vertebrates—among insects, for example. Whenever social animals are discussed, people usually think first of the famous insect states, those of the termites, ants, and bees. Termites are sometimes called "white ants," but they have nothing to do with the highly developed ants; rather they are fairly primitive insects, closely related to cockroaches. In their states the king survives together with the queen, with whom he founded the state, whereas in the states of *Hymenoptera* ("membranous wings") such as ants, bees, wasps, hornets, and bumblebees, only the queen survives. All insect states are structured according to a very definite system. There is only one animal who sees to reproduction; the others, sometimes numbering hundreds of thousands, serve the state as workers, brood-tenders, soldiers, builders, etc. One of the largest insect states is that of the leaf-eating ant *Atta cephalotes,* whose subterranean nests can extend to a depth of five or six meters in the ground and span a distance of more than one hundred meters. Five or six million animals live here with a queen, who lays twenty million eggs in her lifetime. If she dies, the whole state perishes with her. For nest-building, these animals move some forty tons of soil, construct thousands of chambers, and breed fungi in them on chewed-up leaves. For the defense of the state they have large soldiers; for bringing the pieces of leaf, leaf-carriers; for protecting the carriers, "foot-soldiers"; the foot-soldiers ride on the piece of leaf and drive off the flies that try to attack the busy leaf-

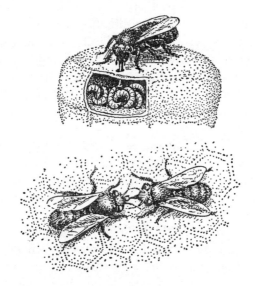

Above: bumblebee feeding the larvae. Below: a worker bee feeding another.

bearer and lay their eggs on his neck.[29] This solidarity among so many and differently specialized individuals has always excited the admiration of observers, and researchers have tried to find out what it is that holds the animals together. They found that there is a nest scent varying from state to state and that the animals drive away or kill any individual with a different nest scent. But this only means that the right nest scent protects from attack. What actually holds them together, as far as we know, is primarily social feeding. The insects continually beg their companions for food and are then fed with a regurgitated drop of food. Two animals can beg at each other too, or try to feed each other reciprocally.

This social mouth-to-mouth feeding derives from brood-tending behavior too, for the insects also feed their larvae mouth-to-mouth. This has come from various successive stages of development. As with the ichneumon fly (*Ichneumonidae*), the mother can sting a grub or other animal and lay an egg in it, or, like the digger wasp (*Sphecoidea*), she can build a chamber in the ground, drag several victims into it, and lay the egg on them. In the most simple case, for instance among potter wasps (*Eumeninae*), these brooding chambers are amply provided with food and are closed up after the mother has laid the egg. We find a higher stage of specialization among some kinds of potter wasp from Africa. Here the mother begins by dragging only one grub into the chamber and laying an egg by it, but she leaves the nest open and brings more grubs from time to time so that the larva is continually provided with new food. Among even more highly specialized kinds, the mother chews the food destined for her larva into a pulp. Since all these species form a very closely related group, it is once again very easy to reconstruct the gradual changes of behavior, finally leading to a "subsocial" behavior that already fulfills many of the requirements of social life although the animals do not live socially yet. When adult, the offspring scatter. But in the wasp genus called *Stenogaster* there are, besides some species that behave as we have just described, some where the mother animal feeds and rears several young at the same time in one nest; at first the young stay with her and help to feed the next brood. After a while they are replaced by the new brothers and sisters and leave the maternal nest to establish their own. So they are fully developed young wasps by then; some build their own nest immediately next to that of their mother.

Only the true social wasps (*Vespinae*)—i.e., our common black-and-yellow wasps—have succeeded in forming social communities in which most of the individuals spend their whole life—although only as workers, for they are no longer capable of reproduction. Brood-tending feeding has evolved into reciprocal feeding by all the members of a state, and even the larvae are not only fed themselves but also provide drops of saliva rich in nourishing substances that are important to the survival of the whole community. Under certain conditions the larvae can even serve as food reserves for the adults. Normally the wasp larvae hanging head down in the cells are fed with a pulp made up of grubs and other insects that the adult wasps premasticate in their mouths. As soon as the larvae are touched, they release a drop of saliva from their mouth aperture, which the adults swallow greedily. This saliva provides an essential motivation for the adults to go to the larvae, and it is fairly common for wasps to visit their larvae again and again and incite them to excrete saliva without bringing them any food pulp. So one cannot say that the animals are motivated by purely maternal feelings and devote themselves quite self-lessly to the larvae. Similarly, it is probably the attraction of the larvae's excretions that causes the young wasps to stay with their mother. And if we are right to assume that the excessive exploitation of the larvae by continually inciting them to excrete new saliva weakens the larvae in a specific fashion and inhibits their development into normal sexual animals, then it becomes clear how strongly the development of the individual and the development of society are interrelated here too.[42] Since we are dealing with natural processes, we need not worry about considerations of right and wrong. It would be more rewarding to consider what this adds to our knowledge of the plan of creation.

In the immediate context of our discussion, it is important to note that wasps and bees have developed this system of states independently of ants; this shows how normal it must be for animals to exploit brood-tending behavior for the construction of a society. Ants have reached an even higher level of individual specialization; we speak of "castes" in their societies. Among honeybees, the different duties in the hive are performed by various old workers, so that each individual passes through a series of different jobs in the course of its life. One or two days after hatching from the cocoon, the female worker begins her job of caring for the larvae; about a week later she spends two weeks or so on general "housework," excretes wax and kneads it in shape for building honeycombs, helps to clean the hive, and also stands guard at the entrance; after this she becomes a forager and brings nectar, pollen, water, resin, etc. to the hive. In case of need she can return to her earlier jobs. But among ants the individuals who do the different jobs are also very different in physique, so they do not, therefore, change jobs. The behavior of the soldiers among leaf-eating ants, for instance, is distinguished by the fact that they never take flight and even attack huge enemies. In order to do so they have developed very large heads and great muscles on their mandibles; but they can no longer eat by themselves with this mouth, so they have to rely on being fed by the female workers. We should really speak of female soldiers too, for these animals are all female in genetic structure, although functionally they are sexless and infertile. They have in fact been sterilized by chemical substances that the queen bee produces. These substances are licked up by the workers and distributed throughout the hive during reciprocal feeding, and their effect is to suppress the development of the reproductive organs. This shows how closely the different behavior patterns are interlinked. The individual animal decides to search for food not because it is or is not hungry; rather it gathers much more food than it can use itself and divides it up among other members of the state. If an ant is hungry it need only beg from a companion. During feeding, both animals act in a community-bonding fashion. The ant that is being fed receives in addition a portion of the substance that makes it into a worker. So this chemical social effect is based on social feeding, which in turn derived from brood-tending feeding.

Such a complex system of social communication and reciprocal influences is, however, liable to what we would call "abuse" in human terms. If an ant can satisfy its hunger by begging from another, a whole group of ants who have fallen on hard times can do the same. But what if they had fallen on hard times because they only had soldiers and had "forgotten" to see to workers? We know what happens then, for we know of species that do precisely that. These are the well-known slave-holding ants found in various ant species. These slave-holding species only have soldier-workers, who cannot eat by themselves. They move in organized columns, often covering long distances, and attack the colony of another species of ant; the workers of the attacked colony usually react by running wildly to and fro and trying to bring the cocoons to safety. But the intruders overcome the workers, take away their cocoons, and carry them home to their own nest. The hatched young do not "know" that they are in the "wrong" nest; they help out just as they would have done at home, working in the state, and looking after the cocoons that are the booty of further raids. The slaves do the building, drag food into it, and look after the eggs and larvae of their robbers. But they have no queen of their own, and gradually the normal death of old age thins out their ranks so that the robbers continually have to see to replacements. For the slaves it obviously makes no difference whether they function as wheels in the machinery of their own state or whether they work as equally responsible wheels in the state of their war-like robbers. These individuals, who are so structured as to react correctly in the interests of the state, are "made" for slavery.

But events need not be quite so warlike. One species of ant without workers of its own can very easily be a parasite on its closest relatives, to whom it is almost identical exter-nally and whose social communication signals are the same. These parasite species are only noticeable because they produce few or no workers, which means that they do not contribute to the preservation of the state on whose po-tential they live. The species have developed as "social parasites from their own ranks," that is to say they have reached a further stage of specialization and broken away from a normal ant species, so that they now live together with and at the cost of this species. The ant state with its perfectly organized care of all individuals belonging to the state is fertile terrain for social parasites; because of the necessary reliability and thus rigidity of its organization the state cannot protect itself against parasites who exploit the state-preserving reactions of the workers in their own interests, while contributing nothing to the preservation of the collective good themselves.[42] Quite different animals can also become parasites in the ant state in this way, for example, mites, bugs, spiders, or beetles.

Of course it may be that the "parasite" for its part offers talents that are of advantage to the species it joins. An example is the cooperation between ants and plant lice.

Plant lice (*aphids*) live off plant juices and excrete the honey as a sugary fluid. They do this increasingly as soon as they are disturbed, flailing about with their long back legs at the same time. It is quite common for an ant to encounter a plant louse and to "disturb" it. The plant louse reacts by waving its legs about and excreting a drop of this sweet substance. For the ant this behavior is the same as when a fellow ant offers a drop of food while greeting with waving antennae. So the ant sees the plant louse as the head of another ant, greets all plant lice by friendly begging, and is fed by all of them. Sometimes the ant also tries to feed this presumed fellow ant and offers the rear end of the plant louse a drop of food—in vain, of course.[54] The mistake on the part of the ants is to the benefit of the plant louse, since ants keep the plant louse colony free of enemies. For the ants, the plant lice are just as much of an advantage as milch cows are to us. The only one to suffer disadvantages from this cohabitation is the plant. The plant louse, who can suck without being annoyed by ants, normally excretes some three cubic millimeters of the sugary fluid per day but excretes three times as much when visited by ants. The fact that one single state of red ants can devour more than a hundred kilograms of the fluid per year gives some idea how this feeding, which has developed from a brood-tending action into a bond holding the society together, and in which the plant lice have become involved as though by accident, affects the plant world, which originally played no part in the social behavior of ants. We cite this example to show that in nature the simple social behavior of one species of animal can entail quite unexpected consequences and can extend its influence to organisms of a quite different type.

The example can also teach us how difficult it is to establish a suitable criterion for what is natural or unnatural. Can it be unnatural that social parasites live in the ant state in nature?

Perhaps the termites can come to our aid again in this train of thought. It is not that they give us the key to what is natural and what is not. But a careful study of the social life of termites might perhaps explain how social parasitism can be avoided. No case of social parasitism is known among termites. They too have social castes that are interdependent, and they too practice reciprocal mouth-

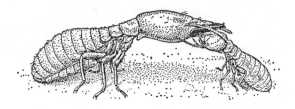

Termite worker feeding one of the large soldiers.

to-mouth feeding among adults—a social bond that derives from brood-tending behavior. For, as we showed for wasps, among the insects closely related to termites there are many species where the mothers care for the eggs and lick them, like the earwig (*Forficula*), and others where the mothers feed the larvae, like some cockroaches. And termites, like social wasps, have made use of this brood-tending behavior as raw material for building up a highly specialized society.

Even among spiders there are species that live socially. Very often, all that is generally known of the life of the spider is that it can be dangerous for the males to come close to a female, for the females are often much larger and treat the male like prey. Not all spiders live in strict solitude; there are some who work together in large groups and get on correspondingly well. In recent years a number of such spiders from Africa have been closely examined, above all a "round" spider (*Achaeranea disparata*) and a cellar spider (*Agelena consociata*[18]).[68] Both build large communal webs on shrubs. If a fairly large prey such as a grasshopper is caught in the web the spiders rush up, carry it away together, and then feed on it together too. Since spiders have a very narrow mouth they cannot devour their food bit by bit; nor do they have chewing mandibles, so they have to suck in their food. This is why they mash up their prey chemically, by spitting digestive juices onto it. The disintegrated predigested prey is then drunk. Individual spiders of the above-named cellar spider family have been made to eat from a radioactively marked prey and then put back on the communal web. After all of them had captured and eaten a new prey together, the radioactivity was traceable in the other animals too. So it must have been spat in the digestive juices of the animal first infected with it and then imbibed by all the others. In fact, the animals eat as though from one large bowl; none of them, so to speak, cooks its own dinner for itself alone. Whether this exchange of substances has any social significance is not yet known. But it is interesting to note that among spiders, who are generally known as greedy and food-jealous animals, a fairly intimate form of social life goes together with a reciprocal grant of food comparable to the early stages of pair-bonding among gulls we described earlier (see p. 128). Admittedly both types of spider form anonymous open societies into which conspecifics from other webs can be admitted without difficulty, and in fact one can even form a new community made up of animals from altogether different webs. It is known that among some other comb-footed spiders of the *Theridion* species, including those native to Europe, the mothers share their meal with their children. One can see a mother with some thirty offspring "eat" from one large fly. And the mother does not only tolerate her young here but even bores a number of holes into the prey for them so that they can eat, for the jaws of the babies are still too weak. When the mother eats alone, she only bores one or two holes. The very small baby spiders are fed mouth-to-mouth by the mother. She regurgitates food from her stomach and offers it to the children in drop form; they come to her one after the other and take the drop from her mouth. The young are cared for in this way from the first day after they hatch from the egg-cocoon until, a few days later, they can take part directly in the mother's meal and later even help the mother to tie up her prey with sticky threads.[9] This collaboration between mother and child is largely the same as the collaboration among adults

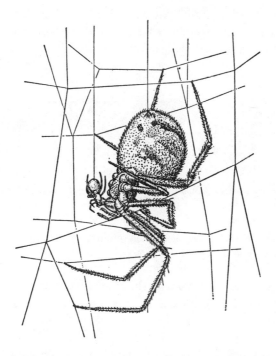

Comb-footed spider mother feeding a young one mouth-to-mouth.

in the related species described earlier, who always live in communities. But hitherto all we know is the correlation between the two; whether social life grew out of brood-tending behavior here too still has to be investigated.

These few examples from the great kingdom of lower animals suffice to show how much even they can tell us about the basic questions of communal social life. Further research in this field is looked forward to with great expectation. Here we will confine ourselves to the observations we have made about fish and birds and now turn to mammals, among whom there are again species that characteristically live in firm pairs or in larger compact groups.

The tree shrews of Southeast Asia, who are very curious animals in many respects, have already become familiar to the reader from the discussion on social stress (see p. 64). In systematic terms they are very primary mammals. In

Tree shrew mates lick each other's snout (right) just as infants do to the mother (left).

contrast to earlier views, they may not after all belong among the close relatives of primates, yet they have some things in common with hares and rabbits. This can be seen, for example, in their brood-tending behavior. Rabbit mothers only visit and suckle their young once every twenty-four hours, tree shrew mothers only once in forty-eight hours! The tree shrew offspring, usually numbering two or three, are quite full up in a few minutes, when they are left to their own devices again for another two days. True, the mother builds a nest for her young, but she does not stay there. She spends the night in the special "parental sleeping nest" together with her mate, with whom she lives in firm monogamy. The young are neither warmed nor covered with nesting material nor cleaned by the mother, and she would not bring them back into the nest if they left it; in fact, they never do so at this stage, and only man or some other disturber could throw them out. Martin, who was probably the first to observe the entire social behavior of these animals carefully,[77] described what happens during the visit of a mother to her young. She stands over the young with straddled legs, and neither looks at them nor licks them. The young lie on their backs diagonally to the mother and suck rapidly. They thrust against the mother's stomach with their front paws. After a short time they move from one teat to the next. After sucking they move forward to the mother's head and lick her mouth, which she inclines down to them. Occasionally the mother offers her mouth directly for licking. After this she leaves them again.

After thirty-three days the young leave the nest, but still return to it in the following three days in cases of danger and at night. After this time they follow their mother into the parental nest and sleep with the parents, until, aged some ninety days, they reach sexual maturity and leave their parents. Shortly before their first excursion out of their own nest the young are occasionally suckled every day. Outside the nest they sometimes suck every six hours, but probably cease to do so entirely as soon as they live in the parental nest. During the transitional phase mouth-licking also occurs more often. At times one young tree shrew sits to the left and another to the right of the mother and they lick up a clear fluid that emerges from the corners of her mouth. Occasionally the young also lick the mouth of the father. When they move into the parental nest, mouth-licking gradually becomes more rare. What its purpose is has not yet been established. Perhaps it provides the young with some nourishing substance or with the necessary digestive bacteria. Or perhaps it provides them with particular olfactory substances. But whatever its significance, it is no doubt an important pattern of behavior between mother and child because it plays such a large part in brood-tending, which has very few other notable features among tree shrews.

Later, this mouth-licking occurs again constantly, but only between the partners of a pair (and probably only when other adults live in the same area). When a male and female who are paired meet, they can sniff at each other just as they sniff at every other member of the species; but here one licks the mouth of the other, just as the children do to their mother. The licking can be initiated by the male or the female, but it is seen more frequently between the parents themselves than between them and the young, who may still live with them. Again it is not certain what its purpose is. Perhaps it serves to transmit scent signals, or it could equally well be a pair-bonding rite.

Intensive reciprocal mouth-licking, in which the young eagerly swallow the maternal saliva, also occurs among golden hamsters (*Mesocricetus*), harvest mice (*Micromys*), spiny mice (*Acomys*), and dormice (*Glis*); they do not live in a state of marriage but sometimes form loose groups. Mouth-licking has never been observed among adults.

One predator that lives in firm monogamy for some years at least is the African black-backed jackal (*Canis mesomelas*); sufficiently protracted studies are still required to determine whether the pair-bond lasts a whole lifetime. Both partners share the brood-tending. As soon as the young begin to eat solid foods the parents go on the hunt and bring prey to the young from far away. They do not carry it in their mouth but presumably in their stomach. While the parents are hunting, the young often play with one another, but they immediately beg at the parents on their return and even venture a little distance to meet them. The young jackal raises its head up steeply toward the mouth of the parent animal and even nuzzles its lips. The parents then regurgitate the food they have brought: whole mice or a rather liquid dark mass that consists of beetles and other insects. Sometimes the young do not wait for the prey to be dropped on the ground but take it out of their parents' mouths, into which they can stick their heads quite far.[123] Adult jackals greet their pair-partner with the same begging gesture, crouching down a little and nudging the lips of the other with their mouth.

The same is known of wolves and domestic dogs. They

Adult jackals (top) and hunting dogs (bottom) nuzzle
the jaws of their partner in greeting in the same way
that their young beg food from adults.

too bring food to their young; the young beg at the parent
by nuzzling its jaws, and adults greet each other in the
same way. But they do not live in firm pairs. So this greeting borrowed from the food-begging of the young animal
can—as with the wood swallow among birds—acquire a general social meaning. This has been studied carefully for
hunting dogs. The African hunting dog (*Lycaon pictus*)
is the predator with the highest success rate in hunting.
Hardly a trip ends in failure. These animals live in packs of
several adults of both sexes (in one carefully studied pack
there were six males, two females, and fifteen young in all,
from two litters).[61] They hunt every morning and evening,
in small groups. As long as the pack still includes dependent
young, the females stay with their offspring and the males
hunt alone. They tear pieces the size of a hand off the prey
and devour them; only the head and skeleton of a thirty-
kilogram gazelle remain after five minutes. Then the hunters
trot home and feed their young by regurgitating the meat in

large portions. When the young are full and will eat no more the adults eat the meat again themselves. If the young become hungry again and beg, more food is regurgitated. Often they regurgitate what they have just begged from one animal for another begging animal. In this way all the members of the pack are provided with meat. This "meat-spitting" is a very effective brood-tending measure. In a pack of hunting dogs that had lost all its females through accidents, five males brought up the nine five-week-old young alone. Such a feeding community also enables the animals to divide up the work in a society in which some members at least "earn their living" indirectly at times. When the pack becomes active again after its night or midday rest, or before it sets off on the hunt, or when some members of the pack meet again after a short separation, intense greeting takes place. The animals go up to each other in a tense attitude, just as they do when other large animals disturb them in their territory, and then lick each other's face and nuzzle their nose against the corners of their partner's mouth in the same way as the young do to the large adults or hungry adults do to returning hunters. So this begging behavior is also addressed to members of the pack who are themselves hungry. But the behavior does not only serve for food-begging; it is also a greeting, and it removes social tensions within the group. When the young are five weeks old they also begin to use this gesture of greeting.[61]

Sea lions (*Zalophus californianus*) live in herds on the coasts of the Galapagos Islands during the mating season. The herds always consist of one bull and several females together with their young. Each male occupies a strip of coast that he defends against rivals by swimming to and fro in front of it almost all day long and, when he surfaces at certain points, loudly barking. Often this means that territorial neighbors emerge next to one another in the shallow water to strengthen their common boundary. Young animals who want to go into the deeper water are cut off from it by

the bull, who pushes them back into the shallow waters
again. In the evening, the bull drives all his females and
young to the shore and is the last to land. Females among
themselves only defend their current territory against other
members of the harem when they are on dry land. Yet this

Left: greeting between mother and child of Galapagos
seals. Right: between male and female Galapagos sea
lions.

fairly often leads to disputes. In that case the lord of the
harem immediately comes to land and separates the disputants by pushing his way between them and then greeting
both sides until the ladies have calmed down again. The
greeting consists of waving his outstretched neck from side
to side and touching the snouts of the ladies. The females
greet one another in the same way, as do mothers their
children.[26] Presumably this greeting has derived from the
food-begging of the young. But hitherto it has not been
fully proved, for young sea lions are not fed by the parent
animals. Here, as with the cuckoo (see p. 133), the behavioral pattern may have survived as a social greeting
while the original function—i.e., feeding the young—has disappeared; for sea lions are predators, among whom feeding
the young is very common; this applies not only to dogs and
jackals, as we have seen, but also among smaller predators,
such as polecats or mongooses. But the food is not always

regurgitated for the young; often it is simply brought to them in the parents' mouths, as with meerkats (*Suricata*), a kind of mongoose that lives in Africa. Here the mother brings the food to her young, offers it to them in her mouth, and then leaps about in front of them until they obey her and take the food from her mouth. Meerkats will eat animal and vegetable foods of the most varied kinds, and in addition they are "food jealous" and try to grab food from the jaws of others. When the mother brings food to the young

A young brown rat snatches a bit of food from its mother.

and then incites them to take it from her she is teaching them which foods are suitable. And indeed this creates eating traditions, for the young learn to choose the diet the mother prefers.[31] Similarly, young squirrels, rats, and other rodents who are just beginning to learn to eat alone try to steal bits of food from the mother's mouth.[28] All this is reminiscent of the snout-nudging that occurs in the greeting of various sea lions. Yet this is only a reference to its possible origins.

This manner of feeding that we have shown among many birds and some predators also occurs among the manlike apes, the chimpanzee, gorilla, and orangutan, who also feed their young mouth-to-mouth with regurgitated food. Even small chimpanzee and gorilla children take bits of food from their mother's hand or even from her mouth. And they also use their own hand or mouth. It is known of gorillas, at lease in captivity, that the mother takes food between her lips and then offers it to her child directly. Chimpanzees do this too, and we know that they also do so in the wild.[72] Even two-year-old children beg at their mother by presenting their pursed lips to her; then the mother pushes a lip full of chewed food directly into their mouth, for chimpanzees have a very wide lower lip, which can be filled with food like a large spoon. As with many birds, and with jackals and hunting dogs, this feeding gesture also appears among adults, namely for greeting purposes, and in particular when two animals have not seen each other for several days, for instance because the pack had split up.

In addition, all chimpanzee mothers gently press their lips onto various parts of the body of their babies and small children (up to the age of one year old). They take the child's hand and touch the palm with their lips. The lips are not pursed for this but remain close to the teeth. The mouth is usually open. Adults touch each other in the same

Mouth-to-mouth baby-feeding (left) and "kiss" of greeting between adult chimpanzees (right).

way, pressing their lips to an arm or a shoulder, at times even to their own hand. A worried child can touch its mother in this way, or even an adult male chimpanzee while he is copulating with the mother. So the kiss of greeting between chimpanzees could also stem from the rather groping contact of the lips which, like mouth-to-mouth feeding, is equally typical of mother-child behavior.

In terms of reciprocal feeding and the social actions derived from it among mammals, there are obvious analogies with the bird behavior we described earlier. The jackal lives in monogamy like the raven and has turned feeding the young into a greeting between partners; meanwhile the actual transmission of food has disappeared, leaving only a ritual. The hunting dog lives in fairly large communities like the wood swallow and treats all the members of the group in the same way as monogamous species treat their mate. The sea lion seems to correspond to the cuckoo, not because it has no brood-tending behavior but insofar as mouth-to-mouth feeding has disappeared here too, while the greeting ritual derived from it has survived. As with birds, however, many other typical brood-tending behavior patterns exist among mammals, and they also play a definite role in social life.

Hungry fawns squeal or utter the somewhat softer contact sound. This brings the mother to them, and she may utter the same sound. Later the same sounds no longer serve to call the mother but to keep mother and child together. The doe in heat also entices the buck with the same sounds.[66] Moreover, she summons him to follow her in the same way as the fawn did, remaining standing in front of him, turning back her raised head, and uttering contact sounds.

If two chamois or goat antelopes of different ranking order come into contact, the lower-ranking animal will usually demonstrate its inferiority "spontaneously." It crouches down, stretches out its head low and horizontally, and occasionally also lifts its nose slightly. In addition it cocks its ears forward and raises its tail above the horizontal. In this posture the chamois slinks or trots to the superior

Fallow-deer doe approaching the buck (top) and low-ranking chamois approaching a higher-ranking doe (below).

partner on bended legs. Animals of all ages and of both sexes do this. Usually they aim for the side of the high-ranking animal, in particular its flanks or head, or more rarely, they come from behind to the rear, i.e., the scrotum for males, the teats for females. Young animals prefer to aim for the body zone of the partner, where the breasts lie on the female, and it can quite often occur that they then subside on their carpal joint ("kneel" on their front legs) and raise their snout conspicuously. This humble attitude is not always released by aggressiveness on the part of the high-ranking animal; often the inferior one will spontaneously go up to the other, in particular among young animals again. These are fairly clear vestiges of child-ish behavior toward the mother, although combined with other elements. For instance, fawns never run to their mother with bended knees nor do they then emphatically cock their ears.[67] If a doe approaches a stronger male she will come with out-stretched head and slightly open snout, while making licking tongue movements, diagonal, upward-thrusting movements with her head, her tail standing on end, and sometimes also uttering a short call. A young fawn coming up to its mother to drink behaves in exactly the same way.

22. *The Social Significance of Maternal Signals*

Adult African hunting dogs, whose group behavior we described in the previous chapter (see p. 165), use various gestures of greeting or appeasement that derive from childish behavior. The young suck from their mother in a lying,

Young hunting dogs sucking from their mother (left) and adult hound licking the teats of a female in greeting (right).

sitting, or standing position. But, as we showed, they do not only receive milk from her teats but are also provided with meat—in part undigested—regurgitated from the mouth of both parents. They beg for both by nudging with their noses, but do not aim specifically for one or the other. It may happen that they obtain milk by bumping their nose against the lips of the mother, or they may obtain meat by knocking against the middle of her body. Young dogs aged three to five weeks prefer to direct their begging movements at the middle of the mother's body between the front and back legs, and do the same to males too. For her part, the mother invites them to suck either by lying down on her side and offering her large right-hand teats or by walking backward with her head held low some meters in front of the whelps, as for regurgitating food, and then letting them suck.

So mouth and teats have a food-presentation significance. At the same time they have a social significance derived from this. On p. 166 we described how these dogs nuzzle one another's lips in greeting. Besides this we also find adults addressing childlike behavior at the female's teats: During the violent greeting after the midday rest and before departing on the hunt the dogs can lick the female's teats. A remarkable feature of this predator notorious for its cruelty toward its prey is the almost unsurpassed friendliness between the members of a pack. There is no apparent ranking order among them, and instead each tries to outdo the other in displays of humility. For this they use gestures of greeting and appeasement derived from childish behavior. So nuzzling and licking of the mouth and teats are not only interchangeable begging movements, but both are also transferred into the social behavior of adults.[61]

The males of the Indian flying fox (*Pteropus giganteus*), a large, fruit-eating bat with a wingspan of up to eighty centimeters, which lives in large colonies, also lick the female's teats, in particular during the foreplay to copulation. There are no firm pair-bonds among these animals; the females are usually rather on the defensive so that the young males have to make great efforts before managing to mate. This is probably why an element from childish behavior, which can put the female into a tolerant frame of mind, appears during their foreplay to mating.[83]

At first the female bat tries to resist the courting male; but among other animals the female more often tries to run away from the male, and the male can counteract this by childish behavior too. An example are the waterbucks of Uganda. Comparison with related species helps to clarify in which functional context this specific behavior benefits the antelope.

The group of ungulates, which is very rich in species, includes many different forms of corporate life between male, female, and young. The bonds between the sexes range through nearly every possible gradation. We find a minimum of solidarity among giraffes, where not even mother and child remain together for long, and the maximum with some duikers, who are monogamous throughout their life. Among most of the species, however, the sexes only meet for mating. It is very common for the females to live in fairly large herds, together with their young, and for the males either to form their own herds or for each male to defend his own territory. When in heat, the females then come into these territories.

The male who succeeds in mating with most females has most progeny, and is therefore favored by selection. But in each reproductive cycle the females are mated several times; so several males can come in question as the father. The probability of a certain male conceiving his progeny with a particular female naturally increases with the number of potential copulatory acts he himself manages to perform during her cycle. This means that he must do his best to prevent rivals from getting at the female. His primary weapon is his territory, in which no male will tolerate rivals. The boundaries are established beforehand by combat, and even when a female is in a neighboring territory, another male will not try to cross the borders. However, this is only half the problem solved. Since the territorial borders only apply to the males, a female could decide to move in with a neighboring male instead. The males of all species try to prevent the female from doing so by various means. Usually they circle around the female or females—who often arrive in groups—try to bar their way or to impress them, and even threaten them. Among the defassa waterbucks (*Kobus defassa ugandae*), the males hold territories extending from twelve hectares to two square kilometers, each closely bordering on the next, in which young males and all the young females wander about. The calves are also born in the territory of an adult male. During the first two to four weeks of its life the calf remains hidden in a special place; this keeps its mother tied to the area too and thus to the territory of the male where her calf was born. Since the next reproductive cycle begins during this same period, although it only lasts a day, the respective territory-owning male has no difficulties in keeping the female in heat close to him.[110]

The Uganda kob (*Adenota kob thomasi*) is closely related to the defassa waterbuck. But the males' territories are extremely small and only have a diameter of fifteen to thirty meters or even less. They too are closely adjoining, thus creating a male colony of mating territories that is fairly large at the borders and becomes smaller and smaller

A young Uganda kob sucking from its mother (left) and
adult bucks in the sequel to copulation (right).

toward the center of the colony, until eventually fifteen or more territories are crowded together in an area of a diameter of about two hundred meters. The females prefer the center of the colony with the smallest territories; most mating occurs in the inner three or four territories. But here the danger of the female moving over to a neighboring male is very great. The Uganda kob bucks counter this by a special behavior. First, no feature of the foreplay of mating of this species looks at all like a threat that could drive off the female; since the foreplay to mating of most antelopes is full of threatening gestures, this "foresight" on the part of the Uganda kob is very striking. In addition, he is the only one to have a special sequel to mating, which can last up to five minutes (copulation itself lasts at most two seconds). While the female stands quiet the buck licks her teats or the inguinal glands, which are directly beside them; he does so by pushing his head either between her straddled back legs or under her abdomen from the side like a suckling calf. This behavior also contributes toward preventing the female from crossing over into neighboring territories and enables the same male to copulate again after a brief pause. Consequently most females only visit three or four males, i.e., much fewer than would be expected at first.[12]

There is no doubt in these cases that the maternal source of milk has a social significance for the adult animals. It can already acquire it for the animal in its early youth. For among mammals, the mother, who at first is the only one to provide food, is therefore also the most important social partner of the newborn animal. Generally, those maternal signals that herald food also acquire the additional significance of marks of protection and security, above all among species who suckle their young for a long time. One can observe this among ungulates. Young antelopes who are suddenly frightened often run to the mother and grasp her teats, even at an age when they would not normally drink from her any more. This "comfort suckling" is also known of the European deer. When the doe, alarmed by a cry of fear from her young, has freed it from an enemy or even fled with it, the young animal will suck briefly and be licked intensively by the mother. Drinking and cleaning are typical of every encounter between mother and offspring in the first three to five months after birth. The doe licks the fawn, particularly around the rear, and this light "massage" intensifies the young animal's search for the teat and desire to drink. Licking reappears later in a different context: After copulation the buck and the doe lie down for a while, then stand up and lick each other reciprocally. This contact behavior corresponds entirely to that of the male Uganda kob after mating; among deer it also serves to keep the partners together, for the buck remains with his doe for a long time, up to nine months.[66]

Young marsupials are born fairly unformed; the offspring of the giant kangaroo are born after only one month of pregnancy. They continue to grow in the pouch, where they sometimes remain for six months and into which they manage to crawl from the birth aperture without help. In the pouch they take the teat into their mouth and cling to it firmly. Later, when they occasionally peer out of the pouch, they still keep the teat in their mouth most of the time. Young kangaroos who have already left the pouch flee back into it at the first sign of danger. But when they have reached a certain size the mother no longer allows her young to return to the pouch; then the young kangaroo confines itself to sticking its head in it (see p. 73). The "comforting effect" of this behavior is not so obvious here, however, since the young are not weaned until after sexual maturity; so it can happen that a female animal already has one young one in her pouch while she herself still sucks from her own mother, and, in the meantime, a "little sister" is already clinging to the other teat. In the foreplay to mating the male sniffs the genital zone and the pouch aperture of the female. He finds special scent glands there which, as far as we know, play a part in mating behavior.

As a rule mammals have scent glands both in the genital region and also beside the teats, whose smell is automatically learned by the baby; later, this scent can become fairly important to mating behavior or even in more general social life.

Man also possesses a scent-producing organ, namely the axillary organ. It is particularly highly developed among women and consists of an extensive complex of scent glands under the arm. This scent organ is not so well-developed among any monkeys, so it is certainly not a mere remnant left to us by our prehuman ancestors, but an evolutionary feature typical of man. This suggests that it is of significance in the social communication between mother and child and between man and woman. Indeed, we already know that olfactory signals play a considerable role for man and that the sensitivity of women to certain scents varies with the menstrual cycle. It would be important to discover more about this, and to compare it with the olfactory signals of animals. Unfortunately this is difficult for us, because we are unable to perceive many chemical stimuli and because analysis of chemical substances is very time-consuming as well as being more awkward than that of sounds or colors, for example. That is why the following examples are probably easier for us to understand, concerned as they are with sight-oriented animals, i.e., those who are guided predominantly by their eyes. But the nose still plays a part, even with man ("He stinks." . . . "This stinks."); only there are clearly visible signals besides the smells.

The young of the gray woolly monkey from South America (*Lagothrix lagotricha*) are suckled for eighteen months. During this time the main purpose of suckling gradually shifts from feeding to comforting. By the age of six months, the young monkey is only suckled before going to sleep and two or three times during the day, usually to console it after some excitement or shock.[127] For a young monkey six weeks old the maternal breast already represents a signal, which the mother uses deliberately when she calls it if it sets off to seek adventure. She lifts her arms and shows it her rather large, full breast. (The young monkeys will also go to other well-known females and occasionally also suckle there.)

It is fairly certain that an olfactory component enters into play here too. The body odor of woolly monkeys is strongest on the breast. In the first four weeks of its life, the baby clings to the dense breast fur of the mother and learns its smell. Later, when the young monkey makes friends with other members of the colony, it begins by seeking out the highest-ranking males and cuddles up against their chest. According to observations made by Williams, the familiar smell of the breast plays an important part both in the relations between mother and child and also in mating, and even in the greeting between adult males. Moreover, the entire living area, in particular that of the adult males of a colony, is marked with "chest rubbing"; the monkey smears saliva on certain places and objects with the lips, and then spreads it around with upward thrusting movements of the chest until eventually his chest is dripping wet. Females do this much less often, the high-ranking ones slightly more often than others. The chest of the male is usually matted and has bark-colored spots from his habit of marking trees.[127]

Many young monkeys of all kinds can be seen sleeping with their mother's teat in their mouth. But even when they are awake, they seek shelter there. If they have strayed far from their mother they rush back to her in face of an often imaginary danger, hold onto her, and grasp a teat with their lips; they do not then suckle, however, but instead twist their head around far enough to be able to see in the direction of the danger. Rheus monkeys, African tree monkeys, and baboons, to mention only a few, all do this. The children often hold the teat in their mouth without sucking even when no danger is looming. This is known of the ring-tailed lemur (*Lemur catta*), a half-ape, too. The maternal teat simply has an appeasement effect. This is why it is difficult to say exactly how long baby monkeys continue to drink from their mother. Observations made in the wild by Jane van Lawick-Goodall[72] have taught us that chimpanzee

A young African vervet seeking shelter at its mother's
breast.

babies drink every ninety minutes up to the age of a year
and a half. But one still sees six-month-old chimpanzee babies drink much more often, every quarter of an hour, in
fact. That is because this is the age when they begin going
out on short forays, and since they are still frightened of any
number of things, they keep running back to the mother to
seek comfort at her breast, often only for a few seconds.
They also grasp the teat when a playmate tries to pull them
away from their mother or to annoy them in some other
way. Three-year-old chimpanzees are still suckled about
once an hour. The children are weaned automatically when
they are 3½ because the mother is then able to conceive
again and her milk dries up. The children still try to drink
from the mother a few times and then give up. Sons leave
their mother off and on for a few days when they are about
six years old. But close relations are maintained between

mother and son even when he is adult; the son comes to his mother's aid if she is threatened by other chimpanzees and the mother shares her food with her son.

Among chimpanzees, then, the female breast has a social significance for the child, but not, so far as we know to date, for adults. But there are signs that it has among other monkeys, such as some African tree monkeys, where the female teats are strikingly colored in certain phases of her cycle, no matter whether she has offspring or not. Since monkeys are very sharp observers, one must assume that the males at least learn to value the teat coloring of the female as an indication of her readiness for mating. This has not yet been studied. There is one monkey, however, for whom the female breast has become an unmistakable social signal. This is the red-chested gelada baboon (*Theropithecus gelada*), who is not in fact a baboon at all but more closely related to the African tree monkeys. The importance of the breast as a signal is evident among other primates too. The breast of the female ring-tailed lemur is almost hairless while she is suckling, so that a black patch of skin is visible in her fur, which is otherwise light gray. Among female tree monkeys who have already borne young, the teats always jut out from the fur; they are red and placed so close together that the baby can suck on both at the same time. The red-chested gelada baboon acquired its name from a large hairless patch on its chest. The patch is divided up into two zones by the fur that grows in from the side. The smaller upper zone is like an inverted triangle, with the lower point touching the point of the inverted heart-shaped zone below it. The naked skin varies from pale red to bright blood-red, and surrounding fur is gray brown. The whole effect can become extremely striking, for on the border of the fur the "*décolleté*" is entirely surrounded by wrinkled folds of skin that can turn almost white and then look like a *ruche*. Again both teats lie close together in the lower heart-shaped area and can, according to the phase of the sexual cycle, become bright red in contrast to the paler skin.

The gelada baboon lives in the mountains of Ethiopia at a height of some three or four thousand meters. It forms bands consisting of harem groups, i.e., a male and several females with her young. They seek their food on the high plateaus, preferably while seated. In this position the chest is very conspicuous. We know that these baboons do not merely carry this physical signal about on them and let it have its effect, but exploit it deliberately in face of conspecifics, pushing out their chest at a partner from the group in a similar way to woolly monkeys. Several observations also suggest that they can underline this by pointing their finger at their own breast. Since these animals have not yet been sufficiently well studied, we do not know yet what effect this signal has on the partner—perhaps it is appeasing, or promises protection and comfort. We can assume that the baby is automatically exposed to this signal when it drinks, like the babies of other animal species who are exposed to the scent signals near the teats. What is certain is that the female breast is a socially important signal for adult gelada baboons and that it has even undergone certain changes in the service of this function, namely becoming more conspicuous. It has acquired a new significance without losing the old one, and the new significance is built up on the old.

There are numerous examples to show how the outer form of an organ changes when it acquires an additional function. Organs and the responses addressed to such organs by the members of a species are quite often to a large extent emancipated from their original purpose in the animal kingdom. Nature or the Creator sees no reason not to introduce an existing "invention" elsewhere too if it can be of use there. Often this upsets the attempts at classification of men who would like to separate organs neatly according to their functions. In the end there will presumably be nothing for it but for man to accept the natural order he finds and to adapt his classifications to it.

Originally, no doubt, breast and teats only served to nourish the infant. They have now acquired not only an additional function in social life but have been exploited in other directions too, for instance by bats, in particular the small insect-eating bats. This order of mammals, very rich in different species, includes the group of horseshoe bats (*Rhinolophoidea*), to which the native European horseshoe bat also belongs (*Rhinolophus*). The animals took their name from the curious "sonar" system on their nose, which serves them for ultrasonic echo-location. In general bats only produce one young, which is why they only have one pair of teats. Formerly, mammals had a number of teats, like pigs, arranged in two rows along the abdomen, and the milk gland formed a long milk line. Among many mammals the length of the milk gland together with the number of teats decreases according to the number of young. The remaining teats can be located near the back legs as with cows, goats, horses, and antelopes, or in front on the trunk as with monkeys, elephants, and bats. In fact, horseshoe bats have another pair of teats between their back legs too; the milk gland beneath them has shriveled up, but among some species the teats themselves are very large and jut far out of the fur. These teats have become specialized as dummies; the young bat takes one of them firmly in its mouth and then rests upright against its mother, who is hanging head down. For drinking, it turns around and goes to one of the front teats, which provide milk. The mother can already take the young bat with her on excursions in the first days after birth, when it attaches itself to one of the dummy teats. Young kangaroos hang onto a teat continually too, but they are also attached to the mother by her pouch. The "dry teats" of horseshoe bats no longer serve for feeding, but in a sense replace the pouch, by keeping the young firmly attached to its mother; they have even become specialized in terms of this attachment function.

The basis for this specialization is the fortuitous "transportation by teat" of the offspring, which we also know of various rodents. Female rats, mice, and squirrels who have had a sudden fright often drag their brood along with them for a certain distance simply because the young do not let go of the teats but remain hanging from them. Usually they fall off after a little while and are then brought back into the nest in the mother's mouth. Among one kind of vole, however (*Microtus incertis*), the female is said to sit over the young in cases of danger and to summon them to suck her teats, and then drags off the whole brood while they are suckling. The young of the wood rat (*Neotoma fuscipes*) hold onto the teats so firmly that the mother can make long leaps with them; the milk teeth of these young are bent into special gripping organs, which fit the teats exactly.[27] Since these animals have many offspring, all the teats are used for suckling; horseshoe bats, by contrast, can leave some teats for conversion into organs of transport.

Infant baboons, rhesus monkeys, and langurs do not only cling to the fur of the mother when she sets off but also hold onto a teat with their mouth. These examples show once again how physical structure depends on behavior: When the mother has to take the young with her and they hold onto the teat, the teats, which were originally meant for suckling, can be transformed into organs of transport. But the same also applies to the original function. Female mammals have not become the more important of the two parents in the care of the newborn baby simply because they possess milk glands; rather the milk glands have become fully developed on the female because it is she who is bound most closely to the young, for the males are also equipped with milk glands.

23. Special Behavior Patterns of the Infant Animal

It is common to classify young animals as either nest-huggers (nidicolous) or nest-fleers (nidifugous). Nest-huggers come into the world relatively undeveloped, often with closed eyes, without fur or teeth, and unable to walk. Nest-fleers, by contrast, are so well developed that they can follow the parent animal or even live by themselves. Kangaroos, bats, and monkeys, however, do not fit either of these categories; their young are born unfinished, but they are not placed in a nest; instead they remain on the body of the mother or of other adults, who carry them around. Manlike apes build sleeping nests, but they never leave the young in them. Chimpanzee babies remain in constant contact with the mother's body during the first four or five months following birth![72]

This very close contact between parents and offspring has given rise to several other behavior elements besides the significance of the maternal breast; these elements acquire an important role in later social life. For example, among monkeys, this includes the well-known reciprocal "delousing" or allogrooming. Originally this was a behavior pattern the mother addressed to her child. Among gorillas, three times as much allogrooming occurs between mother and child as between adults. Among chimpanzees, however, it is the reverse—not because chimpanzee mothers care less intensively for their young but because grooming between

Male doguera baboon performing brood-tending ("delousing") on a young one (left); social grooming between
adult female hamadryas baboons (right). The grooming
female has a large estrus-swelling (see pp. 208f.).

adults has increased to a corresponding degree; one-third
of all allogrooming actions among chimpanzees takes place
between adult males and adult females.[95]

This mutual fur-care is known to anyone who has ever
watched zoo monkeys, such as macaques or baboons. A
more exact analysis will show that the "delousing" partners
do not meet haphazardly. Among rhesus monkeys, for instance, it is mothers and their offspring who prefer to
delouse each other, even if the offspring is already adult.
They can be joined by good friends of the mother, and
this creates loose- or tight-knit grooming communities within
the society.[96]

Among adults, allogrooming appears to inhibit attack and
is used in those situations that could easily lead to disputes,
in order to appease a higher-ranking animal; it occurs very
often between the female and her mate during the mating
season. There are distinct postures for the invitation to
allogrooming, but the males can also respond to presentation (see p. 207) by allogrooming. The more fully these
conditions are studied on increasingly numerous species of
monkeys, the more clearly we discern the great social sig-

nificance of this action, which also derives from brood-tending.[63, 109]

The same evolution has occurred independently among the half-apes. They too have converted the maternal grooming of young into an important social action, but they groom predominantly with their teeth, while the higher monkeys use their hands.[51]

When a baboon or macaque mother has weaned her offspring and no longer lets it drink from her breast, one sometimes sees a young one sitting in front of its mother

A young doguera baboon trying to reach the mother's teats.

and stretching its hand out to her breast. I saw doguera baboon children in the wild who reached out for food that the mother had in her mouth or was taking into her mouth. Occasionally they also reached for the mother's face, which was then turned to them. From these gestures there has now developed a "begging gesture," like that of zoo mon-

Hamadryas baboon (above) and chimpanzee stretching
out an open hand in "begging."

keys toward visitors. The animals learn to convert the original grasping attempt into a calm, expectant raising of
the hand. Macaques living in the wild use this as a begging
gesture toward conspecifics; chimpanzees too, both young
and adult, stretch out their hand to a member of their
species who has food, and some of what they desire is

then placed in their hand. Even high-ranking chimpanzee males beg lower-ranking ones who had a lucky hunt for meat.[72] An adult male hamadryas baboon in Munich Zoo did not only employ the usual pasha methods but also used his hand, laid open on the ground in the direction of his female, as an invitation to her to come to him or to stay with him. Chimpanzees eventually command agreement or social support with this gesture; a lower-ranking animal who wants to go past a higher-ranking one to a tree with fruit stretches out its hand to the higher-ranking one and waits until the latter lays its finger on the hand or some other part of the body of the beggar in agreement. Opening up the hand, stretching out the hand, and, finally, pressing the hand, give encouragement or support in tense situations.[72]

It is tempting, although not yet clearly proved, to assume that these manual gestures go back to early childhood when the young one grasps its mother. More exact long-term observations will no doubt tell us more. It is already known that hand-foot contacts act as encouragement and signify agreement and greeting among chimpanzees, as does reciprocal touching of the genitals. The following social behavior patterns are more obviously derived from childhood.

For a mother-hugger like a young monkey it is particularly important to hold on and, if danger threatens and it is far from its mother, to rush back to her immediately and cling to her so that she can carry it with her on her flight. This behavior survives into old age: Adult male baboons and chimpanzees who are scared or faced with danger or an unknown thing that frightens them look around for a friendly comrade, go up to him, and embrace him. Before an attack on an enemy predator or at the onset of a violent quarrel within the herd one can see large male baboons falling around each other's necks uttering soothing sounds. Even the young animal who has been weaned, first seeks refuge with another female and larger males; this can lead to individual friendships, in which gestures of greeting taken from brood-tending behavior play an important role. The success of such friendships is based on the mutual "protective help" that often lasts well into old age. Gestures of embrace and clutching to the breast derive from maternal behavior, which one partner uses in response to the other's search for refuge.

Among hamadryas baboons, other brood-tending elements besides these play a major part in the structure of the harem society.[63] Males also take part in brood-tending (see illustration, p. 187), particularly the young males. Orphans are usually adopted by half-grown males and brought up by them. At the onset of sexual maturity, the males take young females to themselves and treat them like a mother her child: They carry them against their body, take them on their back to jump over crevices in the rocks, guard them, and continually clutch them like a mother her child (males punish adult females with bites if they stray too far). These young females flee to their male protector in case of danger, cuddle up to him like children to their mother, and also call him with the call of the lost child. The male builds up a firm relationship with females who are not yet sexually mature with the help of this mother-child behavior; sexual behavior can remain absent for years, until the female is sexually mature.

By contrast, the young male can take up sexual relations with the females of an existing harem (see p. 227), and it is easier the younger he is. This way of life as an additional male on the borders of a harem group is extremely advantageous, for it means that the young male acquires the varied experience of paths and places of the old pasha and finally takes over the whole harem when the pasha abdicates and gives up his monopoly over the females. Yet the old animal continues to remain in the group, which is now led by the younger male, and he is still of use when situations crop up with which the young baboon cannot yet cope, perhaps because he has never before encountered them. Then the young baboon does not precede the troupe as leader but waits for the grizzled expasha to take over the leadership again. We find the same principle among doguera baboons: These animals have a "council of elders" who are no longer the highest-ranking group leaders and no longer have a prerogative in reproduction.[63]

24. Change of Function of Sexual Behavior

Permanent corporate life between two or more individuals is obviously a recent stage of development and, as always in evolution, the necessary adjustments are not "invented" *ad hoc* but derive from existing behavior. Behavior patterns taken from brood-tending are addressed to conspecifics; they agree neither with aggression against these conspecifics nor with flight behavior before them but are well suited for neutralizing aggression and flight tendencies in a society. Lorenz has stressed *redirected aggression* as another pair-bonding mechanism, which plays a role in the mating behavior of cichlid and graylag geese pairs.[75] Redirection means that the aggressive tendencies of one partner toward the other are deflected from the latter to a third party; the first partner is often infected and joins in too. This "come on, let's both get that one" behavior has some drawbacks, however: It binds two individuals at the price of their good relations with a third one and very often requires that a third be there in the first place. There are cases, again among monogamous cichlids, where a pair disintegrates for lack of such an outside "whipping boy," because the partners now direct their aggressive tendencies at each other after all. Now the different forms of pair-bonding are not mutually exclusive, and the same animal can exhibit both redirected aggression and functionally changed brood-tending actions.

There is a third root of pair-bonding behavior, namely the

sexual relations between the partners. Sexual behavior is also addressed at conspecifics, and it is equally irreconcilable with open attack or open flight. Australian finches offer a good example of the role that functionally changed sexual behavior can play in pair-bonding and social life.

Tropical finches are clearly followers of civilization and are therefore fairly easy to observe in the wild. In addition, they stand out by their very sociable way of life, which aroused the interest of behavior researchers. Immelmann has devoted extensive studies to the eighteen Australian species of this finch, and found, among other facts, the following.[48]

Far from the brooding places the animals live in flocks in which unmated animals of both sexes find their partner. Pair-bonding is usually initiated by the male with his song and preliminary courtship displays. If a male sings to a female who is already mated and at the same time slowly hops up to her, either he is attacked—or the female flees. But a female ready for mating shows her agreement by responding with weak greeting or courting movements. Among the zebra finches (*Taeniopygia guttata*) and the star finch (*Neochimia ruficauda*) pair-formation has taken place as soon as the partners cuddle up to each other or allopreen. In every case it is the female who decides whether to accept the male's advances or not; females who particularly want to mate can also invite the males to court. Most species seem to live monogamously, but the degree of cohesion of the partners varies: Diamond finch, red-eared finch, fire-tail finch, gouldian finch, and crimson finch are largely solitary, and the partners remain fairly independent even in the brooding time; however, among long-tailed and masked finches (*Poephila acuticauda* and *Poephila personata*), both partners always follow each other blindly, even when they are in flocks outside the brooding time. The flocks or groups are most characteristic of the steppe species, least so of the species that live in forests.

Shortly before sunset, the groups dissolve. Group coherence is an advantage for life in dry regions where the animals can only brood at certain times and sometimes have to go far afield to find food, and this coherence contributes much to the reciprocal stimulus and synchronization of the brood-pairs. Most species, therefore, continue to live socially during the brooding season. In many colonies real friendships come into being between pairs of neighbors.

Above all it is the special "social hours" of the day that serve to keep the group together; these periods are partly devoted to a communal search for food. The "socials" of masked amadines are the most highly developed instance. They are held at any desired spot as soon as several pairs from the large brooding colony meet: First the partners of each pair sit together allopreening, at a distance of a few centimeters from the next pair. After several minutes, isolated animals separate from their partner, hop up to a neighboring pair, and begin to "help" preen there. Gradually the whole group comes into motion, new partners keep coming together, and in the end almost every member of the group has preened every other one. This "social," in which six to ten pairs usually take part, lasts from thirty to sixty minutes. Eventually the brood-pairs come together again and the partners fly back to their nest together.

We have already spoken of the social significance of allopreening (see pp. 145ff.). The masked finch displays other special behavior forms during its "socials" too. Each newly arriving pair is greeted by rapid movements of the tail feathers, which quiver up and down vertically; all the pairs greet one another by quivering their tail feathers in this way. But this tail-quivering also occurs in a quite different behavior context, namely at the end of a series of courtship displays as the female invitation to copulation. This invitation to copulation, which is unusual among small birds, is peculiar to all tropical finches. Tail-quivering is widespread in this context, so it is no doubt the earlier behavior.

The tail-quivering of the masked amadine is both a female invitation to copulation and a general social greeting.

Among masked finches it has also become a gesture of greeting; this means that, although it looks identical in the two cases, it serves two entirely different purposes. But there is a difference in the choice of addressee: Between marital partners, tail-quivering occurs at the end of courtship as an invitation to copulation, and the female directs it at her male. As a gesture of greeting within a group, it occurs exclusively between members of the species who are not partners. When marital partners greet each other in a group, they perform a very low courtship bow. For tail-quivering to act as an invitation to copulation, the animals must, therefore, know each other as intimately as only the partners of a pair usually do; otherwise it will have the effect of a greeting. The partners of a pair have evidently chosen a different behavior pattern as greeting—namely the courtship bow—because they always see tail-quivering as an invitation to copulation. But masked finches bred in captivity consider all tail-quivering, even when meant as a greeting, as a summons to copulation. Perhaps this is because they are all compelled to know one another only too well in the confined space in which they live. Hereupon the males try to mate with each female who greets them. What is also striking is that only the female uses tail-quivering as a prelude to copulation, whereas both sexes use it for social greeting. So it can mean two things if done by the female, but if the male does so it can only be a greeting.

How has it happened that what was originally a purely sexual pattern of behavior occurs in group situations at all? So far we have only begun to answer this problem. It is likely that group life as such, which as we know serves the reciprocal stimulus and synchronization of the brood-pairs, is slightly sexual in tone. The "socials" we have described give the animals an opportunity for a kind of social courtship, and individual courtship actions have become freed from this context, which was originally strictly sexual, and become emancipated—now they serve to keep the group together. Some even occur more frequently outside the reproductive season than during the brooding period, so they must have become fairly independent of sexual mood.

The social groups of tropical finches, as we have shown, consist in part of young animals who have not yet mated, but also usually of firm pairs, who stay together outside the brooding season too. And if the solidarity of the group is strengthened by functionally changed sexual behavior patterns, the same applies to the solidarity of the pair. There are some behavior patterns that clearly serve pair-bonding, such as the courtship bow toward the partner, with the tail often turned to the partner too. This bow derives from nest-building behavior; it is a firm component of the foreplay to copulation, but also occurs throughout the year as an exaggerated greeting between the partners of a pair, and in rather weaker form as a general greeting between the members of a group.

The same applies to song, which primarily serves as a form of address to a female. It has a purely sexual significance and in a pair-bond it serves to stimulate and woo the female. Besides this there is the so-called "undirected song," which indicates a very slightly sexual mood, differs from the courting song only in its slowness and the longer intervals between the individual phrases, and is never directed at a conspecific. But among many species it serves to keep the group together. First, it has an infectious effect, so that other males also start to sing, preferably while perched close beside the first singer. Females do this too, and adult males even sit beside young birds who have not yet molted but who already sing. So we are evidently not dealing with "singing lessons." The listening attitude is very strongly marked among spice finches, mannikin finches (*Lonchura*), and some other kinds. While the singer continues its song as though alone, other members of the species sit down in front of and beside it, stretch out their neck till their head is close to the beak of the singer, as though actually lending an ear, and remain motionless in this position for a time. Sometimes the listeners quarrel about the best seat or even stand in a line so that if one bird flies off another can move up. Some singers are clearly favorites, and they are usually closely surrounded, while others almost always sing alone. Females listen only to males, not to their own sex. This behavior is not found among masked amadines.

I have listed in the bibliography other examples of originally sexual behavior patterns that have been transferred to the general social field among birds.[48] The examples quoted here may suffice to clarify the general principle.

The transfer of sexual behavior patterns into the social realm is not, of course, confined to the kingdom of birds. It also occurs from the lowest to the highest vertebrates, i.e., from fish to monkeys. But unlike brood-tending, which is often easy to observe in captivity, higher forms of social life can only be adequately studied in the wild, since the conditions of captivity can falsify normal behavior. But observations in the wild are usually very difficult to achieve, and this is why we have sufficient details of the social behavior of only comparatively few animal species; however, results so far show that this will be an extremely fascinating field of inquiry.

Among fishes, we again know most about a family that the amateur loves very much. These are the cichlids (*Cichlidae*), of whom we have already discussed one representative, the orange chromide (see p. 149). In the last twelve years, we have examined forty-five species of cichlid from twenty-three different families in the Max Planck Institute and have compared their fights, their brood-tending, and their social behavior. Besides the harem-formers, the monogamous, and the nonmonogamous types, we also found a cichlid (*Tropheus moorii*), from Lake Tanganyika, who forms compact groups of several females and males and wanders along the wide, rocky shores of the lake in such shoals. If unknown members of the species come into the vicinity of the shoal, they are attacked and driven off, while the members of the shoal seem to keep peace among themselves. Exact observations under conditions as close to normal as possible in large aquaria showed, however, that members of a shoal are not quite as peaceful among themselves as would seem at first sight. Unless the animals are just taking a siesta, it may even happen that every few minutes one will swim up to another and threaten it with outspread fins. The strongest male does this most frequently. Normally such behavior will not lead to a fight, for the threatened fish reacts by placing itself broadside in front of the aggressor, turning its head diagonally up, dropping its tail and bending it slightly away from the opponent, spreading its pelvic fins out to brake, and gently shaking the tail end of its body from side to side or quivering its entire body. This "tail-beat" (*rütteln*) appeases the partner, who thereupon desists from further attack and swims on its way.

Anyone familiar with the over-all behavior repertory of this fish will have come across the "tail-beat" before, al-

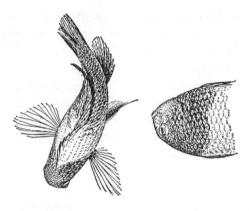

The tail-beating of the *Tropheus* cichlid is both a male display movement and a general social appeasement gesture.

though in a totally different context. Indeed, it is one of the most frequent behavior patterns of the courting male and also occurs when he ejects sperm after the female has deposited the eggs. It occurs as a courtship movement among many related kinds of cichlid too, but always on the part of the male and only if he owns a territory, if he is ready to spawn, and if in addition a female who is also ripe comes to him. This clearly shows that tail-beating is a sexual behavior pattern. More distantly related cichlids, for instance the *Pelmatochromis* species, where it is the female who courts, have taken these movements very far. Here the female bends herself into a U-shape and stretches out to her partner her convex flank, which is marked with a bright red area of color. This colored mark on her abdomen has a bite-inhibiting effect, as experiments have shown, and the whole "belly dance" has the effect of appeasing the male, who is generally fairly aggressive. The relatives of the *Tropheus* cichlid we mentioned also have a red or yellowish-red spot of color on their flank; in this case the males are also the ones to do the courting. The *Tropheus* cichlid itself is black with a yellowish-red band of color around the middle that can light up in the space of seconds if the animal is courting, and disappears again equally rapidly after the reproductive act.

In all the species we have just discussed the sexes are easily distinguished because of this courtship coloring or display dress. But this is not so for *Tropheus*, where the females also have a display dress. They do not in fact court, nor do they need this display dress for their reproductive behavior. But here the typical courtship movement, tail-beating, also serves to create agreement within the group, as we have seen, and in this context the female certainly does need it. Males and females tail-beat as often as they are threatened by fellow members of the group and quite independently of whether there are or are not any animals in the group ready to mate. In addition, appeasement tail-beating occurs among young animals, long before they reach sexual maturity. This proves that tail-beating has become largely if not completely divorced from sexual excitement. Anyone who expects early progeny after the violent "courtship" of these animals will discover this to his disappointment—for it cannot even be said with certainty whether both sexes are in fact represented in the group. I was disappointed too until I understood the circumstances, which comforted me very soon, since the animals did eventually reproduce.

Within the social group, *Tropheus* uses tail-beating in order to inhibit aggression. The male *Tropheus* tail-beats both in a sexual context, i.e., during courtship and insemination, and in a nonsexual context, in order to appease an aggressor. In both cases the movement looks the same. The female *Tropheus*, who does not court, only uses this movement for appeasement in a social context. For the behavior researcher this means that behavior sequences as a whole must be kept in sight if he wants to decide whether the same movement means courtship or appeasement. In addition, he must remember that externally the female resembles the male. This is remarkable because the male and female *Tropheus* often play very different roles in their reproductive behavior and because all cichlids where this is the case have very distinct males and females. The more difference there is between the behavior of male and female, the greater are the sexual differences. Among species where the female alone tends the brood while the males court, fight for a mating territory, and inseminate the eggs, this has led to males and females being described as belonging to different species simply because they look so very different. With *Tropheus* too, only the male courts; the female takes the eggs into her mouth, broods them there for some forty days, and later also takes the young into her mouth in cases of danger, while the male pays no attention to them. But in spite of this great difference in behavior, the sexes look the same. This makes it clear that there must have been a strong evolutionary tendency against the formation of sexual differences. Everything points to the fact that this tendency derived from social life. So far *Tropheus* is the only species of cichlids to lead this kind of social life. In it the male courtship movement plays a special, secondary role; this applies not only to the movement itself but also to the display dress accompanying it. With the help of the physiological color changes that are so common among fish, the display dress can change; yet special color cells must exist for each coloring as well as for the corresponding nerve fibers. That the female *Tropheus* possesses both can only be explained by the fact that she needs both for social life within the group.

It is now possible for us to give a rough estimate of how important this functionally changed courtship movement is to the species. Tail-beating in a social context must be just as important as the great external difference between the sexes is among related species; for this tendency toward distinct sexual differentiation among nonsocially living species is balanced out by the other tendency to eliminate sexual differences among species where tail-beating, which is socially important, occurs. Later we shall cite examples of comparable cases where sexual differentiation can even be eliminated retroactively in the interests of social life. This could also be true of *Tropheus*, i.e., that with its ancestors who did not yet live socially males and females were clearly distinguished from each other and that the females only came to resemble the males afterward. From what we know of these animals now, however, this is unlikely, nor would it make much difference in the problem discussed here in any case. So we find the same principle of sexual behavior forms transferred to the social field even among cold-blooded vertebrates. The following examples will show that the principle is also valid for the most highly developed vertebrates.

The spotted hyena (*Crocuta*) from Africa is a very curious mammal. It is ugly and branded as a coward, and from among the very many different sounds it utters people always stress the "demonic" laughter to which it gives vent when excited. If we add to this the sinister teeth that act like shears and that are capable of breaking apart even the thickest bones, we gradually create a picture of a truly horrible nightmarish monster. This supposed "monster" is in fact very easy to tame and when adult will remain trustworthy as a dog. This alone goes to show that the spotted hyena is a social animal, for only they can attach themselves to man as a substitute parent and accept him as a social companion. (Besides the spotted hyena there is also the striped hyena, but it has none of the following features in common with the spotted hyena.) Studies made in recent years by Kruuk have adjusted the image we had of this animal a little.[70] The spotted hyena is a very social animal; it lives in fixed territories in packs of ten to a hundred individuals, and each pack has a central resting place and hollows in the earth where the young are first lodged. Contrary to popular belief, hyenas do not only eat carrion but also hunt living zebras and gnus. They assemble into a

pack of several animals, usually toward evening, after spend-
ing the day resting in a mudhole in the shade of a tree or
some other protected place. The members of a pack know
one another and greet whenever they meet, even when they
assemble for the hunt in the evening. The members of a
group stay peaceful among themselves when devouring their
prey, but if animals from another group come up there will
immediately be quarreling or even open warfare.

Since the time of Aristotle, legend has had it that spotted
hyenas can change their sex at wish, which is why they
laugh so often. Even today the Bantus and some white
hunters still believe that these animals are hermaphrodites.
The reason for this error is that in fact males and females
can hardly be distinguished externally, since their sexual
organs look the same from the outside. Older females who
have already had several litters have much larger teats
than males and the birth opening is enlarged; but this is
not very noticeable because it is not located where one
would have expected to find it. The females also have two
clearly visible scrotum pouches immediately under the anus,
just like the males, except that they do not contain testicles
but simply fatty and connective tissues.[19] In front of this,
on the abdomen, the female has a penis just like the male;
because of its somewhat different anatomical construction
one should really call it a pseudopenis, but in this context
the following is more important: The pseudopenis of the
female can hang just like that of the male with its tip
almost touching the ground. In addition it can be erected.
The skin of the pseudopenis surrounds the birth passage,
which therefore opens in front at the tip. This seems highly
impractical, for normally young mammals leave the body
of the mother by the shortest possible route after they have
passed through the pelvis. But hyena babies can only reach
the open via a birth passage that curves 180 degrees forward. What is surprising is that these babies are extremely
well-developed for a predator. Their eyes are already open,

The external genitals of the male and female spotted
hyena look almost the same (below). They play an important role in the socially appeasing greeting ceremony of
these animals (above).

they have cut their incisors and canines, and they can walk,
albeit somewhat shakily.

Hyenas are probably relatives of the larger cats, which
include civets. Among these cats there are several species
where the differences in the external male and female genitals are very slight. But the coincidence is never as great
as with the spotted hyena. And it is very likely that this
coincidence developed in connection with their social life.
In any case it plays a large part in it. The external genitals
have a decisive importance in the friendly greeting between
members of a group.[120]

If two spotted hyenas who know each other meet, they persistently lick and sniff each other's genitals, at the base of which also lie the teats and special scent glands, so that the whole area is socially very significant. This area is displayed conspicuously to the partner: the animal lifts the hind leg nearest its partner and at the same time the penis or pseudopenis juts far out. So at first one cannot tell whether two males, two females, or a male and a female are greeting each other; one also sees this form of greeting between young animals and adults. It has an important appeasing function and is in effect a greeting of peace. A hyena who refuses this greeting to another runs the risk of being violently attacked or driven off.

This greeting derives from the pair-bonding behavior of the male, for the genitals of the female are, of course, not erect during copulation. But the position of the female genitals requires the male to adopt a special posture preparatory to mating, which we need not discuss in detail here either. Before mating the animals also sniff each other's anal zone, which is only vaguely hinted at during greeting. It is evident that part of the male foreplay to mating became a social gesture of greeting for both sexes here and that the reproductive organs play an important part in it. How the form of the females' organs changed for this purpose is not yet known, since no comparative observations have been made on related species of predators.

We know more about comparable greeting ceremonies among various Old World monkeys, i.e., all the monkeys that occur outside the Western Hemisphere. (They are sometimes called small-nosed monkeys in contrast to the wide-nosed monkeys of the New World.) It is presumed that the New World monkeys have retained more primitive traits, and that the Old World monkeys are therefore more modern and more highly developed; all the manlike apes also belong among them. The most familiar from our zoos are the baboons, in whose social behavior sexual signals play a very large part. Most mammal females adopt a typical posture when they invite the male to mate. They turn their hindquarters to him and bend their tail to the side or upward. But anyone who carefully observes a band of baboons will soon discover that by no means every individual who presents in front of another is female, and that the individuals to whom they present also react variously to it. This is because, as has been known for some time, presentation also acts as a gesture of social appeasement or as greeting by a lower-ranking animal to a higher-ranking companion. This greeting can take many different forms. There are all manner of transitions, from a brief swaying of the hindquarters during walking, to a short pause, during which the tail is slightly or very markedly bent to the side, and finally to the most remarkable position of all in which the animal puts its behind directly under the other's nose, looks at it backward over its shoulder, and sometimes even bends its forelegs and raises its hindquarters skyward. These considerable differences correspond to the rising intensity of the greeting, which in turn depends on how much higher in rank the greeted individual is and how close to the greeter. It makes no difference whether the greeting or greeted animal is male or female. Lower-ranking animals, whether male or female, present in front of high-ranking ones, no matter whether they are male or female. Since baboons live in compact bands, one can tell the ranking order of the members among themselves by observing how often each individual presents in front of each other animal.[63] The higher the rank of an individual, the more rarely will it present in front of others and the more often will they present to him.

One can tell the ranking order of a group of *Tropheus* cichlids in exactly the same way. The higher the rank of a fish, the more rarely will it tail-beat in front of the others and the more often will the others tail-beat in front of it. However, this tail-beat of *Tropheus* cichlids derives from male sexual behavior, while the presentation of baboons derives from female sexual behavior. But just as a female *Tropheus* will very rarely court, a male baboon will very seldom present before copulation. So, in the sexual context, these behavior patterns are confined to one sex in each case, whereas both sexes use them in a general social context. And just as very young *Tropheus* cichlids already tail-beat, baboon children who have not yet reached sexual maturity can be seen presenting. Here too the greeting behavior has been removed from its sexual context and has become largely emancipated. When a baboon approaches another, stops in front of it, turns its hindquarters toward it and lifts its tail, remaining in this posture for a moment and then sitting down, this is not an invitation to mating that received no response, but a greeting to a superior, an acknowledgment of rank. Directly afterward, the animals will often begin to delouse each other's fur, which is to say, a social behavior pattern derived from brood-tending follows directly upon one derived from the sexual field. But the animals have not experienced a change of mood in the meantime; they have simply remained, so to speak, in a social mood.

We find presentation as a social gesture of greeting among nearly all Old World monkeys, that is to say, baboons, macaques, who include the rhesus monkey (*Macaca mulatta*), langurs (*Trachypithecus* and *Presbytis*), and also chimpanzees. This behavior is always ambivalent. It can be a female invitation to mating, but usually it is a social gesture of greeting that is not "meant" sexually.

During the rutting season the females of many species develop a large red swelling of the naked areas of skin around the genital orifice. This estrus-swelling reaches such proportions among some baboons that the animal can hardly sit down properly. The naïve observer often thinks that animals in this phase are ill because of their curious "growth" (see illustration, p. 187). In fact it shows the male of the same species that the female is ready for mating. Naturally this signal is presented to the male very insistently during the invitation to copulation. If we compare this with conditions among *Tropheus,* who also present a special color signal during courtship, we might ask whether it would not also be in the monkey's interests to use the same color signal for social greeting. Here the female fish imitates the male courtship dress when she uses the male courtship movements as greeting. In terms of their purely functional coincidence, we could deduce a working hypothesis from this for monkeys and expect the males to imitate the female rutting signal when they use the female invitation to copulation as a greeting. And, in fact, so they do.

This is easiest to see with the hamadryas baboon (*Papio hamadryas*) we very often find in zoos. Doguera baboons (*Papio doguera*) have a brownish-gray rump on which the red swelling only shines forth on rutting females. This color signal fades almost entirely as soon as the rutting period is over. The estrus-swelling of the hamadryas baboon, who is more highly specialized on the whole, is larger, and the rump remains red all the time. Among these animals, social presentation plays a very important role—more, it would seem, than with the doguera baboon. And this is why male hamadryas baboons have an equally bright red backside in imitation of the female rutting signal, although they use it not in a sexual connection but merely in a general social context. The females of many macaques, of the mangabey (*Cercocebus*), the gelada baboon, and the chimpanzee, also have striking genital coloring or swellings. But the hamadryas baboon is not the only monkey whose females have an estrus-swelling. And since most Old World monkeys can present as a gesture of greeting, one could expect the males of other species to imitate the female rutting signal too. Or, in simpler terms: If the striking coloring of the rump of male monkeys can be traced back to an imitation of the female rutting signal, then it should occur only among those species where the females have a colored rutting signal in the genital zone. This is indeed so.[124] Cases where only the females of some species of a fairly large related group have an estrus-swelling and where the males of these species, and only these species, have a very similar coloring or even swelling in the anal region, are particularly convincing. Among the many leaf-eating monkeys—guerezas, langurs, dusky langurs (*Semnopithecus*), long-nosed monkeys (*Nasalis*), doucs or variegated langurs (*Pygathrix*)—only a few have a female genital swelling, namely the green and the brown guerezas (*Procolobus verus* and *Colobus badius*). And the males have a swelling of the same shape! Young males, in particular, have such a good "imitation" of the

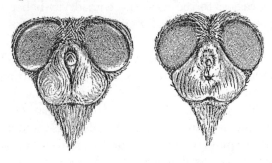

View of the buttocks of a red colobus monkey with genital swelling (left) and imitation of these female genitals on a young male (right).

female genital region that they are not easily recognized as males. Since, moreover, they often display to the adult males of their group,[62] nature seems to have attempted to make them mistakable for females here too, which can mean that young males are tolerated and not harmed in a group of adult males. At any rate there is no doubt that this signal is also borrowed from sexual behavior and put in the service of corporate life.

Plausible as it seems that monkeys should notice such a striking rutting signal with their sharp eyes, it seems equally implausible to many humans if they are told that these

monkeys all allow themselves to be misled by an "imitation" of this signal to such a degree that they can take a
male for a female. In fact it is due to the "poster" effect.
It has been shown that when we buy goods even we humans prefer those car tires or beers that are offered to us on
a poster or advertisement with an attractive girl in the back-
ground. Naturally we do not take the paper girl for a real
girl, but she "pleases us"—the girl-signals she emanates put
us in a more kindly, positive mood, which is in the interests
of the offered object, that is to say of its manufacturer (for
such automatic responses to signals, see pp. 262f.). And this
is precisely what is achieved in the animal kingdom by the
exploitation of certain signals. It is particularly clear with
monkeys how effective this use of "imitation" is when we
note that they are specially "manufactured." Since there
are enough opportunities for comparison with other species,
we know that the aforementioned coincidences between
males and females are not by any chance due to the fact
that they were never formed differently in the first place.
Normally the differences are very much there, and they
are only subsequently eliminated among some specialized
species. Sometimes the signal is even produced on the male
by other means: A red area of color, consisting of naked
skin in the case of the female, can be imitated by red hair
on the male.

We can observe what responses the signal elicits in the
social partner. A baboon, macaque, or other species either
does not react visibly at all to the presentation of a conspecific or gives a brief glance, or touches the proffered behind with its fingers, or sniffs it briefly, or cleans it, or stands
up and takes it between its thighs, or mounts and makes
a few copulatory movements, or actually copulates. This is
a series of mating actions of increasing intensity. Which one
will occur depends on many contingent circumstances. But
it shows that the signal, even if not intended sexually, can
still be taken sexually. It is very rarely meant sexually in

a monkey society. But the more certain it is to elicit sexual responses, the more surely will it also suppress aggressive tendencies on the part of the receiver of the signal.

It is fairly certain that presentation does not have only the effect of appeasing aggression. If a member of the group is afraid of a higher-ranking member and would like to flee, the same signal can have a calming or even enticing effect because it recalls a female in rut, and it can even override the tendency to flight. Indeed, it can be observed, though more clearly for some species than others, that high-ranking animals sometimes present in front of lower-ranking ones, and that the latter then mount them. It is impossible to list all the possibilities registered so far; many of our investigations are only in the early stages. All we want to show here is that behavior elements and signals from the sexual realm can acquire new meanings in social life. For instance, presentation can appease aggression when addressed to a higher-ranking animal, or help overcome tendencies to flight when directed at a lower-ranking one, and, as a further step in this direction, it can finally become a social invitation to follow, that is, a quite general signal serving the coherence of the group, as when the pasha sets off and entices the others to follow him by motioning with his "female poster." High-ranking hamadryas baboon males do this during their so-called "swing step." They lift their tail and sway their behind from side to side in the rhythm of their big steps, and this can make the entire group suddenly set off after them.[64]

The more such new functions a signal or behavior pattern acquires, the more often will we see it occur. We have already shown this with "delousing" (see p. 209), to which the human observer usually reacts neutrally, simply registering it. Of course, the same applies to functionally changed brood-tending actions; but man usually sees billing and kissing take place with such an obvious social function that it requires some effort to convince him that what he is seeing are in fact derived brood-tending actions that orig-inally had an entirely different function. The reverse is true of functionally changed sexual actions; they are always taken in their original sense, and it takes great effort to explain that they have other functions too. These various attitudes on the part of the naïve beholder are prejudices that can very easily lead to misunderstanding.

25. The Value of Greeting

In very simple terms, a form of behavior has an appeasing effect when it awakens a behavioral tendency irreconcilable with aggression in the aggressor. Here it is enough if the tendency is strong enough to inhibit aggressive behavior. The other, counteracting behavior need not even be visible externally. So the appeasing presentation of the genitals need not elicit sexual behavior on the part of the partner; it is enough if the partner desists from further attack. This is called "change of mood." Fortunately this minimal requirement is very often more than fulfilled, that is to say, it does lead at least to incipient sexual actions or, if we are dealing with appeasement food begging, at least to incipient feeding. So it is easy to determine which behavior has in fact been stimulated in the partner; if nothing was visible from the outside but an absence of attack, it would be more difficult to interpret.

It is not even necessary for all attack to be halted by the appeasing behavior. *For appeasement to acquire a biological social value, it is sufficient for it to make attack less probable.* It is important to realize this, for in the case of baboons one can fairly often see an animal who is presenting violently being bitten by a higher-ranking one in spite of it. This is always a punishment, i.e., an aggressive reaction toward an individual who has behaved counter to the norm. Two examples should suffice to explain what we mean. Male hamadryas baboons keep their harem together by force. If a female roams too far away from the others she is threatened, and if this does not work, she is attacked by the pasha and bitten in the neck; usually not even presentation will help. Moreover, baboons are known to have a fairly firm ranking order when feeding. Now it can happen that visitors try to distract the attention of the pasha for a moment in order to quickly give a lower-ranking animal a tidbit. By doing so they are of course tempting this animal to act against the pasha's prerogative. In any case, the pasha usually notices. There have been cases where the pasha sat in a different section of the cage, from where he could not even see the "culprit" directly, yet he could see its hand, which was stretched out through the bars. This was enough: The pasha rushed up and punished the lower-ranking baboon even though the latter presented very intensely.

But monkeys, as well as less highly developed vertebrates, do not only use appeasement afterward, when the partner has already been provoked to attack, but also beforehand, as introduction to an action that will presumably incite the partner to attack. In the simplest case, a lower-ranking animal will not simply pass close by a high-ranking one and appease it in case it feels irritated by this proximity; instead the lower-ranking animal performs the gesture of appeasement before setting off, as though to "beg pardon" in advance for an action to follow. This anticipatory appeasement has very much of the character of a greeting. We do not yet know whether this behavior is always a matter of instinct or whether it is the result of an intelligent view of the situation and of behavior planned in advance; monkeys, at least, are known to be quite capable of doing this.

But if they are capable of this, one would expect them also to "abuse" this greeting, which protects them against attack; for instance, in order to protect themselves from punishment. As was shown above, however, this does not usually seem to work. It would be amusing to imagine the entire order of a baboon troop breaking up simply because each member could avoid punishment by a humble greeting. At least this kind of functional consideration shows why it would in fact be a disadvantage if presentation were always sure to inhibit aggression. Yet there are fairly common situations in which our human sense of justice does suspect an abuse of the gesture of submission. In technical language this situation is called "protected threat." This can be explained by the following example.

Three monkeys are concerned, of whom one is of very high rank; the other two can be of almost equal rank. For some reason, one of these two violently threatens the other with shrieks, threatening gestures, and all the other movements that belong to aggression. But it places itself in such

The "protected threat" of the hamadryas baboon.

a way as to present its hindquarters to the high-ranking animal at the same time. This achieves two things: The actual threatener who is presenting toward its superior protects itself against attack by the latter. The threatened animal cannot also present toward its superior unless it wants to withdraw, so it cannot secure itself against attack. If it wanted to do so it would also have to present toward its aggressor and thus declare itself its inferior. Added to this, however, is that the high-ranking monkey usually intervenes in quarrels between its inferiors, often simply separating the disputants by passing between them. Often, however, it also threatens one or both and drives them away. But in the case of "protected threat," the disturber of the peace has already presented toward the high-ranking animal "in anticipation," whereupon the latter has to attack and drive off the threatened animal if it wants peace. That happens often enough in this situation to give the impression that by its submissive behavior the disturber is forcing the high-ranking animal to become angry with a third animal who has not in fact given it any cause for anger. In this way even a low-ranking animal can have a fellow member of the group who is superior to it driven away by the highest-ranking animal. We know this behavior from captive and wild rhesus monkeys, from wild doguera baboons from various regions of Africa, and from hamadryas baboons in captivity. Curiously it has never been seen among hamadryas baboons living in the wild in spite of careful observation.[64]

One could perhaps take this as an indication that "protected threat" is not an innate behavior form among any of the animals and that instead they "invent" it and learn to use it from personal experience. In any case, "protected threat" gives the best proof of the strong inhibiting effect presentation has and of how far an originally sexual behavioral element has changed function here. It also shows the danger inherent in this behavior. The animals may rely so heavily on protection by presentation that they exploit it for their own interests, which, as far as we can judge, do not serve the community. An aggressive animal can play out its aggression and alter the responses of the community in such a way as to spark off new aggression in the remainder of the community. This is the first small step on the road to putting self-interest over the interests of the community.

As we showed, the animal at whom presentation is directed can react in different ways, even with mounting and incipient or actual copulation. Then it looks as though the lower-ranking individual were offering the higher-ranking one an opportunity for sexual activity and thus gaining some advantage for itself—whether to evade a threat, temporarily remove a rival, or obtain a tidbit. Occasionally this is described as prostitution. Whether this term is right depends entirely on how we define prostitution. However, we would then have to call the entire appeasing behavior of presentation prostitution too, since the reaction of the partner can range through all possible transitions from the almost invisible inhibition of attack to complete change of mood together with normal copulation. But if prostitution, as we understand it, means wrong behavior, then the term cannot apply to monkeys. For here we are dealing with a behavior pattern that is biologically justified. Nor does it matter that rutting females may perhaps have more success with presentation as a means of appeasement and that they also learn to exploit this because the males like to copulate with them.

26. Hypersexualization?

If we start by making an inventory of the behavior at the disposal of a particular species as the necessary basis for more exact behavior studies, we are proceeding like any naïve observer. First he distinguishes between typical recurrent and recognizable behavior patterns and classifies them according to their biological function. Growling and baring the teeth on the part of a dog belong to aggressive behavior. Prowling on the part of a cat belongs in the functional circle of foraging; the nest-building of the blackbird, rook, finch, and starling belong to brood-tending, and so on. Usually we try to make do with as few functional concepts as possible. This is good scientific strategy. However, we must take care not to put too much trust in these first attempts at classification. In other words, we must be prepared to consider the order we have set up as a provisional one, and alter it as soon as new discoveries require it.

It can easily happen that the observer has already been careless in the naming of the behavior patterns he has recognized; for example, he may have used interpretative names instead of neutral descriptive ones. The first researchers to observe the behavior of the orange chromide began with young animals, who acted out territorial flights and pair-bonding before they reared offspring themselves. One pattern was striking in the behavior of the partners of a pair. One animal would ram its mouth against the flank of its partner. But the ramming was not violent and never led to wounding. Later, among the young who had just learned to swim, the researchers saw a behavior pattern reminiscent of this ramming of adult fish: The little fish also swam up their parents' flank as though to ram it. The form of the movement, added to the consideration that the small fish could not yet fight, led to this behavior on the part of the young animals being entered into scientific literature as "apparent ramming." In fact, the sequence according to which this researcher assembled his observations clearly had an unfavorable effect on his interpretation and naming of the action; for, as we have shown (see p. 150), what the young animals are in fact doing is feeding from their parents; the parent animals continue to use this behavior pattern among themselves in a derived form, and it is this that ought to be called "apparent *feeding.*"

So it is only to be expected that the presentation of baboons, the tail-beat of *Tropheus,* and the penis display of the spotted hyena were formerly interpreted uniformly as sexual behavior. This sexual behavior occurred, however, with surprising frequency; more often, at any rate, than among many other species. And it also occurred distinct from direct reproductive behavior, whereas the other species with whom they were compared only behaved sexually in the context of reproduction. So it was more than tempting to speak of hypersexualization here, above all for baboons, who were particularly easy to observe in zoos. Even today many zoo visitors not only find baboons droll but also excited by their strong sexuality. Closer observation and study of typical sequences of behavior will soon show that presentation, penis display, and tail-beating, like the "tail-flirtation" of masked amadines, can all occur in various typical sequences. One of these sequences always leads to mating (or spawning in the case of fish), while the other does not. Continuing from this point, we will soon discover differences in the situations and social constellations that lead to the respective behaviors. Eventually, the word "sexual," in the context of a situation that does not lead to mating, will be left in quotation marks for the sake of caution, and then replaced by another word, which, experience has shown, is "greeting."

At this stage of our research at the latest we will have finally dismissed the thesis of hypersexuality. But could we not retain it? All this would require would be to place a higher value on the form of the behavioral pattern than on the inner drive responsible for its appearance. We might well decide that everything that looks sexual should also be called sexual; in consequence, however, we would then also have to ascribe everything that looked like brood-tending to brood-tending and, accordingly, speak of "hypertrophied brood-tending" for the social grooming actions of the monkeys, the billing of crows, parrots, pigeons etc., which we described in detail earlier. This procedure is generally rejected, because we know that what adults do among themselves is plainly not brood-tending. The case is very clear with those cuckoos who have dropped brood-tending but retained pair-feeding (see p. 133); for brood-tending cannot at the same time disappear and be hypertrophied. The name we give a behavior does not, therefore, depend on the form the behavior takes but on the situation that elicits it, on the inner drive behind it, or on the biological consequence of the behavior. Unfortunately we find no such good arguments for reproductive behavior as in our example of brood-tending, because although a species can abandon brood-tending it can never abandon reproduction. Yet here too, for the sake of the uniformity of the system, we must look at more than the mere form the behavior takes. Then the totally different biological function of this behavior will compel us to find another name for it and to give up the naïve idea of hypersexuality.

I shall deal with the situation among humans in a moment. Here I would merely like to remark how surprisingly often points of view related purely to man, what are called "anthropomorphic" ideas, play a part in descriptions of animal behavior. This can lead to calling the behavior of animals "perverted" whenever it would be called perverted between humans. This is why baboons in particular often seem rather "perverted" to many people. And the impression is even heightened in a zoo situation, where baboons, like men in a large city, are densely crowded and lack the distractions that wild life and their natural habitat could offer them. Yet to proceed from man to animal is just as dangerous as to proceed from animal to man. Even if we can show that the so-called perverted sexual behavior of baboons is seen more often in captivity than in the wild, this could easily be explained by the lack of space in the zoo, which does not permit the animals to keep the prescribed distance from certain other individuals; and if they continually have to fall short of this distance, they are also forced into continual "polite greeting." So what is abnormal is the frequency of the greeting, but not the greeting itself.

Sexual behavioral patterns do not increase in frequency only in the context of social greeting. There is a widespread view that, in the animal kingdom, mating and the foreplay to mating are confined to the times favorable to reproduction. We know that among species who reproduce only at certain times of the year the gonads are set in action by outside signals, for instance by rising temperature or the longer daylight in spring, by rainfall, or such. In this way the reproductive behavior of both sexes is at least roughly synchronized. But among species who can rear offspring throughout the year, like many inhabitants of the tropical zones, there are still times when mating with a female would be of no advantage, namely as long as the female is pregnant or so fully occupied with brood-tending that a new birth during this period might endanger both litters. Indeed, among many animals the female emits signals that show her readiness for mating and upon which the males begin their attempts to mate. There are even indications that the females are not alone in having a cycle of alternate phases of readiness for mating and rejection of mating; male rats, rabbits, cattle (and humans) also have a cycle. Moreover, the length of the cycles of males and females of the same species seem to be adjusted to each other and the males, if they always live together with the same female, eventually become ready for mating at the same time as the females.[53] The sexual behavior of male rhesus monkeys largely coincides with the various phases of the estrous cycle of their females.[80] The frequency of copulation and the corresponding number of ejaculations is greatest in the fertile phase, but sexual behavior does not fade out entirely in the remaining time either. We know that among monkeys and other vertebrates mating also occurs with pregnant females. But it is not even necessary for there to be variations in frequency.

Those species of animal where the males are continually seen courting the females represent an extreme; but the success rate seems to bear no relation to the trouble taken, since the females usually take no notice at all of the males' efforts. A typical representative of these animals is known to every aquarian, namely the guppy (*Lebistes reticulatus*). Other toothed carps behave in the same way, and—from an entirely different group of fish—so do the South American swordtail characins (*Corynopoma riisei*) and related species. In both cases these are fish who fertilize internally, i.e., where the male introduces the sperm into the sexual passage of the female with a copulatory organ. Now one cannot simply say that constant courting is unnatural; rather we must try to find the reasons for it. An exact analysis of the inner and outer causes of this endless courtship and its effects on the female has led to the following conclusions to date.[82]

Most fish eject eggs and sperm at the same time; the water brings them together and it is enough if the readiness to spawn of both sexes gives rise to sexual behavior, and in particular to bringing them as close together as possible. Among fish with internal fertilization, however, either the female keeps the sperm in her body for a fairly long time, or, if we are dealing with fish who bear live young like the guppy, the development of the embryos in the mother's body takes some time. In each case the female must be mated at a time when she is incapable and therefore not even ready to deposit the eggs or the finished young. Now, by nature the female is only inclined to tolerate the approach of a male when she is ready to spawn herself. Outside this time she keeps the males at a distance. But precisely among those species who are fertilized internally this time-lag must be overcome entirely, since direct bodily contact is necessary. The problem is solved here by the male, who so to speak bombards the unwilling female with courtship in order to make her change her mind. Swordtail characins are so eager to mate that not even successful copulation will lead to an interruption in courtship; immediately afterward the male will continue his efforts with the same violence.

While female toothed carps usually try to evade and remain passive, the females of some species of characin become aggressive toward the males. It is interesting to note that these males have developed a form of courtship feeding, in the course of which, incidentally, the females are misled (not to say cheated). None of these species tends or feeds its young, so there is no brood-tending feeding that could be exploited for the introduction to mating. But in spite of this the female is occasionally hungry, and then searches for something edible such as a small *Cyclops* or other small plankton-crustacean. Now the male swordtail characin has a small bony knob on a long stem on the cover of his gills, which looks like a *Cyclops* and in addition is moved like a *Cyclops* when the male spreads his gill cover and parades the *Cyclops* snare in front of the female while executing sporadic courtship movements. When the female snaps for what she supposes is a morsel of food and bites it, she comes close enough for the male to carry out mating in a split second.[125] Such examples do not, of course, mean that hypersexuality does not exist; but they do show how cautiously we must apply the concept.

27. Emancipated Copulation

Where does the procreative process begin?

As we have seen, what is commonly called the foreplay to mating often does not have the aim of creating new life but of binding the partners of a pair more firmly together. An incipient or fully performed act of copulation can still serve this purpose even if ejaculation, the ejection of the sperm into the female sexual passages, is lacking.

To start with, copulation can not only send the sperms on the way to the ova or egg-cells but among some animals it can also send the ova to meet the sperm. Besides those species of animal whose females ovulate spontaneously, and whose egg-cells, when ripe, automatically leave the ovaries, there are some species where the egg-cells are liberated only during the foreplay to mating or during copulation itself, for instance by the stimulus of the contact of the penis with the vagina. Rabbits and cats belong to this category. Repeated copulations often also serve to make the female responsive. With the diamond dove (*Geopelia cuneata*), the male pigeon mounts the female seven or eight times, begins to copulate, then hops down again, courts, mounts, etc., and each time the female opens out the feathers around her cloaca further, until she is finally ready to mate, and the union then takes place.[86] The Indian flying fox (*Pteropus gigantëus*) requires three to seven copulations before he can ejaculate. One only sees a complete copulation sequence during the reproductive period, but individual copulations occur throughout the year, even with pregnant females.[83] It is also known that mice perform a series of copulations before ejaculation. Naturally this is related to the duration of each individual copulation, which is extremely short for mice. Among other animals it can take hours (for instance, the pouched mouse, *Sminthopsis*, takes eleven hours); the male gapeworm (*Syngamus tracheae*), which lives in hens, actually lives in a state of permanent copulation with his female.

Some monkeys, such as rhesus monkeys and baboons, also require a series of copulations, which are separated from one another by an interval of a few seconds to a few minutes, before they can ejaculate. Usually one only sees such a series of copulations on the part of the highest-ranking male, such as the pasha who is the sole owner of all the females in the harem among hamadryas baboons. Yet a group of hamadryas baboons will also include young males. They make friends with one or another female and occasionally copulate with her too. These isolated copulations, to which the female can even incite the male, affirm the bond between the respective individuals, but hardly ever lead to pregnancy since the young males never reach the number of copulations necessary for ejaculation.[63] The isolated copulation has thus become free to acquire a new social function here.

We could perhaps speculate why so many copulations are required before ejaculation. Then it becomes tempting to assume that once again it may have a social significance; for example, the first copulations may not only serve to prepare the partner or make her agree, as we showed earlier, but over and above this also serve to tie the partners together more closely. There have been no studies of animals in this context yet. But we know that in man a union where ejaculation is often postponed for over an hour (*Carezza*) can greatly promote the pair-bond between individuals. The role that orgasm plays here is much disputed.

What is certain is merely that the function of copulation has been extended or even entirely transformed among humans too, so that it is comparable to a ceremonial banquet, which of course does not primarily serve to feed the participants but to strengthen the bond within the community; or it is comparable to the kiss (p. 237), where the feeding function has lapsed entirely.

If a female baboon has mated with a male other than the pasha, one of the two concerned often runs up to the pasha—as though "plagued by a guilty conscience"—and presents to him. The pasha reacts in the same way as to all social presentation, i.e., he may mount briefly and copulate, or at least attempt to do so if the presenting animal is a male. This situation shows the appeasing effect of mounting and copulation, an effect which, as in the presentation of the hindquarters (see p. 207), can be independent of the sex of the participants. The effect becomes clearest when the mounted animal is a male, who naturally obtains no sexual satisfaction from the act but presumably does achieve social satisfaction. But copulation between male and female can have the same social effect. Among rhesus monkeys, if one male mounts another it is occasionally an aggressive threat and demonstration of rank, but sometimes it is also the expression of an acknowledged order, which obviously only serves to strengthen the bond between the individuals. Usually the higher-ranking animal mounts first; afterward he in turn is often mounted by the other.

With langurs, it is known that young males continually mount adult males of their group and often embrace them afterward.[50] The significance of this behavior is not yet known. Its form of movement reminds me more of the spreading of urine on the ground as a mark of ownership (which we see among marmosets) than of copulation. At the Third Congress of the "Deutsche Gesellschaft für Psychotherapie und Tiefenpsychologie" (1960) held in Paris, Roumajon told of extensive observations of gangs of young people in France in which the "chief" played the dominant role. In the course of an initiation rite, and later too, the members of the gang submit to anal coition by their "chief." There are girls too in these gangs, so ordinary sexual contact is quite possible for the members. In any case, it is certainly not rape on the part of the "chief." The youth is merely seeking "support" and affection from his "chief," and he clings to him particularly closely afterward. In the games of classical Greece, the victor among the young competitors is also said to have had the right to placatory anal intercourse with his defeated rival. In a more recent Polish novel there is a reference to shepherd boys raping strangers who intrude into their territory.[60] Similarly, male rhesus monkeys of enemy groups mount if they meet. These examples show two things:

1. That even for man, such "sexual" behavior, which is not tied to reproduction, is not a "degenerate phenomenon."
2. That the copulation of higher animals has by nature a pair-bonding function, and that in this context it can be reduced (mating without ejaculation; mounting without introduction of the penis; etc.).

So even copulation does not have to be the "introduction to a procreative process."

IV

28. Pair-Bonding Behavior Elements in Man

We can sum up the facts that have emerged from this wide range of examples.

1. Just as organs can serve different purposes—for instance, the limbs serve for locomotion and for using tools, the mouth for eating and for speaking—so too can behavior patterns and the signals that accompany them. The same behavior patterns can be an essential part of brood-tending while at the same time serving the synchronization and cohesion of the sexual partners, and, in given cases, also serving to change the mood of aggressive conspecifics and to inhibit their aggressive tendencies.

2. For this it is necessary that these behavior elements with their manifold uses should also be available for a corresponding variety of situations. They must not merely be applicable to one specific situation. But they may very well look the same for different situations. This is even an advantage, since the actions are meant to appeal to a very particular predisposition on the part of the partner who will respond by a very particular behavior, and this is best achieved by an unambiguous, unmistakable signal. This brings with it the risk that the observer will overlook the different natural meanings of the behavior or signals because of their similarity of form.

3. There are three focal points in the corporate life of animals: brood-tending, the relations between the sexual

partners, and the alliance of many conspecifics into fairly large groups. Behavior patterns that have proved themselves in one of these fields can be transferred to others too: Elements from brood-tending and reproductive behavior can be put to use to keep the partners of a pair or a larger society together. This produces freely convertible behavior elements, so that one cannot always tell from which of the three fields an element originally stems.

4. If one cannot always tell the origin of behavior elements, this is usually because they lack something that would make their meaning in this special, derived form comprehensible. We can only understand why a bird holding stems of grass in its beak should woo the female and then throw away the grass if we know that this form of courtship derived from nest-building movements. Because the original meaning of the action, which gave it its form, is now lacking, such behavior patterns are called "rituals"; they come about through "ritualization." (Sometimes the term "symbolic action" is also used; for instance, the form of courtship we have just discussed could be called "symbolic nest-building." But this can easily mislead the reader into assuming that the animal is aware of the symbolic character of its actions.) Ritualization causes a change in the frequency with which a behavior pattern occurs and in the inner drive that impels the animal toward this specific mode of action. The same action can be performed in response to various different moods or, in human terms, it can be "meant" differently. In addition, physical structures can appear that underline the new significance of this action (for instance, the color signals we described for the *Tropheus* cichlid and for baboons).

5. All this applies to vertebrates at very varied stages of development, from fish to the manlike apes, insofar as

they lead a comparable social life. So it must have something to do with corporate, social life. And indeed the close analysis we made earlier shows that the aforementioned facts 1–4 are biological adaptations to the conditions of social life—just as the spindle-shaped body with fins that we also find from fish upward to the highest marine mammals is an adaptation to the conditions of aquatic life.

We must note, however, that individually this body shape and the accompanying fins can come about in different ways. Similarly, we must take care to differentiate between the general principles of construction of social life and the specific behavior patterns that play comparable roles therein. For instance, it is part of the general principle of construction that brood-tending behavior patterns are built into the pair relationship, yet these brood-tending behavior patterns have a different aspect from species to species.

We were not concerned in this work with explaining the development of the greatest possible number of highly specialized social behavior patterns; rather we wanted to establish clearly that such social behavior patterns did indeed undergo a development and that they always stem from quite definite roots.

6. The more different the animals are who have independently traversed the same paths of development along parallel lines and in whose highly developed social life we can recognize the same structural principle (although each species has its own species-specific behavior repertory), the more certain we can be of having found a natural law valid for the group of creatures examined. We shall confine ourselves to the realm of vertebrates here, although this natural law relating to the construction of societies goes beyond the boundary between vertebrates and invertebrates—as the examples of insects and

spiders have shown—and although it is legitimate to assume that the same relations between, for instance, brood-tending and pair-bonding behavior will be found again and again among the so-called lower animals too.

7. The laws we have found enable us to predict that any vertebrate that exhibits a firm pair-bond or a complex social life will very probably have taken over behavior patterns and signals that originally served brood-tending or reproduction into the pair-bond and group-bond; as a result these patterns and signals no longer (or not only) serve the production and rearing of offspring now, but (also) serve the cohesion of pairs and larger groups. This is even more probable if the vertebrate in question is closely related to one of the animal species to which the aforementioned laws have already been found to be applicable.

Since man belongs biologically to the vertebrates and exhibits both firm pair-bonds and larger group formations, this natural law should also be applicable to him. We will examine this in the following chapters. And that is why we have given preference to examples that facilitated a comparison with the behavior patterns of man in the preceding section of this work.

29. Social Feeding and the Kiss

In order to make clear this comparison between the changes of function of social behavior patterns in the animal kingdom and in man, we shall begin by examining human behavior patterns in the same sequence. We shall, therefore, begin with brood-tending elements.

Mouth-to-mouth feeding is a widespread phenomenon in the "brood-tending" behavior of man too. It is necessary to man for the same reasons as it is to the manlike apes, namely because the children gradually require more solid food. True, they are suckled for a long time; but besides this they are given more and more other food, which must be rendered as soft as possible at first, and then gradually is left increasingly solid. Our own customary use of baby food—which is soft, made of the best foods, and lovingly prepared—is no more than a highly mechanized form of feeding, as accurately attuned as possible to the biological requirements of the child. It goes far beyond what could be produced by purely natural means and is thus a hypernormal adaptation to the needs of the child. In principle, however, it is nothing new. The Greeks fed their children with premasticated food,[5] and even in the past century, in the rural parts of Austria, it was quite usual for the mother to premasticate food and then transfer it directly into the mouth of the infant. In Holstein, Germany, the grandmothers of thirty years ago premasticated butter dumplings for the older infants.[89] I observed the same in a farm in

Münsterland in 1954. The grandmother premasticated dough or milk rusks, took what she had chewed out of her mouth with a small spoon, and fed it to the baby. Characteristically, it was the grandmothers who still practiced this custom. Toward the end of the Second World War, I also saw mothers use this method of feeding during the refugee treks. Mouth-to-mouth feeding was still a normal feature of child-care among various primitive peoples until very recently; it occurred, for instance, in the Carolines, in

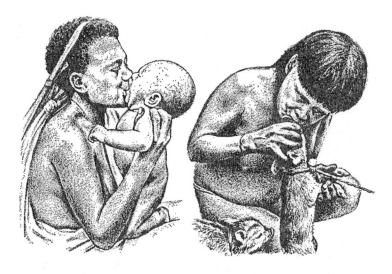

Papua mother feeding her child mouth-to-mouth (left), and Uruku Indian feeding a piglet mouth-to-mouth.

Samoa,[91] among the Naga tribes of Assam,[3] and among the Papua tribes of New Guinea.[103] This method of feeding children was also registered as a normal daily occurrence in Hausa villages on the Niger by Viennese behavior researchers of the biological station of Wilhelminenberg in 1954.

In such cases the premasticated food is transmitted directly from the mouth of the mother to that of the infant.

If the mother approaches her three-month-old infant with her mouth, it purses its lips as soon as she comes close. When the mouth-to-mouth contact has been achieved, the child sticks its tongue out and makes licking movements. Ploog reports that "We repeated this experiment on our own children with the same result."[89] So it is quite certain that the European infant, and probably every infant, is adapted to this method of feeding. It does not have to be forced on the infant, for it already understands it and is probably innately capable of performing its part in it. But infants become adults, and as adults they still retain this ability—and maybe even the need to employ it.

It becomes apparent how firmly anchored mouth-to-mouth feeding is in the brood-tending of some primitive raccs in cases where other living things take the place of children. Harald Schultz has written about the Uruku Indians from the Amazon area, who often kill sows on their hunts. The Indian women lovingly tend the helpless young piglets who are also brought back from these hunts, chew up food for them, and pass it directly into their mouths.[102] Similarly, missionaries from New Guinea reported that women chewed up vegetables and fruit and transmitted them directly from their own lips into the snouts of piglets.[24, 25] These piglets come from the village pigs and are reared in place of the mother's first born, whom she kills immediately after birth. Since this method of feeding even works with animals, who normally never receive their food in this way, it is not surprising that Brandes managed to feed a young orangutan with premasticated and well-salivated bananas and rusks.[89]

Direct mouth-to-mouth food transmission does not take place only between mother and child, but also between adults, both among primitive races and among the so-called civilized peoples. It is most likely to occur regularly in certain rituals, when it is, accordingly, described as a component of the ritual. The Pygmies of the tropical jungle

Mouth-to-mouth feeding of a dog; three-thousand-year-old clay figure from a grave in Tlatilco, a suburb of Mexico City.

of Central Africa, who still live at the economic level of primitive hunters and food-gatherers, live in residential groups of several blood-related families, seldom numbering more than fifty to a hundred persons. The leader of each group is usually the best hunter. The Pygmies are almost exclusively monogamous. Of the various African groups, the Ituri Pygmies are considered the purest race. They live on the Ituri, more or less where it flows into the Congo. Among others, they occasionally kill elephants in pitfalls with poisoned harpoons. How they do this is shown in a film put together from archive material and prepared for secondary school instruction, which can be rented, from the Institut für den Wissenschaftlichen Film in Göttingen.[108] The film also includes sequences showing the dissection and sharing of the prey. Whoever has set up the trap also has the right of disposal; it is he who parcels out the meat. And here a curious ceremony takes place, whose

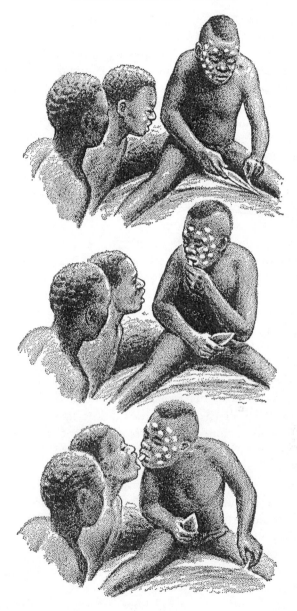

Scene of ritual feeding among Ituri Pygmies.

significance has not yet been understood: A foreman, probably the owner of the trap, cuts pieces of meat from the animals, puts them between his lips, and then transfers them directly, mouth-to-mouth, to a companion. It would, of course, be simpler to pass the piece of meat from hand to hand. The mouth-to-mouth method must surely be a ritual. Unfortunately all we can say at present is that it occurs among adults; from all we know from our comparisons of form and species, it derives from infant feeding.

We can cite another example, from Central Europe this time: In the Ziller valley, the Puster valley, and in Pinzgau, chewed tobacco used to be exchanged as an affirmation of friendship. If a girl accepted the wad of premasticated tobacco, it meant she returned the boy's love. Besides tobacco (and probably the source of the custom, since the use of tobacco only dates from the seventeenth century), they also chewed spruce resin and pitch—at least they still did so in 1912—and these substances were also exchanged after chewing, often during dancing, and in particular between lovers. The young man would let a tip of the piece of pitch show between his closed teeth and invite the girl to grasp it with her teeth—which of course obliged her to press her mouth firmly on that of the young man—and to pull it out. "If the dancer agrees to the invitation of the young man, this is a sign that she feels well-disposed toward him, and often even more," writes Von Hörmann.[43]

Advertising also exploits the motif of mouth-to-mouth feeding, for instance by displaying a friendly man and girl with their faces turned toward each other, and both aiming with open mouth for a tasty morsel lying between them (which the advertisement is extolling), or one of them aiming with open mouth for a tidbit held between the lips of the other.

Bilz defends the rather old interpretation that the human kiss came into being in this way on the basis of ethnological findings.[3] Besides the fact that lovers do indeed feed each other in this way, he also cites a collection of words for "kissing" from different languages that often have the additional meaning of premastication, or a tender gesture. This ethnological interpretation receives strong support from our earlier comparisons with animals. Close bonds between social partners are very generally established and maintained through the medium of transferred brood-tending behavior elements; and brood-tending feeding very often plays a major role in them, although the actual transmission of food can fall away so that a new kind of ritual emerges. This ritual appears most often between the partners of a pair. The same applies to man. The more intimate the relations between two humans, the more easily kissing can turn into feeding-kissing; this transition also goes to show how close the connection between the two is. But quite apart from the "playful" transmission of food, to and fro movements of the tongue can occur that give away the origin of the whole thing.

Primarily, of course, all this applies to kissing on the mouth. Kisses on other parts of the body could have as origin the "tender touching" with the lips that we described for chimpanzees (see p. 169). However, this is also a typical behavior of the mother toward her child and does not, therefore, affect the relation we have established to brood-tending behavior; we can simply say that it did not necessarily derive from feeding here. The kissing that occurs among humans can just as easily turn into nibbling with the teeth, which we find in the primitive grooming of man too. On the other hand, one and the same person can use different types of kiss as greeting, according to the ranking order between him and the person greeted. Herodotus (I, 34) and Strabo (XV, 2, 20) tell of this among the Persians: The Persians greet each other differently according to the rank of each person. If they are of equal rank, they kiss on the mouth; if one is just a little subordinate to the other, they kiss on the cheek; but if one is of much lower birth than the other, he prostrates himself in front of the other. In order to make St. Perpetua recant her faith and to save her from martyrdom, her father kissed her hand, actually threw himself at her feet, and tearfully called her his mistress. When a visitor wanted to kiss the hand of Caliph Hisam (A.D. 724-43), the latter replied that only a coward did this among Arabs. This shows that the kiss can become a fixed social demonstration, in which the presence of a third person can also be of importance. According to Plutarch, Cato the Elder had Pretorius Manilius crossed off the list of senators because he had given his wife a kiss in the presence of his own daughter. It could of course be that the kiss that was originally directed at the mouth was deflected elsewhere because of ranking order. And indeed we know far too little about this extremely common behavior of man, which could be clarified by careful study, to be able to reply to the more specific question about the particular behavior elements within brood-tending from which kissing derives.

The kiss is used for greetings and farewells, for appeasement, and in addition it is one of those actions that occur almost for their own sake and presumably result in strengthening the pair-bond; finally, it is also used in the foreplay to copulation. Furthermore, it plays an important part in religious life. Man worships divine beings by kissing their living representatives (priests), statues, or other holy objects: temple thresholds, altars, the Koran, the Torah, or the Bible. All this is considered part of the veneration, love, or greeting of the godhead; but it can also be used to coax something from it. The Benedictine Father Ohm gives a detailed account, from which most of the examples quoted here were taken, in his modern book on the gestures of prayer.[87]

The kiss can also turn from a greeting into a sign of brothership, of the "union of souls." In the days of the early Christians, the baptist and the assembled Christians would kiss the child to be baptized. Even in Antiquity, the man who was admitted to a council was kissed; and only a few years ago Marlene Dietrich was kissed when she became a Knight of the Legion of Honor in Germany. The *osculum sanctum*, the liturgical kiss of peace, also belongs in this context, and indeed it was not always as pure as the rules would have it. The Church regulations of Hippolytus require that the faithful shall kiss one another; the man shall kiss the man and the woman shall kiss the woman, and the men shall not kiss the women; and the Coptic sources of the Council of Nicea declare: "Thou shalt teach women not to give the kiss of peace to a man except if they are old and if the men are old men, unless they be older women who are very faithful."

We may also note the occurrence among the ancient Indians and Arabs, and in African and other native tribes, of the smelling or sniffing kiss. Presumably this also related to brood-tending; for instance, according to ancient Indian house rules, the father must sniff the head of the newborn child, or of a child returned from a journey, three times.

"Blowing a kiss" very probably also derived from brood-tending feeding. Here one kisses one's own hand and then pretends to throw the kiss to the object of devotion. Indeed, particularly with older children, mouth-to-mouth feeding by the parents is replaced by the transmission of pre-masticated food, which is let fall from the mouth into the chewer's own hand and then given to the child among some native tribes. Since this gesture too is often easily dismissed and not considered worth further attention, these plausible interpretations must remain no more than suggestions for the time being.

What we can maintain here is that the mouth kiss, which has occurred among civilized and primitive peoples from ancient times to today, is a ritualized brood-tending action, and that at least in some of its forms it goes back to the mouth-to-mouth feeding of small children by their mother.

30. The Social Significance of the Female Breast

If we consider the parallels, it becomes clear that it is a necessary consequence of the mother-child situation for the maternal breast to become a place of security for humans too and to acquire secondary meanings in social life very similar to those it acquired among the mammals we mentioned earlier. In the first three days after birth, every newborn baby can be comforted by giving it something teatlike to suck, even if the baby does not receive any nourishment in this way. So even prior to all experience, the maternal breast has a comforting effect. But both animal and human infants also gain corroborating experience of this effect. The following examples will show how great the analogies between men and mammals are here.

Elizabeth M. Thomas described the following scene which she witnessed among the bushmen of the Kalahari:

> When his little son saw what he was doing and realized that his father was preparing to go, he began to cry, saying: "Father, Father," and when Lazy Kwi hesitated a moment, then said he was going anyway, the little boy picked up a handful of stones and threw one at him. This amused Lazy Kwi's wife, who smiled and tried half-heartedly to take the stones away, but it angered Lazy Kwi, who caught his son by the arm and boxed his ears. That made the little boy so furious that he had a tantrum; he screamed and cried and arched

his back to draw away from his mother, who tried to pick him up, both mother and child doing exactly what they had done when the little boy was a baby and no doubt had been doing ever since. His mother always did have a terrible time managing him, and he was still nursing although he was now five or six years old. Before his father left, his mother had managed to mollify him somewhat, and she sat on the ground, letting him sit on her leg to nurse. He drank from one breast and held the other in his hand as he glared over his mother's shoulder at his father, who was already in the Jeep.

Papua woman with her baby at one breast and a piglet at the other.

Another scene:

Hearing me speak of medicine, Little Gashe glared at me balefully. I had treated his eyes before and perhaps he

*remembered that the medicine was painful, or perhaps he
was afraid that I would harm his eyes. He scrambled into
his mother's lap to nurse and, facing toward her for safety,
glared at me over her shoulder.*[113]

Both these scenes show clearly how the child reacts to an
aggressive, or presumably dangerous, and certainly frightening conspecific, whether father or stranger, how the child
then finds itself in a situation of social repression, and thereupon seeks protection with the mother and takes her
breast.

Many observers of such scenes do not mention whether
the child actually drinks or not. Sorenson and Gajdusek,
who studied natives of various tribes in New Guinea, were
able to record similar scenes on film.[107] Among the Fore
in the eastern mountains, the three-to-four-year-olds were
particularly fearful in the presence of strangers and cried
as soon as they were approached, even if they were close
to their mother. But often they would calm down as soon
as they had cuddled up to her and could grasp her breast
with their mouth, even though they did not drink. In this
position they lost their fear and would even begin to throw
cautious, curious glances at the stranger and his camera.

It was clearly apparent to the researchers that the children did not actually drink in this situation, and yet they
spoke of "nursing." One has to be equally careful about the
details given on the periods of lactation of other tribes,
especially since the respective authors often omit to say
whether they observed constant suckling in these cases or
only occasionally saw children at their mother's breast. I
know from my own experience with Africans that frightened children often took the breast without making drinking motions.

Of course the prerequisite for all this is that the children
should have easy access to the maternal breast. If the
breasts are covered up, children who flee to their mother

still press their face against her breast, but it is no longer quite clear what they are actually seeking there.

In regions where the breasts are still kept free of clothing, mothers usually nurse their children far longer than in places where clothing customs make it more difficult and for this reason alone encourage earlier weaning. Kraho Indians nurse their children for several years,[102] and the Nuna of West Africa (Upper Volta) still nurse them until well past the third year. Bushmen children are still nursed until their fourth year, and in the first eighteen months they live on little else but the maternal milk.[105] Gypsies also nurse until into the fourth year if not longer,[17] as do Eskimos, among whom it even used to be common for the mother to go on nursing the child until her next pregnancy. Freuchen, one of the great experts on the Eskimos in their "primitive state," saw Eskimo mothers from various regions give the breast to fourteen-year-old sons.[33] But the children do not only suck, they also play with the breasts. Eskimo children still do so when they are at least seven years old. This is frequently observed among various native tribes too, although again it is only occasionally mentioned in ethnological accounts. Nursing and playing probably also play a part in the children's fixation on the maternal breast as a place of security. At least it is striking that a short lactation period, covered breasts, and the attribution of an excessively erotic, almost fetishistic significance to the breasts tend to go together, just as the reverse is true: Among primitive peoples we find a long lactation period and uncovered breasts, and the significance attached to them in everyday social life often seems astonishingly normal to Westerners. Naturally many other factors come into play too; but no exact comparative research has been undertaken in this field yet, perhaps because no one has ever thought of formulating the question.

Ford and Beach, when they compared many human groups and peoples, found no direct correlation between the custom of covering up the breasts in daily life and the significance accorded to stimulating the breasts in sexual life.[32] However, direct sexual (fore-) play is not the only possible framework and probably not even the right framework for determining the biological and social value of the breasts as signals. That they have such a signal value between adults is general knowledge. And that this signal value is culturally influenced is equally demonstrable. For while no one objects to the sight of an Indian woman, in almost European dress, calmly nursing her baby in front of a shop entrance in Ecuador, or to an elegant young lady doing the same on a park bench in the smart Corso Vittorio Emmanuele in Naples, many European women scarcely dare to nurse their child at home in the presence even of good friends.

Monkey mothers, who are constantly surrounded by "good friends," cannot afford such reticence. But human mothers can offer their babies feeding bottles as breast substitutes. This can largely if not entirely divest the breast of its original biological function. The extreme care that is lavished on the female breast today relates almost exclusively to its social signal value. The manufacturers of creams, ointments, lotions, tablets, drops, special douches, rotating brushes, and even inflatable or foam rubber "falsies" are all striving to make the breasts into "one of the most attractive attributes of femininity," and "the ideal of feminine perfection." They are not concerned with the baby, but with the most perfect *décolleté*, with the breast beautiful, whose praises have always been sung by man, as for instance in the Song of Solomon: "Thy breasts are like two young roes that are twins, which feed among the lilies." The scene in Homer where the beautiful Helen conciliates her angry husband by showing him her breasts can be taken as another example of the breasts' value as signals.

This coincides in many ways with the effect the female

breast exerts in the social life of the gelada baboon. However, we must then ask whether perhaps the human female breast underwent a further development in the service of its function as a social signal, as it did with the female gelada baboon.

Now man is the only living mammal in whom the mammary glands are constantly strongly developed and remain noticeable even when they do not produce milk. The difference in size for different women bears no relation to the amount of milk they produce; small breasts can secrete more milk than larger ones, for the form of the breast depends on the development of the stroma, a connective tissue structure into which the milk ducts of the glands sprout during pregnancy. At the end of the period of lactation, when the gland tissue regresses again, the connective tissue increases considerably instead.[2] In addition, the fatty tissue also has a part in the structure of the breast. But fatty and connective tissue can easily accumulate in any part of the body. They are building materials that can be used anywhere, even for building signal structures. For man often uses formal signals where lower primates use color signals. This applies to the infant schema, in which the chubby cheeks that are also built up of fatty and connective tissues play an important role, just as it applies to the female breast, which admittedly has already developed into a social signal among monkeys but which is supplemented by striking colors. Naturally this does not mean that man could not also turn colors to account. Painting and tattooing are evidence of this among peoples who do not wear clothes, as are the sophisticated fashions of our cultural sphere, where clothes are used like an artificial skin and in the bargain aim at the "gelada effect" by similar neck lines—which has led to the jocular christening of the gelada baboon as the "dirndl monkey."

Now that it is becoming less important, since we have artificial baby foods, whether the female breast can in fact fulfill its original function, while at the same time the breast is assuming increasing importance as a signal in the relations between adults, we might well expect its structure and shape to gradually adapt itself more and more to its new function—insofar as this is not easier to do by cosmetic and other technical tricks. There are several examples to show that races with large breasts prefer these, whereas races with small breasts prefer small ones. Whether this means that the form of the organ has adapted itself to the preference, or on the contrary that the latter is adapted to the existing form of the organ, cannot be determined as yet. But it would be possible to examine what role the experience of the baby at the breast plays in the eventual adult's evaluation of the breast by a comparison between adults who were breast fed and others who were brought up on the bottle alone.

However the specific signal effect of the female breast has come about, what is certain is that it plays an important part in the conjugal and general social life of man. This secondary significance is so commonplace today that the breast even counts as a sexual signal, although everyone knows its original significance. This effect is of course enhanced by the fact that the mother does not only take the child to her breast for suckling, but also as a caress or if the child needs comforting and protection. "Cuddling" and clasping to the breast is the emancipated preliminary to nursing. And this reaction is not only addressed to babies and children. In the Song of Solomon, the girl dreaming of her lover wishes: "O that thou wert as my brother, that sucked the breasts of my mother!," and the mystic Mechthild von Magdeburg sighed: "Oh thou god, reposing at my breasts" to her divine husband. No doubt everyone knows further examples from everyday experience.

That sucking at the breast also appeases the woman, i.e., that it can have an effect similar to that occurring with the hunting dog or the Uganda kob, is evident from the example of a Turkish fairytale[8] that we shall quote in part here. A young man is sent on an adventure on some pretext and encounters a dervish on the way. The dervish asks him what his intention is and after being told says: "Oh my son, he who sends you, sends you to your doom. But only go, Allah will help you." The dervish predicts to the young man that although he will meet with huge demons, called Dev, on his way, he will be able to appease them by a specific behavior: "Take these three okka of chewing resin! And now listen well! On the way you will meet a Dev woman. When flies fly into her mouth and come out of her seat she is asleep. When they fly into her seat and come out of her mouth, she is awake. If she is awake, you must immediately put one okka of chewing resin into her mouth and embrace her right nipple. Then she will show you the way; you can ask her." The young man leaves the dervish, and after a while he meets the Dev woman. Since flies are flying into her seat and coming out of her mouth, he immediately throws the chewing resin into her mouth, grasps her nipple, and sucks it. Then she catches sight of him and says: "Oh you human, if you did not grasp my right nipple I would crunch you between my teeth and mix you with my chewing resin. . . . Where are you going?" When he had answered she sent him on to her elder sister, who in turn sent him on to an even older sister. Both times he behaved as the dervish had advised. Thereupon the second sister said: "Oh you human, what shall I do now that you have become my child? Whence do you come and where are you going?" The third sister said: "Oh you boy, if you did not suck my nipple I would crunch you between my teeth and mix you with my chewing resin! Where are you going?"

Naturally man judges the behavior of spirits, demons, and gods according to his own behavior, that is, strictly anthropomorphically. So such fairytales are not descriptions of the behavior of spiritual beings but reflect the behavior and experiences of man. Since we also know that many women experience a feeling of voluptuousness when nursing a baby or when their partner fondles and sucks at their breast during the foreplay to coitus, and sometimes even have an orgasm, this fairytale account is certainly not implausible.

31. The Infant Schema

Twenty-five years ago, Konrad Lorenz coined the term "infant schema" to describe a special perceptual achievement of man that consists of protective responses toward typical infantile characteristics. The generalized attitude that

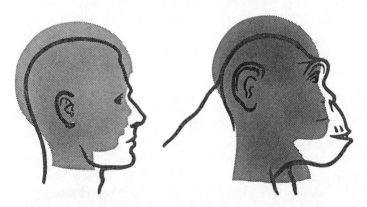

Typical head shape of the human child and adult (left) and the chimpanzee child and adult (right). The eye and ear have been chosen as points of reference, in order to clarify the proportionate sizes of the skull and face.

man adopts toward the still helpless young of his own kind in need of care is characterized on the one hand by certain unmistakable feelings and emotions and connected with a specific experience whose quality is usually conveyed in English by the words "sweet," "cute," and so on. On the other hand it is dependent on surprisingly few character-istics. The characteristics that an object must possess in or-der to elicit the specific experiential quality of "cute" are as follows, according to Lorenz:

1. *A comparatively thick head;*
2. *A prominent cranium with a domed brow out of propor-tion to the face;*
3. *A large correspondingly disproportionate eye situated as low as or below the middle of the entire skull;*
4. *Comparatively short, thick limbs with pudgy hands and feet;*
5. *Rounded body forms in general;*
6. *A very specific, soft, and elastic surface texture;*
7. *Round, prominent, "chubby" cheeks.*

All living things and even inanimate objects that exhibit several of these characteristics have a "cute" effect on the observer. A perfect example is Walt Disney's Bambi. Many pets who, of course, are often treated like babies, exhibit these same characteristics, and Lorenz points out that these are in fact almost dummy infants for childless people.

Naturally man is not the only creature to have these brood-tending responses. Many animals who have a well-marked brood-tending behavior respond to specific char-acteristics that characterize their progeny with brood-tend-ing actions. The turkey hen recognizes her chicks by signs of an acoustic nature; the mother only tends and guards chicks that cheep. Noncheeping chicks are killed, and accordingly a deaf turkey hen who has never heard a chick cheep kills all her progeny.[100] The optical signals that are known include the colored beak flanges and the colorful gapes of many nestling birds, which incite the old bird to feed them. But even among birds we must note that it is certainly not only parents who are in a brood-tending mood who respond to these releasing stimuli; often strange conspecifics who have no offspring of their own, and even juvenile birds, respond in the same way. Herring gulls, who defend food territories outside the breeding season, tolerate and even feed begging young birds in these territories. Although the young birds need not be their own progeny, they still must have the brown plumage of a young bird. Then the adults will at most make incipient moves to drive them away, but they are clearly inhibited in their aggression.[23] Mammals use many olfactory signals that we cannot go into here, most of which have in any case not been sufficiently studied yet. But baby monkeys often have color markings that insure them the protection of the adults.

The fur of the newborn offspring of all African tree monkeys (*Cercopithecus*) has a color that is clearly distinct from that of the adults. At the age of six to eight weeks, the baby color is slowly replaced by the juvenile coat but still remains recognizable until the fourth month. Adult African tree monkeys of both sexes living in the wild react extremely violently if they see a baby-colored young one in danger, for instance if a human holds it in his hand. Large males of the particularly aggressive *Cercopithecus aethiops* species even dare to attack humans in such cases, and utter threatening calls while doing so. It is important that the young animal should move; adults do not react if it is dead. But it does not have to scream, although this tends to heighten the adults' reaction. Adult males and females do not only try to free baby animals in danger; they also take immediate care of an abandoned offspring. When a mother is shot by hunters, unless she dies at once she will push away the baby who is clinging to her, so that it will have to cling to a branch instead, before she falls down. Thereupon it is immediately fetched away by another adult. By contrast, the adults show no reaction at all if a young animal that has already changed color or another adult is captured or wounded.[7] The black-and-white mountain guereza (*Colobus*) responds in the same way to babies who are still colored white all over if they are in danger.

Baboon babies have a black coat for the first six months, while they are still sucking from the mother (adults have brown or gray fur), and so they can play the fool to their heart's content during this period. All the adults, even old males, try to adopt a black-furred baby, groom it, and watch over it. Among hamadryas baboons, the half-grown males in particular are excellent baby-sitters. At first, mother baboons will not normally allow their newborn baby to be touched by others. African tree monkey mothers also guard their baby jealously.

The long-tailed Asian langurs and dusky langurs behave quite differently. Dusky langur babies are almost black, while adults are light gray. Spectacled langurs have a brownish gray to almost blackish-brown fur when adult, but the babies are golden yellow like a teddy bear or almost white. Now, immediately after a langur baby is born, four to ten females from the group, whether adult or still young, seat themselves around the mother, observe the baby attentively, and try to touch and sniff it. Male langurs pay little attention to babies. In the first few hours after birth, the mother tries to turn her back on the other females who are waiting patiently. But once the baby is quite dry she allows the others to touch it carefully, and now it only takes a few minutes before one of the other females has the baby on her arm. Then, as the mother had done before her, she examines the baby carefully, cautiously touches, sniffs, and licks it, in particular on the head, hands, and genitals. As soon as the baby tries to free itself, it is taken over by another female. Many babies are carried in the arms of eight different females on the first day of their life, and sometimes taken up to twenty meters away from the mother. But the mother can take the baby back whenever she likes, especially to suckle it, although the other females also permit the baby to try to drink from them; some females even help it to find the teat and grasp it with its lips. On the other hand, there are also females who are very awkward with their baby and soon hand it over to a neighbor. This interest on the part of all the female members of the band lasts for the first three to five months of the baby's life, as long as it is still characterized by its baby color; then it wanes rapidly. The mother weans it, rather forcefully, in fact, when it is eleven to fifteen months old.[50]

So the langur baby is constantly passed from one female to another during the first three to five months of its life, as though it were common property. But chimpanzee babies constantly remain in direct contact with their mother in the first 3½ to 5½ months, and she forestalls any attempts to take the baby away from her during that time. This builds up a very close mother-child relationship that survives into adulthood, as shown by the fact that the two animals often continue to accompany each other, share food, or come to each other's aid. Chimpanzee babies are not intentionally weaned by the mother; they stop drinking when the milk dries up.

Just when the young chimpanzee occasionally begins to leave its mother and eventually makes more and more distant sorties, it develops a striking color marking, namely the large white tuft of hair that juts out from the dark fur like a little tail. This tuft is small and unobtrusive on the newborn baby and only consists of a few sparse hairs. It is conspicuous by the age of 3½ months, and this is when the young chimpanzee begins to reach out from the mother toward conspecifics. At the age of three years, the white tuft disappears, and from then on the young are repulsed and pushed away more and more roughly by the adults. So the tuft is quite clearly an infant characteristic that becomes most important when the young begin to have dealings with adults, to annoy them, and also to greet them by laying a hand on some part of their body.[72]

These observations on African tree monkeys, guerezas, langurs, and chimpanzees are very valuable because they were all made in the wild, and the animals were therefore living their normal lives. The offspring of all these species grow up in a stable social group, and grow into it. As long as they are still small and need help, they enjoy special protection by the other members of the society. Our comparison shows that this protection is insured by special signals that emanate from the young animal but only appear when it begins to move about freely in the society or when the need for protection by members of the society other than the mother become urgent. We shall now try to examine the infant schema of man in the framework of these findings.

In a fairly wide series of tests of the infant characteristics mentioned at the beginning of this chapter, Nos. 2, 3, and 7 were tried on 330 test subjects aged between six and thirty (male and female children from homes, schoolchildren, and students).[45] They had to choose the cutest, sweetest, or prettiest head from the series of pictures, each of which gave two choices. Most of the drawings were outlines of a child's head, but there were also tests on donkeys' heads with similarly distorted proportions. Our drawing shows a few pictures from various series of tests.

Perhaps it would be advisable for the reader to look at the heads carefully at this point and to try, without much thought, to decide which he himself considers the prettiest, and which, on the contrary, he finds least attractive.

The result of the aforementioned series of tests was as follows:

All adults quite clearly preferred head B2 to head B1; girls already did so at the age of ten to thirteen, boys from about eighteen years old. They never preferred B1.

Adult women also preferred K2 to K1, while male subjects either made no distinction between the two or preferred K1.

Other characteristics were also tested, and this showed that heads with hair were preferred to bald heads (not

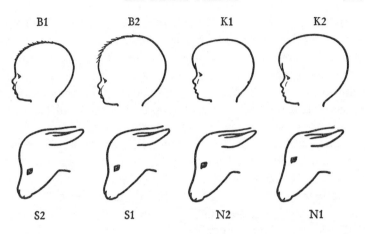

The "infant schema" as shown on children's and donkeys' heads (explanation in text).

shown here), but only if the shape of the head was the same in both cases. Otherwise adult women again preferred a head like B2, but without hair, to the B1 illustrated here.

This is striking because B1 is the proportionally "correct" head of an infant, while B2 is an exaggerated head shape that normally never occurs. Similarly, K1 is the natural head of an eight-to-ten-year-old boy, while K2 is an unnatural exaggeration. The exaggeration always concerns the skull, that is to say, its size in relation to the face and the prominence of the brow. And these exaggerated characteristics are indeed preferred to the natural features, which means that our perception overrates the typical characteristics of an infant and is actually duped by abnormal dummies. The more the dummy seems natural in other respects, the stronger this response becomes. Here we are dealing with simple line drawings. But the doll industry produces much more complicated dummies that play on, and if possible exaggerate, other infant characteristics listed by Lorenz, besides the ones tested here.

This response becomes very clear when the infant characteristics in question are not depicted on a child at all but on some other object, and nevertheless evoke the same evaluation. The curve of the brow and the height of the upper skull were also varied on a donkey's head. With the exception of ten-to-thirteen-year-old boys (who pass through a very realistic and critical phase at this age), all test subjects preferred head S2, where the exaggeration corresponds most closely to the preferred outline in the infant schema. N1 was liked least. And indeed, N1 corresponds to an older, N2 to a younger donkey, while S1 and S2 do not exist in nature. The results of the donkey's head tests are hardly surprising, for they show how Bambi and similar figures came into being.

These tests provide several important points of reference to the social behavior of man. First, it is clear that the response that was tested is peculiar both to young people and to adults of either sex. So it is not purely a maternal, brood-tending response but an important general tendency to watch over children in our society, as baby-sitters do. Since this normally only becomes necessary if the child is outside the immediate vicinity of the mother, it is understandable that only the characteristics of the *infant* release this protective response. For the human infant needs these signals, which elicit a general protectiveness, just as little as the chimpanzee baby—indeed, they could even harm it. If all good acquaintances were to try to caress the newborn infant and carry it about, as among langurs, this could seriously affect the development of the intimate mother-child bond. So biologically speaking it makes sense that the real infant was not often found sweet or cute in these tests. The tested response was not meant for it in any case. (This probably also means that the maternal drive to care for a child depends on other characteristics.)

The infant characteristics do not have to appear on an infant. They are as unlikely to fail their effect on an older child or an adult as on a donkey. This means that we should expect that even an adult man will be driven into the role of friend and protector at the sight of a pretty face with snub nose and saucer eyes, even if the role is quite out of place. It is not difficult to find examples of this. Experience shows that if there are two applicants for a secretarial job, the prettier girl will have a better chance, even if she has made more mistakes in the dictation test. So although we can argue that secretarial work is not only a question of typing and that the ability to work together as smoothly as possible is equally necessary, we must still remember that simple biological signals can evidently influence the evaluation of a purely technical achievement quite considerably. So there is a danger of social injustice here. It can, of course, be eliminated, but only if one is aware of it and knows its origins. The danger becomes greater if a person deliberately exploits these associations in his own interests. The behavior of a pretty, "scheming woman" is often not so very different from that of the baboons described on p. 216, with their use of "protected threat"; in both cases a biologically important social behavior is being misused, and the user is so successful simply because the response to the signal is an automatic one.

This is certainly not confined to the realm of brood-tending signals. Sugar substances are an important food for man. We recognize them by the fact that they taste sweet. This means that our sense of taste is equipped to recognize the characteristic molecular elements of such foods and evaluates them as "sweet." It is possible to build similar molecular elements into substances without any food value by artificial means. These substances also taste sweet and are used as "sugar substitutes," for instance for diabetics. What is important in this context is that such substitutes, such as saccharin, also taste sweeter to the chemist, who knows their chemical structure and is well aware that they are only substitutes without food value. The fact that he knows it neither alters his sense of taste nor does it stop him from preferring saccharin, i.e., preferring it in his mouth, to quinine, for example. Our response to infant characteristics and many other signals from the brood-tending or sexual field is just as automatic, and "knowing better" makes no difference. If we want to guard against the abuse of these responses, for instance in advertising, we must intervene in the response *after* it has made its primary appeal to us, that is, *not* buy a product although the baby face on the package is very cute, not buy a car simply because truly attractive young ladies in the tiniest of bikinis advertise it, etc. For if we wanted to achieve the effect of preventing the baby face from being considered cute (always assuming this was at all possible), we would by the same count have to destroy our natural response to small children. *The primary response to such biological signals is not an ethical question.*

The preceding example suffices to show how deeply our whole social life is penetrated by brood-tending elements. This is, of course, biologically built in to us and not just there for us to misuse. Our comparisons with similarly structured animal societies suggest that this brood-tending response is directed at children while also playing an important part in the relations between the human sexual partners. Now we have long since known that on a purely external basis, woman looks much more "pedomorphic," i.e., more childlike, than man. On an average, in every race, she is 7 percent smaller than he, has relatively shorter limbs and a rounder face, and her nose and chin are less marked. Whatever the reason for this, one result is that it prevents the man from behaving like a rabid aggressor, and makes it easier to him to fulfill his role of guardian and protector.

As we said, monkeys have evolved from smell-oriented to sight-oriented animals, and accordingly an increasing number of optical social signals were joined to the olfactory signals, beginning with color signals. In the course of further developments, the color markings were accompanied by increasingly well-defined formal signals. Accordingly, the more dangerous color signals (more dangerous because more visible to predators) were gradually replaced by formal signals. This does not mean that smells and colors became insignificant in later development; but it does mean that small gestures and forms have acquired a particular importance in intraspecific communication. (Only at this stage of development do we find, for instance, marked facial expressions. This is most highly developed in man. And it also entails the ability to see the play of features and the development of a complex system of muscular activity that produces the manifold forms of mimicry.) While the infant schema of monkeys largely relies on color signals, formal signals play a major role in the infant schema of man and have been adapted to it: The chubby cheeks of the baby, which elicit particularly strong responses, were evidently developed specifically in the service of the infant schema. At any rate they are not necessary for sucking, as we can see from the thin faces of monkey babies, who suck just as forcefully.

32. Mother-Child Behavior in Society

Like the chimpanzee baby (see p. 186), the human baby is neither a nest-hugger nor a nest-fleer but a "mother-hugger" and should be carried against the mother's body continuously in the early days of its life, as is still the custom among primitive races today. The entire behavior repertory of the newborn baby is adapted for this. For man is not physiologically a premature birth, as is often asserted. Rather, from birth on he possesses all the motor patterns that enable him to live on the mother's body. Accordingly, the baby clings to the mother, especially to her hair, as we all know. The baby only becomes "helpless" in the truest sense of the word when it is separated from its mother. It is not biological for us to place our babies in cribs. Symptomatic of this is that the babies cry out of loneliness with abnormal frequency in our culture, while one scarcely ever finds this among the children of primitive peoples. Equally symptomatic are the "contact dummies" that soothe the baby by deluding it that it is in bodily contact with its mother: namely the dummy and the rocking motion of the cradle or carriage. The way the baby clings to its mother in moments of shock or fear corresponds to the need for close bodily contact with the mother that we have already described in monkeys. And this behavior survives into adulthood: Fright makes an adult want to cling to another and embrace him. The same words are also used in the figurative sense, for we speak of embracing or clinging "mentally" to something or someone, just as one clings to one's hanky in moments of helplessness. Adult male chimpanzees sometimes even embrace little chimpanzees if they are suddenly frightened. Monkeys and humans embrace one another in the same way before going to sleep. The mutual grooming of humans also derives from mother-child behavior. Describing the Maku Indians from the dense jungle between the Rio Negro and Rio Japura in the Amazon state, Schultz reports: "The reciprocal extraction of unwelcome living things from the hair of the head is a gesture of friendship that can be observed quite frequently among the Indians. If one sees a young man lay his head confidingly in the lap of a young girl, one can almost certainly regard them as an engaged couple. The virtue of giving reciprocal assistance eventually developed into a kind of caress, owing to man's susceptibility to these little animals (i.e., lice). The lice caught after a successful foray are often eaten."[102] The same delousing can also be seen among women who lie comfortably in their hammocks throughout the procedure. These peoples have no effective household remedy of their own for ridding themselves of this age-old pest. So modern chemical preparations are greeted with great joy, for they can very rapidly free the people of their tormentors. Do they also free them from the kind of caressing connected with it? Almost certainly not; for to groom or delouse the body of a partner is a form of behavior very commonly serving as introduction to a sexual relationship. It is found among the Siriono nomads of eastern Bolivia; the Dusun of northern Borneo, who are farmers, fishers, and craftsmen; the Prairie-Cree hunters of Saskatchewan, Alberta, and Montana; the Trobriand islanders of eastern Melanesia[32]; and on our own beaches. While Siriono lovers spend hours searching for lice on each others' heads and ticks on each others' bodies (and eating them), as well as removing worms and thorns from each others' skin, "civilized" Western lovers rub each other with suntan lotion and squeeze each others' blackheads. And almost forty years ago Yerkes wrote: "They [these actions] may very well be basically natural or inherited and only secondarily cultural; but in either event they are biologically important as conditioning comfort and health, highly socialized, strongly motivated, and accompanied by marked positive effects. The student of phylogenesis, with special interest in the evolution of human social service, may very well suspect that cultural developments and transformations of the variously named forms of grooming in infrahuman primates have given origin to tonsorial artistry, nursing, surgery, and other related social services of man."[128] Whether or not this is true, what is certain is that allogrooming also has an important place in the social behavior of man and has enough elements in common with baby care to enable us to recognize its origins in brood-tending behavior fairly easily here too. The tender caress is also addressed to other species: Man strokes his pets, and Javan monkeys delouse a friendly fox in Zürich Zoo. Some primitive races also use their teeth for grooming, and Eibl-Eibesfeldt has recently filmed a scene of greeting among the Waikas on the Orinoco, where intensive nibbling takes the place of kissing the cheek. Like greeting, tender stroking, pinching, and ruffling the other's hair are emancipated, former grooming actions.

Unlike that of many mammals, the ear of the newborn human baby is already fully functional at birth, and the baby can be soothed by certain sounds, ideally by a pitch around 150 cycles per second, i.e., similar to the tender tones of a woman's voice.[4] Adults still respond to this too. Specific sounds from the mother-child relationship also play a role among, for instance, rodents, although here it is the ultrasonic sounds uttered by the young animal that call the mother to it and make her carry it back to the nest. Similar sounds are also emitted during copulation, and in some species they are uttered by an animal if it is defeated in a fight.[104]

We all know that parents lead their small children by the hand. It is equally well-known that this walking hand-in-hand also occurs between lovers and that "to stand together, hand in hand" is a sign of social solidarity. Stroking, caressing, holding hands, and kissing are typical behavior patterns between sexual partners, which derive from the mother-child relationship. We can add to them the sounds uttered between mother and child. And with forms of address such as "little one," or the more modern "oh baby," language goes out of its way to point to the underlying brood-tending mood. We indicated the significance of the infant schema in this context in the previous chapter.

An important, socially cohesive behavior of man is his smile: "Keep smiling." "Smile and the world will smile with you." But here, as with the preening of birds, see p. 145, it is not yet proved whether the behavior was taken over from brood-tending behavior into social life or the reverse. Child psychologists have long since been aware of the importance of the eye-contact between mother and child during nursing. And it was once assumed that smiling developed in this framework. But even babies blind from birth smile when their mother speaks to them; when she smiles they even stop the rolling of the eyes typical of blind babies and turn their eyes to the source of sound instead, although they cannot see it.[28] Accordingly, the form of the smile and the related turning of the eyes for visual contact are just as genetically determined as the situation that elicits the smile, part of this situation being acoustic contact with the mother.[55]

Most people must be familiar with the role that smiling and smiling back, and the exchange of glances between mother and child as well as between the partners of a human couple play. And a little observation of oneself and others will soon show that at the beginning of a friendship, apparently meaningless chatter, holding hands, or laughing have exactly the same effect as the appeasement gestures derived from brood-tending have among other social creatures. They help the partners to overcome their contact shyness and slight fear of each other.

33. The Pseudosexualization of Society

By now I hope the reader will both expect and take a rather cautious view of the constant lament about the sexualization of our society. On the one hand, presumably man too will have put elements of sexual behavior in the service of social life together, and on the other, these elements will presumably have lost their sexual significance and have become just as "emancipated" as the transferred behavior patterns of many animals. Often we cannot tell this from the form of the behavior, since that must remain the same wherever possible. Otherwise it would lose its potency. Such behavior patterns, which have changed function and moved into the social realm, could be expected to appear most conspicuously in very closely settled areas, just as they are most in evidence among social animals under high population density. Indeed, sexualization is as a whole a large city phenomenon. However, a number of so-called sexual actions and signals in our life are not sexual at all by origin but borrowed from brood-tending. This includes the open display of the female breasts on advertisements, "petting" in public places, and many other things.

Here I do not want to discuss such phenomena, which are more or less typical of fairly large societies, for they involve much more than our heritage as vertebrates alone. But it is fairly certain that much of this "sexualization" has more to do with sociability than with sex. The same very probably applies to the fashion for miniskirts and topless dresses, which presumably help to obviate the tensions in our anonymous society by acting as "friendly" social signals that seem equally anonymous—i.e., by means that are biologically built in, such as we saw for the tropical finches discussed on p. 197. We studied the nonsexual social significance of the male genitals in detail earlier (see p. 51); this too is apparent in the history of Western fashion, in the cod-pieces and flaps of knights' armor and lansquenets' trousers in the fifteenth and sixteenth centuries, in the penis decoration of various primitive races, and perhaps also in some modern trouser fashions and advertisements for gentlemen's underwear in our own society, as well as in the various phallic amulets worn as protection from the evil eye, envy, etc., and finally in aggressive turns of phrase, like the Arabic "a phallus in your eye." The image of Priapus with his gigantic reproductive organ, when set up in gardens and at the boundaries of fields, gave protection from thieves and from the effects of envy. Greek and Roman soldiers chose the phallus as escutcheon and for the emblem of their slingshots. The phallic images in ancient cathedrals are also meant to ban evil spirits. They are just as little a sign of sexualization or sexual excess as was the old custom of laying a hand on the genitals of the other when swearing an oath, as Abraham ordered his oldest servant to do (Gen. 24:2).

The figures on ancient castle and city gates, towers, walls, churches, and monasteries, showing the naked posterior, are also designed to ban evil spirits. They are always found on the outer front of the building, that is, they are directed at the enemy, but not in the inner court or on the back of portals. On very stormy nights, the men and women of ancient Germany would stick their bared bottom outside the front door in order to appease Wotan. This was originally the female invitation to mating; then it turned into a gesture of social submission and defense. It is impossible to retrace the gradual changes of meaning in the long development of this gesture. But the female bottom has also become a social signal in another way.

We are fortunate in the existence of the Khoisanide race. These are Bushmen and Hottentots, who still retain many primitive characteristics. The womenfolk have the so-called "Hottentot tablier," a striking enlargement of the small labia that begins with puberty; eventually the labia hang four or five centimeters outside the genital aperture.[117] Richly provided with blood vessels, they change color during sexual excitement, turning from pink to bright red. They are evaluated as a sexual signal by the partner too, for the men are proud of this feature of their women, and play with the labia before copulation.[115] The women of neighboring tribes—the Batetela, Basutos, and some Bantus—try to emulate this natural formation of the Khoisanides by artificial manipulation, in order to become sexually more attractive. We often find actual genital sexual signals among female monkeys, but not among any other human females.

The Khoisanides are further characterized by "steatopygia," i.e., fatty buttocks. This is in part due to the backward curvature of the spine at the sacrum typical of this race, which makes the pelvis rise almost vertically. The seat, which juts out as a result, is further enlarged by a large accumulation of fatty and connective tissue.[69] That this tissue forms signal structures on the human body is clear from our earlier discussion of the female breast and the chubby cheeks of the little child (see p. 251). As far as we know, the fatty buttocks of the Khoisanides are also a signal structure, which, to judge from cave paintings, already existed among the earliest men and can only secondarily, if at all, serve as reserve fat for times of need.[115]

Now it seems that the men of all human races respond strongly to the shape of the female bottom. European fashions have continually tried to exaggerate the female bottom artificially. This probably reached an extreme after 1880

Left: characteristic fatty buttocks of a Bushman woman.
Right: elegant dress dating from 1882.

with the *cul de crin* (called *cul de Paris* outside France),
and naturally it was designed to please man. Like the products of the doll industry discussed in the chapter on the
infant schema, these attempted snares indicate man's susceptibility to certain signals which, although deriving from
the sexual sphere, are certainly not always evaluated sexually; often they simply make a pleasant or agreeable impression.

Besides shape, motion also plays an important role.
Women has by nature a different form of pelvis from man.
This is the cause of her slightly knock-kneed stance, but it
also results in the familiar swaying movements of her hips
when she walks. Since this is easiest to see from the rear,
and since hints of female flight and male pursuit occur quite

regularly in the course of pair-formation, one can assume that the original signal value of these movements lay in the sphere of the foreplay to mating. We also know that today they tend to promote contact but do not necessarily have the effect of a sexual invitation, even when coquettishly exaggerated. High-heeled shoes, which are said to be bad for the health, are unlikely to die out as a fashion, because this unnatural position of the feet forces the woman to assume the "Khoisanide" posture that we like to see too, pushing out the bottom and underlining its motion. Many primitive peoples exaggerate these movements, especially when dancing, and have accentuated the shaking of the bottom and swaying of the hips by means of grass skirts, or colorful tassels or plumes attached above the bottom. This becomes very striking in cases where long dresses covering up these movements are prescribed at the mission and the women then wear a grass skirt on top of the dress for dancing.

Movements that are clearly copulatory also occur in dances, as much in our culture as among primitive peoples. This can look obscene, but is not intended as such by the dancers. In any case these are not exhibition dances by origin. As far as the performer is concerned, many of the motor patterns are emancipated from the sexual realm. But the observer is often unable to tell the difference from the movement alone, as he is unable in the ambiguous social behavior patterns we listed earlier. And if he does not take account of the mood underlying the performer's behavior, he will wrongly conclude that such behavior and corresponding linguistic expressions are evidence of hypersexualization, as he did with baboons. There is in fact an increasing sexualization in our life; this we do not deny. But we must be cautious about lumping together too much under the same heading.

34. Pair-Bonding and Reproduction in Marriage

What we have said of society also applies to the smallest social group, marriage. Man too has borrowed behavior patterns from the mother-child relationship for the foreplay to mating; besides this he has also put them in the service of pair-bonding, together with originally sexual behavior elements. Again, the outside observer can very easily be misled and take this for a sexualization of marriage, in particular if he has had no direct personal experience from which to understand the mood of the protagonists.

By his technical advances man is influencing marriage; for instance, its potential duration can only be realized today, when women very rarely die before men. More children survive too, and thus pair-bonding as opposed to reproduction comes into the foreground in marriage. Everything that serves its interests, without impairing the value and dignity of the individual or his love, can only be good in ethical terms, even if it is an intervention into the biological processes of reproduction that gives free access to the natural methods of pair-bonding discussed here. Inevitably this will also affect pre- and extramarital social life. The various possible types of partner relationships, whose sequence we can follow through history, and our ethical assessment of them as phases in history, can also occur side by side in the plurality of our society.

The following findings seem legitimate and important to me in this context:

1. Natural inclinations do not have to be resisted on principle.

2. Sexual behavior is closely connected with social behavior and ranking order. If a form of behavior acts as a signal, it must remain the same if it is not to lose its signal value. In nature, this general principle always means that signals do, admittedly, extend or alter their function, but retain their form. The receiver of the signal can be misled if he does not distinguish between different situations where the signal has different meanings. This is also the source of misunderstandings about the significance in each case of apparently sexual human behavior. Some species of animal and plant can mislead others in the same manner and even create advantages for themselves at the cost of these others.[125] But the misunderstanding of "sexual" gestures by the general public and the misunderstanding of the nature of the marital act by moral theology are based on a blindness to detail that is the observer's own fault. He receives the signal, but interprets it wrongly, seeing only one aspect of it, because he has forgotten about the reciprocal relationship between sexual and social behavior. This can be seen elsewhere too: The term "moral corruption" is almost exclusively applied to sexual activities now. If the signs of a "decline of the West" appear to be multiplying, sexual licentiousness is held responsible, although these signs are much more likely to be merely one of the many after-effects of a crisis in society than its source. When told about the initiation rites of primitive races, the general public misinterprets them as a display of a predominantly sexual nature, although they are in fact a

lesson in social science that informs us about tribal divinities and the methods of hunting, about behavior toward strangers, enemies, persons of authority within the tribe, and of course about behavior toward the other sex. Carnivals and Mardi Gras celebrations are often seen as an opportunity for sexual license, although economic and political abuses are denounced during the pageants, and the keys of the city hall—i.e., governmental power—are handed to the carnival prince; this is evidence enough that this is a time when general social criteria are usefully re-examined, when, in the framework of merrymaking and high jinks, the basic principles of our rigorous social order are put in question—i.e., subjected to critical appraisal, lest they should rigidify unchecked.

3. In evolution, behavior determines the structure of organs; changes in behavior entail changes in body structure. This is why we cannot deduce binding "purposive norms" for the future use of these organs from the form of organs (see pp. 38 and 185). Conversely, from the standpoint of current usage, we cannot assert that an organ was formerly used "wrongly" either. The same applies to behavior patterns that have changed function. If, therefore, man has the means of obeying the commandment to love his neighbor by emancipating natural behavior patterns (by methods that are, moreover, laid down by nature), we cannot describe this as in principle contrary to nature. The fact that earlier generations did not yet realize this and that other norms were proclaimed as a result does not mean that people erred. Insofar as ethical norms are based on natural laws, they must be able to change with the progress of our knowledge of natural laws.

4. The use of behavior patterns originally derived from brood-tending or mating for pair-bonding in marriage

or in larger societies is a regular occurrence among social beings. The brood-tending organs can have sexual signal functions, and the reproductive organs can have nonsexual signal functions (see p. 51). The dual functions and change of function of organs and behavior patterns originally serving brood-tending or reproduction that we constantly find in the animal kingdom were listed on pp. 233ff.

5. Mating serves to produce genetic variety, reproduction serves to preserve life, and pair-bonding originally served to maintain species-specific characteristics. All three can occur independently (see pp. 87f.). According to the requirements, they can be combined with one another, or they can be functionally dissociated again in nature.

6. Permanent monogamy has measurable advantages in some cases (see p. 105), which increase according to the number of individual variable characteristics that must coincide in the parents. This includes, for instance, the synchronization of physiological processes, the preference for a particular nesting or breeding place, and traditions. Among many animals, knowledge of the prey, of paths, or of the signals needed for intraspecific communication (e.g., the song of many birds), is transmitted. Tradition makes it possible to "pass down" acquired characteristics, to transmit the knowledge an individual has gained. If the offspring have to rely on learning such things from their parents, it can be an advantage for both parents to agree on what is to be transmitted.

7. The specific types of family and marriage (monogamy, polygamy, permanent or seasonal bonds) are adaptations in the biological sense, i.e., they correspond to the typical living requirements at the time of the species

in question. Permanent monogamy can be a transitional stage in the phylogeny of a group of animals, and some species will deviate from it (e.g., tropical finches); but this is neither regression nor degeneration! Moreover, not all individuals of the same species are as similar as we might assume. We say that the graylag goose is permanently monogamous, yet there are some individuals who do not contract a firm bond, in addition to others who have firm bonds with several partners, and yet others who, besides their firm pair-bond, occasionally enter into a sexual and social relationship with different partners (cf. p. 98), as Fischer discovered in our institute. This does not imply that the nonmonogamous graylag geese are failures, "breakdowns," who do not correspond to the type of the species; rather it means that we will have to check whether this difference is not of advantage to the species, just as sickle-cell anemia, as Lorenz explained in the Introduction, also has advantages in some cases and is an adaptation, even though it counts as a disease in our latitudes. It would be equally careless if we were to describe one of the various current forms of marriage among humans as biologically "right" and the others as "wrong" before checking whether the marital form in question is adapted to the over-all life structure of the respective nation or tribe. And probably the question of whether man is monogamous is wrongly put, seeing that individuals are by nature functionally as different among themselves as the graylag geese.

8. In the case of animals, we content ourselves with simply describing their manifestations of life, and therewith also their behavior patterns. But with man, we also evaluate them; *this does not replace description, however, but presupposes it*. Whether it is possible to arrive at an ethical evaluation from a description of nature—

this is the disputed question of the normative value of
the real, which cannot be discussed here. But if in some
cases a method had demonstrably led to false conclusions, we will have to query all the results arrived at
by this method, even if they seem plausible. That man
should live in monogamy according to the will of God,
because monogamy is the most widespread form of marriage among men, may sound plausible, but it is an in-
admissible deduction; for then we would also have to
posit lying as God's will, since all men lie.

Man is different from animals. His behavior is that
of a thinking being, so it cannot be assessed in terms
of biology alone; but neither can it be assessed without
biology. Findings on animals cannot be transferred—as
findings—either to other species of animal or to man.
All that can be transferred are working hypotheses.
Their accuracy has to be checked anew in every case.
To omit to do this or to fail to transfer working hypotheses is unscientific.

9. Man is an aggressive creature. Presumably primitive
mankind was dispersed in groups and, like animals who
live in groups, knew two kinds of conspecifics, namely
the members of his group and strangers. It was a biological necessity that this should give rise to two different, and in many ways opposed, moral principles: one
applying to the behavior toward one's own social group,
the other to behavior toward outsiders. In adaptive
terms, aggressive animals have aggression-inhibiting behavior patterns (so-called appeasement or submission
gestures), performed by the loser in a fight, by which
it "admits" its defeat and prevents further attack by
the victor. Man can perceive this connection, and as a
result he has put himself in a very difficult position.
For not only does he improve his weaponry, he also
prohibits capitulation to a superior. And another as-

pect of this unbiological attitude is that he does not permit the exploitation of those appeasing behavior patterns with which nature has endowed him and that generally derive from brood-tending or mating behavior. That this is their derivation may comfort those who believed that aggression toward conspecifics is part of an original evil that still has to be combatted by inhibiting mechanisms. The inhibiting mechanisms we use largely derive from reproductive behavior, so their roots are as ancient as those of aggression. It is probably correct that living things could afford intraspecific aggression on top of reproduction, in the interests of extending their territory and colonizing the earth, and that its limits were always fixed by the requirements of reproduction and in given cases by brood-tending—which is why elements from these spheres of behavior are so suitable for inhibiting aggression.

If living things learn much from their parents, or even grow into the parents' group entirely, this promotes the transmission of tradition, but at the same time it increases the risk that the belligerent old males will drive away their own sons as rivals and thus exclude them from the tradition. So it is very important to inhibit the aggression between them, and aggression-inhibiting mechanisms have evolved further and further in the service of social cohesion.

10. Among social animals of less highly developed species, the females are not ready to conceive again during the period of brood-tending; but they become fertile very quickly if brood-tending is cut short owing to an accident. Sexual relations between the parent animals stop during the period when they could disturb the mother-child relationship. But in the case of man, the theologians defend the principle that the mother-child relationship should not affect conjugal relations between

the partners (not more, at any rate, than is inevitable under the circumstances). So man should take active steps to preserve the close conjugal partnership. Many physical intimacies could serve this end besides actual copulation; this is already so in animal societies. There are no indications in biology or ethnology to suggest that the foreplay to mating or even copulation itself are inextricably linked to reproduction—quite the reverse, in fact. Knaus and Ogino have demonstrated that loving union and procreation are not necessarily, by their nature, interconnected for man either. Moral theology even admits of grounds that temporarily or even permanently forbid procreation in a marriage. In such cases, the couple is entitled to desire and request that the natural outcome of marital intercourse should not come about during this period. But the only thing the couple may do besides this is to observe the infertile periods when conception is unlikely, i.e., to avoid conception but not to practice contraception. Circa A.D. 200 the Church father Tertullian forbade women to wear dyed wools, on the grounds that God had not created purple and scarlet sheep. Even in the last century, there was resistance to lighting the streets with artificial gas lights in Cologne, because this infringed the order created by God, according to which the nights are dark. People today are prepared to take deviations from the "natural order" as a matter of course in such cases.

Man must master nature, not become its submissive slave.

Theology has shown itself unable to determine what is natural and what is contrary to nature in love life. It has not proved that the doctrine of salvation is irreconcilable with the following statement—which is not contrary to the nature of man: The morality of the marital act does not depend on the potential fruitfulness of each individual act, but on the requirements of mutual love in all its aspects. The consequence of this statement is that the form of his love life is the responsibility of each individual, that the married couple must decide for itself which methods are acceptable to it, and that these methods can differ from marriage to marriage. Furthermore, each individual must also decide for himself—again given the requirements of reciprocal love in each marriage—what is permissible to him or her in the way of extramarital, so-called "flirtation" as a social bond. In both cases the decision also depends on the consideration of other members of the society who are all more or less affected by it, which makes the question no easier.

BIBLIOGRAPHY

1) *Armstrong, E. A.* (1965): Bird display and behavior. New edition, Dover Publications, Inc., New York
2) *Bargmann, W.* (1959): Histologie und mikroskopische Anatomie des Menschen. Third edition, G. Thieme, Stuttgart
3) *Bilz, R.* (1943): Lebensgesetze der Liebe. Hirzel, Leipzig
4) *Birns, B., M. Blank, W. H. Bridger* and *S. K. Escalona* (1965): Behavioral inhibition in neonates produced by auditory stimuli. Child Development 36, 639–45
5) *Birth, Th.* (1928): Das Kulturleben der Griechen und Römer. Quelle & Meyer, Leipzig
6) *Blüm, V.* (1966): Zur hormonalen Steuerung der Brutpflege einiger Cichliden. Zool. Jb. Physiol. 72, 264–90
7) *Booth, C.* (1962): Some observations on behavior of *Cercopithecus* monkeys. Ann. N. Y. Acad. Sci. 102, 477–87
8) *Boratov, P. N.* (1967): Türkische Volksmärchen, S. 272. Akademie-Verlag, Berlin
9) *Bristowe, W. S.* (1958): The world of spiders. Collins, London
10) *Bruder, R. H.,* and *D. S. Lehrman* (1967): Role of the mate in the elicitation of hormone-induced incubation behavior in the ring dove. J. comp. physiol. Psychol. 63, 382–84
11) *Bubenik, A. B.* (1967): Neues aus dem Leben des Edelwildes. Die Pirsch 19, 322–28
12) *Buechner, H. K.,* and *R. Schloeth* (1965): Ceremonial mating behavior in Uganda Kob (*Adenota kob thomasi* Neumann). Z. Tierpsychol. 22, 209–25
13) *Burckhardt, D.* (1958): Kindliches Verhalten als Ausdrucksbewegung im Fortpflanzungszeremoniell einiger Wiederkäuer, Rev. Suisse Zool. 65, 311–16
14) *Carayon, J.* (1964): Les aberrations sexuelles »normalisées« de certains Hémiptères Cimicoidea. In: Psychiatrie animale (A. Brion and H. Ey eds.). Paris

286   BIBLIOGRAPHY

15) *Cleveland, L. R.* (1949): Hormone-induced sexual cycles of flagellates. I. Gametogenesis, fertilization and meiosis in *Trichonympha*. J. Morphol. 85, 197–296

16) *Coulson, J. C.* (1966): The influence of the pair-bond and age on the breeding biology of the Kittiwake Gull, *Rissa tridactyla*. J. Anim. Ecol. 35, 269–79

17) *Daettwyler, O.*, and *M. Maximoff* (1959): Tsiganes. Büchergilde Gutenberg, Zürich

18) *Darchen, R.* (1968): Ethologie d'*Achaearanea disparata* Denis, araignée sociale du Gabon. Biologia Gabonica 4, 5–25

19) *Davis, D. D.*, and *H. E. Story* (1949): The female external genitalia of the spotted hyena. Fieldiana, Zool. 31, 277–83

20) *Deckert, G.* (1968): Der Feldsperling. A. Ziemsen, Wittenberg-Lutherstadt

21) *Dejung, B.* (1967): Regressionen im Verhalten des Menschen. Juris-Verlag, Zürich

22) *Doms, H.* (1965): Gatteneinheit und Nachkommenschaft. M. Grünewald-Verlag, Mainz

23) *Drury, W. II.*, and *W. J. Smith* (1968): Defense of feeding areas by adult herring gulls and intrusion by young. Evolution 22, 193–201

24) *Dupeyrat, A.* (1960): 21 Jahre bei den Kannibalen. Herold, Wien-München

25) *Dupeyrat, A.* (1963): Papua, Beasts and Men. Macgibbon & Kee, London

26) *Eibl-Eibesfeldt, I.* (1955): Ethologische Studien am Galapagos-Seelöwen, *Zalophus wollebaeki* Sivertsen. Z. Tierpsychol. 12, 286–303

27) *Eibl-Eibesfeldt, I.* (1955): Das Verhalten der Nagetiere. In: Kükenthal, Handb. Zool. 8, Volume 10, 13

28) *Eibl-Eibesfeldt, I.* (1969): Grundriss der vergleichenden Verhaltensforschung. Second edition, R. Piper & Co., München

29) *Eibl-Eibesfeldt, I.* and *E.* (1967): Das Parasitenabwehren der Minima-Arbeiterinnen der Blattschneider-Ameise (*Atta cephalotes*). Z. Tierpsychol. 24, 278–81

30) *Eisenberg, J. F.* (1966): The social organizations of mammals. Handb. Zool. 8, Volume 10 (7), 1–92

31) *Ewer, R. F.* (1963): The behavior of the Meerkat, *Suricata suricatta* (Schreber). Z. Tierpsychol. 20, 570–607

32) *Ford, C. S.*, and *F. A. Beach* (1960): Das Sexualverhalten von Mensch und Tier. Colloquium Verlag, Berlin

33) *Freuchen, P.* (1961): Book of the Eskimos. World Publishing Company, Cleveland, New York

34) *Friedmann, H.* (1960): The parasitic weaverbirds. U. S. Nation. Mus. Bull. 223

35) *Geist, V.* (1968): On the interrelation of external appearance, social behavior and social structure of mountain sheep. Z. Tierpsychol. 25, 199–215

36) *Gwinner, E.* (1964): Untersuchungen über das Ausdrucks- und Sozialverhalten der Kolkraben (*Corvus corax corax* L.). Z. Tierpsychol. 21, 657–748

37) *Haag, H.* (1966): Biblische Schöpfungslehre und kirchliche Erbsündenlehre. Katholisches Bibelwerk, Stuttgart

38) *Haas, G.* (1964): Horst- und Partnerwechsel eines männlichen Weissstorchs innerhalb einer Brutzeit. Jb. Ver. vaterl. Naturkd. Württemberg 118/119, 382–85

39) *Haberland, E.* (1963): Galla Süd-Äthiopiens. W. Kohlhammer, Stuttgart

40) *Harrison, C. J. O.* (1965): Allopreening as agonistic behavior. Behaviour 24, 161–209

41) *Hartmann, M.* (1956): Die Sexualität. Fischer Verlag, Stuttgart

42) *Hassenstein, B.* (1962): Die Spannung zwischen Individuum und Kollektiv im Tierreich. In: Individuum u. Kollektiv. Freiburger Dies Universitatis 9

43) *Hörmann, L. v.* (1912): Genuss- und Reizmittel in den Ostalpen; eine volkskundliche Skizze. Z. Dtsch. Österr. Alpenver. 43, 78–100

44) *Holst, D. v.* (1969): Sozialer Stress bei Tupajas (*Tupaia belangeri*). Z. vergl. Physiol. 63, 1–58

45) *Hückstedt, B.* (1965): Experimentelle Untersuchungen zum »Kindchenschema«. Z. exper. angew. Psychol. 12, 421–50

46) *Hutt, C.*, and *M. J. Vaizey* (1967): Group density and social behavior. In: Neue Ergebnisse der Primatologie (D. Starck, R. Schneider, H.-J. Kuhn eds.), Stuttgart, S. 225–27

47) *Immelmann, K.* (1961): Beiträge zur Biologie und Ethologie australischer Honigfresser (*Meliphagidae*). J. Orn. 102, 164–207

48) *Immelmann, K.* (1962): Beiträge zu einer vergleichenden Biologie australischer Prachtfinken (*Spermestidae*). Zool. Jb. Syst. 90, 1–196

49) *Immelmann, K.* (1966): Beobachtungen an Schwalbenstaren. J. Orn. 107, 37–69

50) *Jay, P.* (1962): Aspects of maternal behavior among langurs. Ann. N. Y. Acad. Sci. 102, 468–76

51) *Jolly, A.* (1966): Lemur behavior. Univ. Chicago Press, Chicago and London

52) *Kaestner, A.* (1960): Lehrbuch der speziellen Zoologie, Volume I. G. Fischer, Stuttgart

53) *Kihlström, J. E.* (1966): A sex cycle in the male. Experientia 22, 630

54) *Klofl, W.* (1959): Versuch einer Analyse der trophobiotischen Beziehungen von Ameisen zu Aphiden. Biol. Zbl. 78, 863–70

55) *Koehler, O.* (1954): Das Lächeln des Säuglings. Umschau 54, 321–24

56) *Koenig, L.* (1951): Beiträge zu einem Aktionssystem des Bienenfressers (*Merops apiaster* L.). Z. Tierpsychol. 8, 169–210

57) *Koenig, L.* (1960): Das Aktionssystem des Siebenschläfers (*Glis glis* L.). Z. Tierpsychol. 17, 427–505

58) *Koenig, O.* (1961): Das Buch vom Neusiedler See, Wollzeilen-Verlag, Wien

59) *Koenig, O.* (1962): Kif-Kif. Wollzeilen-Verlag, Wien

60) *Kosinski, J.* (1966): The Painted Bird. New York

61) *Kühme, W.* (1965): Freilandstudien zur Soziologie des Hyänenhundes (*Lycaon pictus lupinus* Thomas 1902). Z. Tierpsychol. 22, 495–541

62) *Kuhn, H.-J.* (1967): Zur Systematik der *Cercopithecidae*. In: Neue Ergebnisse der Primatologie, Stuttgart, 25–46

63) *Kummer, H.* (1968): Social organization of hamadryas baboons. S. Karger, Basel and New York

64) *Kummer, H.,* and *F. Kurt* (1965): A comparison of social behavior in captive and wild hamadryas baboons. In: The baboon in medical research (H. Vagtborg ed.). Univ. Texas Press

65) *Kunkel, P.* (1962): Bewegungsformen, Sozialverhalten, Balz und Nestbau des Gangesbrillenvogels (*Zosterops palpebrosa*). Z. Tierpsychol. 19, 559–76

66) *Kurt, F.* (1968): Das Sozialverhalten des Rehes. Parey, Hamburg and Berlin

67) *Krämer, A.* (1968): Soziale Organisation und Sozialverhalten einer Gemspopulation (*Rupicapra rupicapra* L.) der Alpen. Dissertation, Universität Zürich

68) *Krafft, B.* (1966): Premières recherches de laboratoire sur le comportement d'une araignée sociale nouvelle, *Agelena consociata* Denis. Rev. Comp. Animal No. 1, 25–30

69) *Krut, L. H.,* and *R. Singer* (1963): Steatopygia; the fatty acid composition of subcutaneous adipose tissue in the Hottentot. J. phys. anthropol. n. s. 21, 181–87

70) *Kruuk, H.* (1966): A new view of the hyaena. New Scientist, June, 849–51

71) *Lack, D.* (1946): The life of the robin. Witherby, London

72) *Lawick-Goodall, J. van* (1968): The behavior of free-living chimpanzees in the Gombe Stream Reserve. Animal Behavior Monographs (London) 1 (3), 161–311

73) *Lind, H.* (1963): The reproductive behavior of the gull-billed tern, *Sterna nilotica* Gmelin. Vidensk. Medd. fra Dansk naturh. Foren 125, 407–48

74) *Löhrl, H.* (1968): Das Nesthäkchen als biologisches Problem. J. Orn. 109, 383–95

75) *Lorenz, K.* (1963): Das sogenannte Böse. Dr. G. Borotha-Schoeler, Wien

76) *Makatsch, W.* (1955): Der Brutparasitismus in der Vogelwelt. Neumann-Verlag, Radebeul and Berlin

77) *Martin, R. D.* (1968): Reproduction and ontogeny in tree shrews (*Tupaia belangeri*). Z. Tierpsychol. 25, 409–95 and 505–32

78) *Mayr, E.* (1963): Animal species and evolution. Harvard Univ. Press, Cambridge (Mass.)

79) *McBride, G.*, Mündl. Mitteilung; work in press.

80) *Michael, R. P., J. Herbert* and *J. Welegalla* (1967): Ovarian hormones and the sexual behavior of the male rhesus monkey (*Macaca mulatta*) under laboratory conditions. J. Endocr. 39, 81–89

81) *Mohr, J. W., R. E. Turner* and *M. B. Jerry* (1964): Pedophilia and Exhibitionism. Univ. Toronto Press

82) *Nelson, K.* (1964): The temporal patterning of courtship behavior in the glandulocaudine fishes. Behaviour 24, 90–146

83) *Neuweiler, G.* (1969): Verhaltensbeobachtungen an einer indischen Flughundkolonie (*Pteropus g. giganteus*). Z. Tierpsychol. 26, 166–99

84) *Nicolai, J.* (1956): Zur Biologie und Ethologie des Gimpels (*Pyrrhula pyrrhula* L.). Z. Tierpsychol. 13, 93–132

85) *Nicolai, J.* (1968): Die isolierte Frühmauser der Farbmerkmale des Kopfgefieders. Z. Tierpsychol. 25, 854–61

86) *Nicolai, J.*, Film on *Geopelia*

87) *Ohm, T.* (1948): Die Gebetsgebärden der Völker und das Christentum. E. J. Brill, Leiden

88) *Parkes, A. S.*, and *H. M. Bruce* (1961): Olfactory stimuli in mammalian reproduction. Science 134, 1049–54

89) *Ploog, D.* (1964): Verhaltensforschung und Psychiatrie. In:

Psychiatrie der Gegenwart Bd. I/1B. Springer, Berlin-Göttingen-Heidelberg

90) *Ploog, D. W., J. Blitz* and *F. Ploog* (1963): Studies on the social and sexual behavior of the squirrel monkey (*Saimiri sciureus*). Folia primat. 1, 29–66

91) *Ploss, H.* (1911): Das Kind in Brauch und Sitte der Völker. Th. Grieben, Leipzig

92) *Pocock, R. I.* (1919): On the external characters of existing chevrotains. Proc. Zool. Soc. London, 1–11

93) *Rauh, F.* (1969): Das sittliche Leben des Menschen im Lichte der vergleichenden Verhaltensforschung. Butzon & Bercker, Kevelaer

94) *Reed, R. A.* (1968): Studies of the Diederik Cuckoo, *Chrysococcyx caprius* in the Transvaal. Ibis 110, 321–31

95) *Reynolds, V.* (1965): Some behavioral comparisons between chimpanzee and gorilla in the wild. Amer. Anthropol. 67, 691–706

96) *Sade, D. S.* (1965): Some aspects of parent-offspring and sibling relations in a group of rhesus monkeys with a discussion of grooming. Amer. J. phys. Anthrop. (n. s.) 23, 1–17

97) *Sauer, F.* (1955): Entwicklung und Regression angeborenen Verhaltens bei der Dorngrasmücke (*Sylvia c. communis*). Acta XI Congr. Int. Orn. 1954, 218–26

98) *Schaller, F.* (1962): Die Unterwelt des Tierreiches. Springer-Verlag, Berlin, Göttingen, Heidelberg

99) *Scheven, J.* (1958): Beitrag zur Biologie der Schmarotzerfeldwespen. Insects Sociaux 5, 409–37

100) *Schleidt, W. M.,* and *M. Magg* (1960): Störungen der Mutter-Kind-Beziehung bei Truthühnern durch Gehörverlust. Behaviour 16, 254–60

101) *Schmidt, R.* (1904): Liebe und Ehe in Indien. Berlin

102) *Schultz, H.* (1962): Hombu; Urwaldleben der brasilianischen Indianer. Belser, Stuttgart

103) *Schultze-Westrum, Th.* (1968): Ergebnisse einer zoologisch-völkerkundlichen Expedition zu den Papuas. Umschau 68, 295–300

104) *Sewell, G. D.* (1968): Ultrasound in rodents. Nature 217, 682–83

105) *Silberbauer, G. B.* (1965): Bushman Survey Report. Bechuanaland Press (PTY.) Ltd., Mafeking

106) *Snyder, R. G.* (1961): The sex ratio of offspring of flyers of high performance military aircraft. Human Biology 33, 1–10

107) *Sorenson, E. R.,* and *D. C. Gajdusek* (1966): The study of

child behavior and development in primitive cultures. Pediatrics 37 No. 1, Pt. II, 149–243

108) *Spannaus, G.* (1949): Urwaldzwerge in Zentralafrika. Hochschulfilm C 567 des Instituts für Film und Bild in Wissenschaft und Unterricht

109) *Sparks, J.* (1967): Allogrooming in Primates: a Review. In: Primate Ethology (D. Morris ed.), Weidenfeld & Nicolson, London, and Doubleday Anchor Books, Garden City, New York

110) *Spinage, C. A.* (1969): Naturalistic observations on the reproductive and maternal behavior of the Uganda defassa waterbuck *Kobus defassa ugandae* Neumann. Z. Tierpsychol. 26, 39–47

111) *Stamm, R. A.* (1962): Aspekte des Paarverhaltens von *Agapornis personata* Reichenow. Behaviour 19, 1–56

112) *Struhsaker, T.* (1967): Behavior of elk (*Cervus canadensis*) during the rut. Z. Tierpsychol. 24, 80–114

113) *Thomas, E. M.* (1962): Meine Freunde die Buschmänner. Ullstein, Berlin-Frankfurt-Wien

114) *Tinbergen, N.* (1958): Tiere untereinander. Parey, Berlin

115) *Tobias, P. V.* (1957): Bushmen of the Kalahari. Man 57, 33–40

116) *Tschanz. B.* (1968): Trottellummen. Parey, Berlin and Hamburg

117) *Villiers, H. de* (1964): The tablier and steatopygia in Kalahari Bushwomen. South Afr. J. Sci. 57, 223–27

118) *Ward, J. A.,* and *G. W. Barlow* (1967): The maturation and regulation of glancing off the parents by young orange chromides. Behaviour 29, 1–56

119) *Weller, M. W.* (1968): The breeding biology of the parasitic black-headed duck. The living bird 7, 169–207

120) *Wickler, W.* (1965): Die Evolution von Mustern der Zeichnung und des Verhaltens. Naturwiss. 52, 335–41

121) *Wickler, W.* (1966): Über die biologische Bedeutung des Genital-Anhanges der männlichen *Tilapia macrochir*. Senck. biol. 47, 419–27

122) *Wickler, W.* (1966): Ursprung und biologische Deutung des Genitalpräsentierens männlicher Primaten. Z. Tierpsychol. 23, 422–37

123) *Wickler, W.* (1967): Vergleichende Verhaltensforschung und Phylogenetik. In: Die Evolution der Organismen (G. Heberer ed.), Fischer, Stuttgart

124) *Wickler, W.* (1967): Socio-sexual signals and their intra-specific imitation among primates. In: Primate Ethology (D. Morris ed.), Weidenfeld & Nicolson, London (69–147), and Doubleday Anchor Books, Garden City, New York

292   BIBLIOGRAPHY

125) *Wickler, W.* (1968): Mimikry; Nachahmung und Täuschung in der Natur. Kindler Verlag, München, and McGraw-Hill, New York

126) *Wickler, W.* (1968): Das Missverständnis der Natur des ehelichen Aktes in der Moraltheologie. Stimmen der Zeit 182, 289–303

127) *Williams, L.* (1968): Der Affe wie ihn keiner kennt. Molden, Wien

128) *Yerkes, R. M.* (1933): Genetic aspects of grooming, a socially important primate behavior pattern. J. Soc. Psychol. 4, 3–25

INDEX